D1035337

KENNESAW
MOUNTAIN   JUNE 1864

KENNESAW

MOUNTAIN JUNE 1864

Bitter Standoff at the Gibraltar of Georgia

RICHARD A. BAUMGARTNER
and LARRY M. STRAYER

BLUE ACORN PRESS

Huntington, West Virginia

Copyright 1998 by Richard A. Baumgartner & Larry M. Strayer

All rights reserved.
Written permission must be secured from the publisher to use or reproduce
any part of this book, except for brief quotations in critical reviews or articles.

Published by

Blue Acorn Press
P.O. Box 2684
Huntington, W.Va. 25726

ISBN 1-885033-20-6

Baumgartner, Richard A., 1953—
Strayer, Larry M., 1955—

Kennesaw Mountain, June 1864

Illustrated.
Includes bibliographical references and index.

History — American Civil War

Manufactured in the United States of America

Design, typography & maps by Richard A. Baumgartner

CONTENTS

ACKNOWLEDGMENTS

Sincere gratitude is extended to everyone who assisted with this book's compilation, especially those furnishing most of the 175 wartime photographs which so greatly enhance the human side of Kennesaw's story.

Michael J. Winey and Randy Hackenburg with the U.S. Army Military History Institute at Carlisle Barracks, Pennsylvania, helped access dozens of photographs from its archives and collections of the Massachusetts Commandery, Military Order of the Loyal Legion of the United States (Mass. MOLLUS, USAMHI). Additional images were made available by Mary Michals, audio-visual curator at the Illinois State Historical Library, Springfield; Norwood A. Kerr, archivist, Alabama Department of Archives and History, Montgomery; and Ronny Mangrum, director of the Lotz House Museum in Franklin, Tennessee.

Private collections provided documents and portraits of many enlisted men and junior officers. Contributions from the following individuals, listed alphabetically, proved invaluable and deserve heartfelt thanks: Beulah Adams, Humboldt, Iowa; Charles Band, North Vancouver, British Columbia, Canada; Gil Barrett, Laurel, Maryland; Franklin Brandt, Stewardson, Illinois; Matt Burr, Bellevue, Ohio; Al L. Camblin, Topeka, Kansas; Richard F. Carlile and Gary Delscamp, Dayton, Ohio; Craig Dunn, Kokomo, Indiana; Larry K. Fryer, Columbia, Maryland; Paul Gibson, Bristol, Tennessee; John Gurnish, Mogadore, Ohio; David and Frances Hall, Clarksville, Tennessee; Roger D. Hunt, Rockville, Maryland; Dennis Kelly, former historian at Kennesaw Mountain National Battlefield Park; Dennis Keesee, Westerville, Ohio; Michael G. Kraus, Pittsburgh, Pennsylvania; Donovan G. Lucus, Lanesboro, Minnesota; Vann R. Martin, Dallas, Texas; Marcus McLemore, Poland, Ohio; Richard W. Nee, Atlanta, Georgia; Howard L. Norton, Little Rock, Arkansas; Janis Pahnke, Chicago, Illinois; Brad L. Pruden, Marietta, Georgia; Irwin Rider, North East, Pennsylvania; Dale S. Snair, Warrensburg, Missouri; Karl Sundstrom, North Riverside, Illinois; Mark Weldon, Fort Wayne, Indiana; George S. Whiteley IV, Atlanta, Georgia; Bob Willey, New Haven, Indiana; and Ray Zielin, Orland Park, Illinois.

Easing the research process were librarians and staff members at a number of institutions, particularly those at Smith Memorial Library, Indiana Historical Society, Indianapolis; the Atlanta History Center library; Woodruff Library's special collections, Emory University, Atlanta; the Ohio Historical Society, Columbus; and special collections at The Golda Meir Library, University of Wisconsin-Milwaukee. Dr. Kenneth T. Slack, curator of the Rosanna A. Blake Library of Confederate History at Marshall University, Huntington, West Virginia, was especially helpful in locating historical journals and microfilm.

Retha W. Stephens, ranger/curator at Kennesaw Mountain National Battlefield Park, graciously granted full access to the park's library files and facilitated photographing several uniforms and artifacts displayed in Kennesaw's visitor center. She also provided insight into the orthography of the name "Kennesaw," which often appears different in Union and Confederate accounts. According to the September 7, 1888 edition of *The Kennesaw Gazette,* "Kennesaw Mountain has always been spelled in Georgia as is shown in this sentence. The Federal commanders during the war, and the northern writers since the war, however, generally spell it Kenesaw. That is and always has been incorrect, and Georgia is bound to down the north in this struggle for Kennesaw."

Finally, special recognition is owed to longtime friend and collaborator Larry M. Strayer, whose perceptive knowledge of Civil War photography, regimental history collection and editing abilities aided materially in completion of the pictorial record and narrative.

Richard A. Baumgartner
Huntington, West Virginia

They said that Fame her clarion dropped
   Because great deeds were done no more —
That even Duty knew no shining ends,
And Glory — 'twas a fallen star!
   But battle can heroes and bards restore.
     Nay, look at Kenesaw:
Perils the mailed ones never knew
Are lightly braved by the ragged coats of blue,
And gentler hearts are bared to deadlier war.

— Herman Melville, 1866

CHAPTER 1

Sherman vs. Johnston: A violent 'chess match' in northwest Georgia

The blue-uniformed soldiers left their entrenchments before dawn on June 1, 1864 with little regret. Faces looked haggard from lack of sleep, nerves taut from the constant whine of bullets and cannon shot. Death stalked friend and foe alike, irrespective of rank, for the past seven days. The wild, densely wooded country east of Dallas, Georgia was dubbed the "hell hole," and all who survived its horrors were glad to be leaving it behind.

Twenty-five days earlier these troops, a majority of them veterans of nearly three years' hard service, embarked upon one of the most arduous campaigns of the Civil War. Three Federal armies, comprising 110,000 men, stepped off from the environs of Chattanooga, Tennessee and headed south into the rugged terrain of northwest Georgia. The objective of their wiry, 43-year-old commander, Major General William Tecumseh Sherman, was the Confederate Army of Tennessee encamped at Dalton. The Southerners had occupied the fields and hills surrounding the small Western & Atlantic Railroad town since the dark days of late-November 1863, following their demoralizing loss of Lookout Mountain and Missionary Ridge at Chattanooga. At the head of the Rebel army was General Joseph Eggleston Johnston, 57 years old, a native Virginian and victor at the first battle of Manassas in 1861. Although despised by Confederate President Jefferson Davis, Johnston was chosen to replace Braxton Bragg, the Army of Tennessee's ascerbic, unpopular commander who resigned shortly after the Missionary Ridge debacle. Within weeks of arriving at Dalton, Johnston restored discipline, improved rations and morale, and infused new confidence in the Rebel ranks as they prepared for the invasion everyone knew was coming. "The approach of warm weather told us that our work for the summer would soon commence," wrote a non-commissioned officer from Tennessee. "Near the latter part of April everything was made ready for action, and every day we listened for the sound of cannon at our outposts." [1]

Johnston's strength at Dalton was about half that of Sherman's. His two infantry corps were commanded by Lieutenant Generals William J. Hardee and John Bell Hood, while the Army of Tennessee's cavalry corps was led by diminutive Major General Joseph Wheeler. Some 20,000 reinforcements, in-

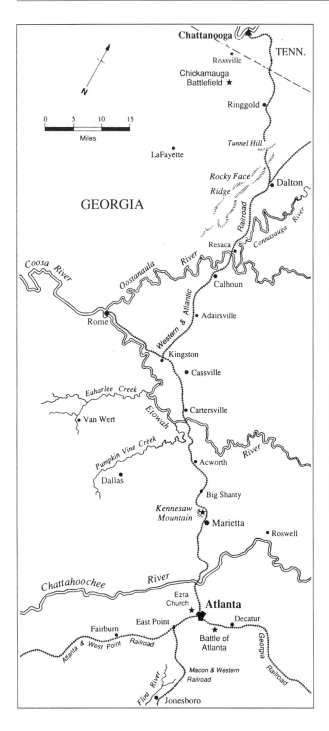

At Sherman's disposal were 18 infantry divisions, four cavalry divisions and 254 guns belonging to Major General George H. Thomas' Army of the Cumberland, Major General James B. McPherson's Army of the Tennessee, and Major General John M. Schofield's 23rd Corps, styled the Army of the Ohio. All except the bulk of Schofield's command were hardened veterans inured to battle. Eighty-eight percent of the Federal troops poised for the campaign hailed from the Midwest, with Ohio, Illinois and Indiana furnishing 65 percent of the total force. Both Sherman and McPherson were natives of the Buckeye State.

Following two days of skirmishing south of Ringgold, Georgia, Sherman pushed forward on May 7. His mission, as outlined by orders from the U.S. Army's commanding general, Ulysses S. Grant, was "to move against Johnston's army, to break it up, and to go into the interior of the enemy's country as far as he could, inflicting all the damage he could upon their war resources ...."[3] Marching with a minimum of baggage, the Union columns attempted to envelop Johnston near Dalton, but the Confederate commander evaded being trapped at Snake Creek Gap after sharp fighting at Rocky Face Ridge and Buzzard's Roost. Dalton was abandoned and the Rebels withdrew south to entrenchments at Resaca, which also was evacuated following three bloody days of heavy skirmishing and fighting, May 13-15.

Johnston fell back across the less rugged countryside between Resaca and the Etowah River, searching for an advantageous position to make a stand. Below Adairsville he temporarily divided his forces, then ordered them concentrated again at Cassville with hopes of pouncing on the Federal left wing. While Hardee and Wheeler's cavalry checked pursuit by Thomas and McPherson from the north and west, Hood on the Confederate right was to fall on Schofield's 23rd Corps before help could arrive. The plan went awry, however, when Federal cavalry unexpectedly appeared on Hood's right. The Confederate corps commander, crippled at Gettysburg and Chickamauga, declined to attack, perceiving a threat to his own flank. Hood's delay proved fateful, for Johnston was forced to scrap his promising plan and order another withdrawal. By May 21 the Army of Tennessee retired into the Allatoona Mountains south of the Etowah, threw up breast-

cluding a corps commanded by Lieutenant General Leonidas Polk brought by rail from Mississippi, reached Johnston by the end of May, but the Confederates still faced superior numbers in manpower and weaponry.[2] If he hoped to combat the unequal odds, Johnston had to rely on efficacious generalship, smart defensive use of terrain, and the fighting spirit of his Southern soldiers.

General Joseph E. Johnston

L.M. Strayer

Major General William T. Sherman

works and waited.

In the meantime, Sherman rested his troops for three days near Kingston. He decided to strike directly across country, leaving behind his railroad supply line and skirting Johnston's stronghold at Allatoona. The small town of Dallas, 16 miles west of Marietta, was selected as the next objective. On May 23, the blue columns crossed the Etowah and marched south and southeast.

Wheeler's watchful cavalry scouts observed the Federal movement, which Johnston divined as an attempt to reach the Chattahoochee River, the last major water barrier in front of Atlanta. The Confederate commander immediately slid his army southwest and hurriedly entrenched again along a heavily wooded line running east-northeast of Dallas. After Sherman's forward elements arrived in the vicinity at 2 p.m. on May 25, they were stunned when their progress was abruptly halted by Johnston's butter-

nut-clad soldiers. Beginning late that afternoon at New Hope Church, and continuing for the next week and a half, heavy cannon and musket fire reverberated through the rocky ravines and dense pine thickets east of Dallas. Wrote a Wisconsin soldier: "It was no safer to follow close upon [Johnston's] heels than to fool around the hind feet of an army mule." [4]

Two days passed before Sherman realized he faced Johnston's entire army and that his long-range flanking move to reach Marietta via Dallas was stalled. He now proposed a short-range one to re-position his forces on the Western & Atlantic Railroad above Marietta. "We don't want to turn the enemy's left flank but his right," Sherman communicated to McPherson on May 27, "so as to put our concentrated army between [Johnston] and the railroad." [5] At the time, McPherson's 15th and 16th corps' divisions were located in breastworks and

War Scenes, Views and Pointers on Western & Atlantic RR

• *Attacking Federals faced withering, nearly point-blank fire on May 27 near Pickett's Mill, as depicted in this engraving based on an Alfred R. Waud sketch. A Rebel cavalryman fighting on the skirmish line recalled: "The enemy ... could not see our men until they were in about twenty yards of them, when they came into the open, and our men were ready, and there was nothing to do but shoot them down. It was most destructive — the greatest loss of life that I ever witnessed. I doubt that there was ever, at any time during the war, as many men killed by so small a force as we had there that day."*

rifle pits east of Dallas on the Federal right flank. Further northeast, the line already was being shifted with a division from Major General Oliver O. Howard's 4th Corps groping through the trackless forest to locate and attack the Rebel right flank. Two late-afternoon assaults, which one Yankee participant described as "a swarm of men struggling through the undergrowth of the forest, pushing and crowding," [6] were bloodily crushed near Pickett's Mill by dismounted cavalry and veterans of Major General Patrick R. Cleburne's division, Hardee's corps. Six-

teen hundred Federals were killed, wounded or captured in little more than an hour and a half. Afterward, a Texas company commander wrote in his diary that "dead men meet the eye in every direction, and in one place I stopped and counted 50 dead men in a circle of 30 ft. of me." [7] An Ohioan whose regiment suffered 104 casualties, including six members of the color guard, commented simply: "This is surely not war, it is *butchery*." [8]

On May 28 McPherson was ordered to vacate his lines that night and march to a new position on the right of Thomas. The 14th Corps under Major General John M. Palmer correspondingly would take over the 23rd Corps' sector with Schofield moving to cover Thomas' left. The pullout was postponed, however, when one of Hardee's divisions commanded by Major General William B. Bate charged a portion of McPherson's entrenchments late in the afternoon. The fierce but uncoordinated assault was met by Federal rifle and artillery fire that literally piled Confederate bodies in heaps. A few members of the famous Kentucky "Orphan" Brigade advanced to within 50 yards of the Union fortifications, but could go no farther. Fifty-one percent of the brigade's 1,100 men engaged were lost. One Kentuckian declared that the attack was among "the most wicked and stupid blunders of the war." [9] The result further underscored to soldiers on both sides the futility of frontally assaulting strong earthworks held by a resolute enemy — a lesson seemingly forgotten by Sherman just four weeks later.

Between May 29 and June 1 the opposing armies faced each other in stalemate along a twisting, nine-mile front running from Dallas to northeast of Pickett's Mill. Along some sections a labyrinth of trenches, traverses and ditches was carved into the landscape, resembling those constructed on the Western Front during World War I. Heavy details of pickets and skirmishers occupied pits dug closer to their opponent's line, and the peculiar sound of bullets zipping through the woods never ceased. Sharpshooters concealed in treetops or thickets attempted to pick off anyone caught in an exposed position, even for a moment. Favorite targets were officers and artillerymen. The latter added to the din and destruction by sometimes unleashing full-scale bombardments, which caused the shells' recipients to dig all the more and improve their defenses. Unrelenting toil, hunger and the constant threat of death strained even the veterans' nerves to a frazzle. The Dallas line had become, as Sherman's soldiers christened it, "the hell hole."

Not until the early morning hours of June 1 was McPherson able to extract safely his divisions from the fortifications on the Federal right and begin the side-stepping movement toward Acworth, a village roughly 10 miles by rail south of the Etowah River. Union cavalry under Major General George Stoneman occupied the deserted town of Allatoona, while engineers went to work rebuilding the Etowah railroad bridge, destroyed during the Confederate retreat.

During the day Johnston learned that the Federals had withdrawn from the Dallas area and were shifting northeast. At first he was inclined to believe the Yankees were retreating, then considered it more likely Sherman again was trying to turn his right flank. As a counter measure, Cleburne's division was transferred to the far right. The giant "chess match" continued, much to Sherman's frustration, as Johnston refused to permit him to break free.

Along the front lines, where bullets and shrapnel flew unabated, the fighting men guessed what was taking place. In the 29th Georgia, Sergeant John W. Hagan wrote to his wife on June 1: "We beleave the yankees are eather trying to flank us & march on Atlanta or they are falling back. We have had Some heavy fighting within the last 9 days & we have in evry case whiped the enemy & I beleave they will be retreating in a few days if they are not on the back track now. I think we will leav here soon. If the yankees are flanking us we will march to cut them off & if they are on a retreat we will persue them." [10]

On the same day, Lieutenant Colonel Columbus Sykes, 43rd Mississippi, informed his wife Pauline: "The enemy ... are all the time shelling and sharp shooting, but nothing more. I am unable to conjecture what can be Sherman's policy. He is lying still in our front, doing apparently but little, yet time must be precious to him as it must be exceedingly difficult for him to feed his army and to keep a full supply of ordnance stores. Sooner or later his plans must be developed and then will come, I imagine, the tug of war in deadly and terrible earnestness. But come when it will, we are ready for him. The army is strong, jubilant and confident, with mutual confidence between commander and troops." [11]

Not far away, the Union 15th Corps shifted to relieve the 20th Corps on June 1. Captain John M. Carr of Company G, 100th Indiana, took stock of his new surroundings. "Am quite unwell today," he confided to his diary. "Was overcome in the morning by the heat. Skirmishing here is very brisk and near." Late that night Carr wrote, "one of the skirmishers fired his gun and then the whole line of skirmishers fired and we all jumped and slung our blankets and the firing comm[enced] from the works on my left and we were sure that the rebels were upon us but we were prepared. They do not catch us naping often. The woods are musical with the birds that do not seem to mind the warfare that is going on between man and man. If it was not for the constant firing one could not realize that this is indeed a terrible conflict." [12]

CHAPTER 2

Plenty of mud for our beds tonight

The second day of June, wrote Captain James L. Burkhalter in his journal, "began almost as usual. Much picket firing had been kept up all during the night and continued on into this morning, but with little damage on either side." [1]

Burkhalter's regiment, the 86th Illinois, had pulled out of line the previous morning with the rest of Colonel Daniel McCook Jr.'s 14th Corps' brigade, relieving one belonging to the 23rd Corps three miles closer to the railroad. [2] As commander of Company F, Burkhalter was especially anxious and concerned for his men's welfare. "Very little sleep was afforded us for several days in front of Dallas," he recorded. "The men are now totally exhausted and nearly dead for want of rest. A position like the one held by this brigade fully taxes the physical endurance of the American Soldier. The loss of six consecutive nights' sleep, even though the men have nothing else to attend to, is enough to prostrate any person of ordinary constitution, and the soldiers have spent much of this time in strengthening this fortification and breastworks. They did it besides fighting by regular turns, which was by alternate days first — one day on, then one day off. I often feared during that terrible enemy musketry fire that many of our men would be killed needlessly, for they appear to have grown entirely indifferent to their personal safety. They were frequently exposed, when they might just as easily have kept under cover." [3]

Further to the left along the new line occupied by Brigadier General William Harrow's 4th Division, 15th Corps, another Illinois company commander noted that casualties and the campaign's rigors already had reduced the 103rd Illinois by one-sixth. "This is getting on the Vicksburg order," wrote Captain Charles W. Wills of Company G, "[but] the troops are in splendid spirits and everything is going on as well as could be wished." He optimistically believed "that to be connected with such a campaign as this is well worth risking one's life for. It occasionally gets a little old, but so does everything in this life, and altogether I don't know but that it wears as well as any of life's pleasures." [4]

In the same division, Private Andrew Bush's viewpoint was far more tainted. A member of Company H, 97th Indiana, Bush was detailed to General Harrow's headquarters after suffering a chin wound

• Lieutenant Generals William J. Hardee, right, and John Bell Hood, below, commanded two of the Army of Tennessee's three infantry corps in June 1864. Known to his troops as "Old Reliable," Hardee was the author of Rifle and Light Infantry Tactics, *a manual of arms used to drill many soldiers on both sides. In 1863, Hood suffered a shattered left arm at Gettysburg and lost his right leg to a bullet at Chickamauga.*

Museum of the Confederacy

Miller's *Photographic History of the Civil War*

in May. He informed his wife that "all our soldiers are very much fatigued and careworn with long watchfulness," and lamented his perception that "those at home ... never for one moment take a thought of how fast our nation is wending its road down toward ruin. It no doubt cheers the hearts of many when they hear of us gaining a great victory, which it should. But do those ever think of what it costs to gain it? The bodies of many brave men are lying on the open field at this time who have been dead for eight days belonging to the enemy. Whenever the rebels make an attempt to get these dead our boys always have a slug ready for them which only adds to the number of dead men and increases

the stench."[5]

Rank provided no immunity from the battlefield's bullets and smells, as Brigadier General Alpheus S. Williams, commander of the 20th Corps' 1st Division, explained in a letter to his daughter: "The days were exceedingly warm and the air filled with the noisome odors of the dead, man and beast .... All the days and nights the same incessant rattle of musketry, so close to us that it seemed in our very camp. About midnight both parties would open in volleys, which in the reverberation through the woods would be redoubled in volume and sounded like a tropical thunder storm twenty times increased in noise."[6]

Greg McMahon

Mass. MOLLUS, USAMHI

Major General John Schofield

Major General James B. McPherson

• *Of Sherman's three top subordinates, Major General George H. Thomas, left, was the most experienced. The native Virginian endeared himself to many enlisted men in the Army of the Cumberland, acquiring the nickname "Old Pap." He also earned the sobriquet "Rock of Chickamauga" following his solid performance during that savage battle in September 1863.*

Janis Pahnke

On June 2 it began to rain, softly at first, then increased to a torrential downpour punctuated by flashes of lightning and cracks of thunder. With few intermissions during the next two and a half weeks, rain cascaded from the sky — deluging the tangled Georgia wilderness and the soldiers trying to maneuver and survive. Creeks swelled over their banks. The woodlands' rough roads and entrenchments were transformed into soupy, viscid mud, and Sherman's sidesteps to the railroad slowed to a snail's pace. Both sides wallowed in the muck for several days after the rain began, although gunfire continued without letup. Describing the discomfort in his diary, Confederate Major General Samuel G. French, one of Polk's division commanders, wrote early in June:

2d. An awful thunderstorm came up, the peals of thunder were frightful, and the Yankee tried to drown it with mimic artillery, as if one at a time was not divertisement enough. Some people can't be satisfied. The ditch is filled up to some depth with water. Over this I sleep on one board with my face turned up to the glare of the shells that shine through the closed eyelids.

3d. Firing as usual, and the enemy moving to our right. Another heavy thunderstorm is in progress. The roar of artillery shakes the rain out of the clouds. We drove in the enemy's skirmish line. One consolation the staff says we have is that no one comes to see us; the ride is not interesting. We see no one, and get no orders. That there is good in everything, including shells, is their doctrine. This battle has now lasted ten days.

4th. Rain again this morning. It was a disagreeable night in the trenches. There is firing in front. At 4 p.m. I received orders to withdraw our lines. It is raining to-night. This, with previous rains, rendered the roads as bad as they can well be, and the night was very dark. Mud, mud everywhere, and the soldiers sink over their shoe tops at every step.[7]

One of French's line officers was especially miserable. First Lieutenant John M. Davidson of Company C, 39th North Carolina, cursed the rain that intensified his aching rheumatism. In a letter to his wife Julia, who was living in Atlanta, he opined:

We are the dirtiest and filthyest looking creatures you ever saw. We are in the reserve ditches and have been for 8 days .... The fireing never ceases and the minney balls are constantly whizzing over our heads & once in a while a man gets shot .... We are so tired of the ditches, almost all are anxious for the fight to come off & yet we all dread it, for many will fall, never to rise in this world.[8]

Davidson probably was unaware that Julia's brother, David White, was only a few miles away in a Federal camp, and perhaps just as wet. White was serving as chaplain of the 107th Illinois, a regiment belonging to the 23rd Corps.

By June 4, recalled General Johnston, "it was evident that the great body of the Federal army was moving to its left rear, toward the railroad, the movement being covered by its long line of intrenchment." Johnston countered Sherman's shift by vacating his breastworks that night and marching to positions previously marked out by his chief engineer, Major Stephen W. Presstman. The new line's left was anchored at Lost Mountain, its center near Gilgal Church, with the right extending beyond the railroad behind Noonday Creek.[9] Darkness, rain and claps of thunder masked the Confederate pullout, but the realignment required great exertion.

"The rain continued all day and we are drenched," wrote William L. Trask, a native Kentuckian and former steamboat pilot serving as an enlisted courier on General Hardee's staff. "We have plenty of mud and nothing else for our beds tonight. Our army moved still farther to the right amidst a heavy rain and were in mud to their knees. At 10 p.m. our party reached the new bivouack but on account of weather conditions there was no sleep for any of us. The infantry marched the whole night in the rain and mud and the roads were almost impassable."[10]

Captain Elbert D. Willett's Company B, 40th Alabama, left its trenches at 1 a.m. on June 5. Willett believed that his men "never had so disagreeable and fatiguing [a] march. Never halted until seven. Greatly exhausted. It is known as the *muddy march.* Rain has fallen three days and the roads were nearly impassible. Rested balance of day on Lost Mountain. Washed mud off clothes. Drew a whiskey ration."[11]

Private Samuel Robinson of the consolidated 1st/27th Tennessee remembered that his comrades "trudged through the rain along the road, with the mud shoe-mouth deep, through the woods, scattering headlong, pell-mell, every man for himself it seemed; but on the army went, a scattered, helter-skelter, uncontrolled mass. When day broke, such a sight as the First and Twenty-seventh, at least, presented! We looked at each other in astonishment. Muddy from head to foot, wet to the skin, guns half full of mud in many instances, hungry — but with all this not demoralized, yet terribly scattered."[12]

Numbed by a dose of opium, Private William O. Norrell of Company B, 63rd Georgia, struggled to

Gary Delscamp

Brigadier General Jacob D. Cox

Lost Mountain by alternately sloshing "up to the ankles in mud, slippery as glass" and riding in an ambulance. He was suffering with a severe bout of diarrhea, which magnified the trek's hardships. "It was the most trying time we have had since our advent into the army. Nothing we have ever done was at all comparable to it." [13]

The 39th North Carolina's rheumatic lieutenant, John M. Davidson, informed his wife on June 6:

We have changed our position and have fallen back to Lost Lountain and are quite busy today fortifying. We commenced leaving our ditches at 10 o'clock Saturday night [June 4], the darkest night I ever saw and the rain pouring down in torrents

all night and — the mud! Oh, you have no idea — it was like batter & from 3 to 12 inches & no chance to shun it. It was slosh, slosh all night. We spent most of yesterday resting & having our positions given. We have a splendid position for Polk's Corps but we are fearful the enemy will not attack as I have just been on top of the mountain and can see the Federal wagons moving to the East and to our right. I am greatly worn out but feel thankful that God has spared my life. [14]

When it became light enough to see on June 5, Federal pickets began banging away for the 11th straight day. But as Captain John Carr of the 100th Indiana discovered, "Our skirmishers commenced firing and got no answers. We smelt a mice and in a few minutes advanced a line and found the rebel rifle pits and works all deserted, the Greybacks all gone. Great rejoicing in our line." [15] Captain John W. Tuttle of Company G, 3rd Kentucky Infantry, was awakened by the cheering. He "found it caused by the nocturnal departure of the rebellious gentlemen. Never felt more relieved in my life as I had become heartily tired of them as neighbors. Visited the rebel fortifications this morning. Found them very strong." [16]

Brigadier General Jacob D. Cox, commander of the 23rd Corps' 3rd Division, was equally impressed by the enemy's strengthened lines. He wrote in his diary: "The works found [were] very strong, both for artillery & infantry, with abattis carefully sharpened & staked down. They have never before shown so much industry & finished their defensive works with so much care. The whole line which they have fortified must be six miles long." [17]

Illinois Captain Charles Wills agreed when he inspected the Confederate entrenchments. "The Rebels run last night. Everything gone this morning slick and clean. Our regiment was the first in their works. I was over their works to-day and find three lines, two of them very strong. A number of dead men lay between their lines and ours, which neither side could bury." [18]

Hastily mustered burial parties scoured the rain-soaked ground for decomposing bodies from both armies. One of these was led by First Lieutenant Willis J. Nugent of Company D, 78th Pennsylvania, who explained that "I took some men, soon after [the Confederates] left, and went out to that part of the battle-field where our regiment fought on Friday, May 27 [near Pickett's Mill]. We found [Privates]

James Little, Ebenezer Mahan, and Thomas Kerr, the three men of Company A that were killed. The rebels had covered them with a few inches of earth. We dug graves and put them in and put up head and foot boards with the name and regiment cut on, and built a rail fence around the graves. We spent the balance of the day in cleaning our arms, drawing rations and ammunition." [19]

The next five days, though awash with rain, provided a welcome respite from the constant firing for many of Sherman's men. Their commanding general's objective, Marietta and the Chattahoochee River, remained the same. But in failing to flank Johnston at Dallas he now revised his strategy to push straight forward, keeping his army in contact with the railroad. Before another advance could commence, however, the destroyed Etowah River bridge had to be rebuilt — a task Sherman's chief of railroad construction assured him would be completed by June 12. Once finished, the bridge would permit trains carrying ordnance, commissary and quartermaster stores to travel all the way to Acworth, with fortified Allatoona Station providing a secondary base. [20]

Sherman also awaited the arrival of reinforcements. These appeared when two divisions — 9,000 troops of the 17th Corps, most of them hardened veterans of Shiloh, Corinth and Vicksburg — marched into Acworth on June 8. Their journey, following furloughs to veteranize in March and April, had begun on May 10 at Cairo, Illinois. Transported by steamboats to Clifton, Tennessee, the 17th Corps then tramped 300 miles via Huntsville, Alabama, on foot. According to Private John Gaddis of Company E, 12th Wisconsin, the final 12 miles to Acworth were "lined with troops, some in camp, some on the way back to the railroad station [at Cartersville, Georgia] with wagon trains after supplies. Saw many wounded men lying in the shade of trees, and under the care of surgeons. General McPherson and staff visited our Corps. As he passed along, each regiment cheered him loudly, flinging their hats high in the air." [21]

Ordered to the army's extreme left, the new arrivals under Major General Francis P. Blair Jr. encamped in thick pine timber near McPherson's headquarters. Little comfort was found after the weary soldiers plopped down to survey their surroundings. "It rained again at night," concluded Private Gaddis'

Tom Molocea

Major General Francis P. Blair Jr.

diary entry for June 8. "None of us, except the officers, have any tents; tents take up too much room in the baggage wagons, so we must do without. We do the best we can to fix some sort of shelter from the storm." [22]

The relative quiet between June 5 and 10 also gave hundreds of men an opportunity to investigate the country behind the lines. Despite special field orders issued by Sherman that were designed, in part, to curtail wanton plundering, rear areas were combed for anything edible. "My bunk mate went out a foraging," wrote diarist Jesse B. Luce on June 6. "He got some mutton [and] I had a good supper." Luce, a 22-year-old private in Company B, 125th

Ohio, had been in the army only five months and was glad to have a friend so adept at supplementing their usual rations of hardtack, bacon and coffee. On the 7th, his "pard went foraging again. He got back at dark with Mutton, beets, onions, vinegar, meal-flour. We live fat now."[23]

That same day, Private William Wallace of Company E, 3rd Wisconsin Infantry, reported that "the boys went a forraging and got pork, chicken and mutton which came in good time for we were out of meat." In addition, there was "a good mess of new potatoes last night for supper, [while] I had a good mess of wheat today. I bruised it between two stones and boiled it in my big tincup. The boys was all then at the same process in a short time. It was as good as barley broth .... My tincup serves for all kinds of cooking purposes — makes coffee, beans, rice, peas, potatoes, boils meat, stews apples in it, and in fact everything that has to be cooked has to be done in it. It and the tin plate, which is all the cooking utensils I possess, spoon, knife and fork is all I have, and it is enough."[24]

Wallace rationalized stealing from the hostile Georgia countryside by explaining that "the inhabitants has all left this part. We dont see neither white nor black males, and when the boys goes to their home for a sheep or a pig, they will all say that we ought not to take from them as they are all widows. The fact is their slaves and husbands has gone along with the rebel army, and their property is compleetly destroyed as far as our army goes, as nothing can escape the scrutiny of the boys. Yesterday when we were busy building our breast works, a big flock of sheep came along screened by the fencing, but they were not long on the land of the living."[25]

Other Federals, like Captain Tuttle of the 3rd Kentucky, trekked back to Pumpkin Vine Creek to bathe and wash clothing. For three days he fought off boredom, passing time by writing, sleeping and playing chess with a fellow officer in an Ohio regiment.[26]

Sergeant Hamlin Coe of Company E, 19th Michigan, noted in his diary on June 9: "We have been in camp again all day. Although I have been busy, the time passes slowly. In fact time has been a drag today. I have had company inspection, which occupied some time, and the remainder of the day has been devoted to the interest of the company and in writing letters home .... This morning some of our boys had quite a time exchanging [news]papers with the Rebs, and they seemed to have a good time between themselves. It commenced by our boys asking the Rebs to exchange papers, when both parties started with a paper waving over their heads and without arms. The Rebs were eager to exchange tobacco for coffee. Among other agreements was one to discontinue firing upon pickets."[27]

New Yorker Edwin Weller also noticed the near cessation of picket firing on the 20th Corps' front. Although first lieutenant of Company H, 107th New York, Weller had been commanding Company F since May 25 when that company's three commissioned officers were killed or wounded at New Hope Church. By June 9, he was happy for the respite. "We are all pretty well fatigued out having been marching and fighting for nearly forty days now, Weller informed his future wife. "I expect to see considerable more hard fighting before this campaign is over. But I have every confidence in our success."[28]

There was scarcely a man in Sherman's ranks who did not share this feeling. Some Confederates were aware of it, too, especially those serving on General Hardee's staff. "Yesterday [June 6] we captured a mail containing several thousand letters," wrote Orderly William L. Trask. "Last night and this morning we have been busily engaged reading them. The letters are of every imaginable style of composition and chirography, but not one contains a single sentiment indicating a desire to close the war by granting the South her independence. All seem determined to subjugate us. Their greatest hope seems to be centered on Grant taking Richmond, and all say when they reach Atlanta and capture Joe Johnston, the war will be over. They will then be permitted to return home and enjoy peace once again. None seem to think it possible they will be longer than the 4th of July reaching Atlanta. Nearly every letter is filled with the most abominable lies imaginable concerning immense rebel losses and fancied victories for them. One scoundrel had placed a lock of hair in his letter which he says he cut from a rebel girl's head. All appear highly elated at their success so far."[29]

The Yankees had good reason for elation. In one month they had penetrated into Georgia some 80 miles, three-fourths of the way from Chattanooga to

Courtesy George S. Whiteley IV

• *Pictured above as a captain early in the war, Lieutenant Colonel Columbus Sykes, 43rd Mississippi, wore the coat at right during June 1864. In a freak accident seven months later, Sykes was fatally injured by a falling tree while sleeping in bivouac.*

Atlanta. Their opponents were forced or flanked out of six defensive positions, and lost in the process about one-seventh of the Army of Tennessee's aggregate strength as casualties. But Johnston had thwarted Sherman's progress along the Dallas line, and continued to possess his soldiers' high regard. "It is said that Gen. Johnston has said that it is the best and bravest army he ever saw," crowed Lieutenant Colonel Columbus Sykes. In an impassioned June 8 letter to his wife, the Mississippi officer wrote: "Let Sherman move as he will. Gen. Johnston is cognizant of it, and is as ready to meet strategy with strategy as he is to return blow for blow. The troops still retain almost unlimited confidence in their chieftain."[30]

Kennesaw Mountain
National Battlefield Park

With each Union move, the Confederate commander reacted by shifting or extending his troops toward the east. The Southerners immediately set to work felling trees, building breastworks, digging trenches and scooping out rifle pits in the mud. Tremendous effort was expended to construct defensive positions, which often were abandoned when another shift in the line required the labor to be repeated all over again. On June 7 at Lost Mountain, Private William J. Watson of Company E, 53rd Tennessee, penciled in his diary that "We finish our works this morning and are waiting for the enemy to come   in the evening we move to the extreme right and build more works and [are] ready for them again." Captain Elbert Willett's Alabama regiment vacated a reserve position at daybreak on June 8 and with Hood's corps, "marched East towards R. Road. At noon bivouaced ... one mile west of R. Road. Went to front and built works, finished them that night." The following morning Willett's company "worked on trenches until noon then moved to E. side of R. Road, to new position there that night." Anxious for some rest, Willett instead was detailed for skirmish duty in the dark with 150 rain-soaked men. Lieutenant Colonel Sykes' Mississippians also shifted to new works on June 9 and 10. "If you could see us this morning," he told his wife, "you would see a pretty rough set though I look and feel tolerable as I put on clean underclothing last night. As long as this unprecedented Campaign continues we will have to rough it in the same way, marching, lying and sleeping in line of battle ready to move at a moments notice, day or night." [31]

By June 9 the Confederate right was anchored on Brushy Mountain east of the railroad, and the left at Lost Mountain. Cavalry guarded both flanks.

Near the center and a mile forward of the main line was Pine Mountain, on which Bate's division of Hardee's corps was posted along with four batteries. The imposing mass of Kennesaw Mountain loomed behind Johnston's 10-mile-long defensive line. Formed of three distinct "knobs" of varying height, the mountain shielded Marietta from the northwest and blocked direct access to the Chattahoochee via the railroad. Big Kennesaw, at the northern end, rose 700 feet above the surrounding forest and fields. Slanting southwest, the ridge sloped to 400-foot-high Little Kennesaw at its center and terminated 2,600 yards to the south at what today is known as Pigeon Hill, 200 feet in elevation. From the crest of Big Kennesaw, Confederate signallers could see 20 miles or more in every direction. Below them, facing Sherman's Yankees, the mountain descended steeply. Thick timber and large rocks studded the northwest side, contributing to the position's natural strength. Some already were calling the place "the Gibraltar of Georgia."

"I expect the enemy to fight us at Kenesaw Mountain," Sherman had informed Washington on June 5, "but I will not run head on his fortifications." Four days later the Federals were poised to resume the advance and force the Rebels from Pine, Lost and Kennesaw mountains. Their determined commander later wrote: "On each of these peaks the enemy had his signal station, the summits were crowned with batteries, and the spurs were alive with men busy in felling trees, digging pits, and preparing for the grand struggle impending. The scene was enchanting; too beautiful to be disturbed by the harsh clamor of war; but the Chattahoochee lay beyond, and I had to reach it." [32]

CHAPTER 3

Cheering and huzzahing like so many devils

The resumption of Sherman's advance began on June 10. From right to left, Schofield's, Thomas' and McPherson's mud-smeared columns were preceded by strong detachments of skirmishers and an artillery battery. "The teams were all left in the rear," recorded Corporal Alexander Downing of Company E, 11th Iowa. "Our army is prepared for a big fight." [1]

Downing's regiment passed near the railroad depot at Big Shanty [present-day Kennesaw, Georgia, and site of 1862's celebrated hijacking of the locomotive "General" by Andrews' Raiders]. He noted that all the surrounding shanty houses were burned. The previous afternoon, Big Shanty was occupied after two brigades of Brigadier General Kenner Garrard's cavalry division drove off an equal number of Confederates during an armed reconnaissance. "We had not went far out side of our lines until our advance run on to the rebel pickets," wrote Corporal Ambrose Remley of Company E, 72nd Indiana. His regiment belonged to Colonel John T. Wilder's hard-hitting "Lightning Brigade" of mounted infantry, and carried Spencer repeating rifles. "Our brigade was dismounted and formed in line of battle .... When every thing was ready we was ordered to advance and we run the rebels out of four lines of breast works and about two miles on the other side of Big Shantee Station. The rebel force was the same as ours. One brigade of Infantry and one of Cavelry and them in breast works. They ought to have whipped us but they run like tow heads." [2]

From Big Shanty McPherson's Army of the Tennessee headed south astride and east of the railroad toward Marietta. The Army of the Cumberland, under Thomas, obliqued right and deployed against Kennesaw and Pine mountains. Schofield's Army of the Ohio, now composed of only two large divisions, faced Lost Mountain. But just as the movements got underway, it started raining again. For the next three days downpours — torrential at times — soaked the already waterlogged earth. The advance slowed to a crawl and temporarily stopped when the leading elements lapped up against their entrenched opponents. Instinctively, the Federals began fortifying.

"We have no tents that will turn anything but dew," 18-year-old Private Chauncey H. Cooke of

• *Brigadier General Alpheus S. Williams, seated, with staff officers in Atlanta, September 1864. Standing from left: Major James Francis (2nd Massachusetts), assistant inspector general; First Lieutenant George Robinson (123rd New York), aide-de-camp; unidentified. Image by S.D. Phillips, 14th Army Corps photographer.*

A native of Connecticut and Yale University graduate, Williams moved to Michigan in the late 1830s. He successively served as a probate judge, newspaper owner, lieutenant colonel of a Michigan regiment during the Mexican War, and Detroit postmaster.

Courtesy Walt Rudecki

the 25th Wisconsin told his mother. "Everything that we have, but our powder, is soaking wet. We are in a great flat field and all about us is flooded with water. We have to lay on raes and brush and logs to keep off the wet ground." [3]

The 12th Kentucky Infantry did not possess any tents and, as First Lieutenant Thomas Speed of Company A explained, "we could not have used [them] if we had them, as we were all the time actively engaged in skirmishing, fighting and advancing from point to point in the face of the enemy. The ground over which we passed was soaked with rain, and the dense undergrowth in the woods and

rank vegetation of the fields were kept constantly wet. The little streams which had to be crossed were all overflowing their banks, so that altogether we were wet to the skin nearly all the time. Sometimes for a number of days we could not take off our boots, nor any of our clothes, and I remember our pants became mouldy in our boots." [4]

Illinois Captain Charles Wills wrote descriptively in his diary: "Everything and everybody thoroughly soaked. Strategy! We moved out into an open field. You can imagine the amount of comfort one could enjoy so situated, after two days' constant rain, and the water still coming down in

Richard F. Carlile

Captain James L. Burkhalter, Company F, 86th Illinois

sheets. The field is trodden into a bed of mortar. No one has ventured a guess of the depth of the mud. It is cold enough for fires and overcoats. My finger nails are as blue as if I had the ague."[5]

In a letter to his daughter, 20th Corps' division commander Alpheus Williams complained: "The ground is saturated from surface to center and the roads, of course, 'awful.' It is so cold that I have on my winter coat. Of course, changing camp under such circumstances is no joke for man or beast. All of us have to take to the deeply saturated ground and as our bedding consists of blankets with now and then a buffalo robe you can fancy we sleep rather moist. If we don't all come out 'rheumaticy' it will be indeed strange."[6]

The rain, decried Sergeant Israel Correll of Company A, 51st Ohio, "will it ever cease? On account of the wet weather and being confined to our works so close, the boys begin to show the same colors on their clothes as the rebels, that of the yellow earth."[7]

Captain James Burkhalter of the 86th Illinois was even more anguished. His journal entry for June 10 crystallized the experiences and feelings of literally thousands of comrades:

The weather was rather nice when we moved out, but soon a heavy shower of rain came down. That made our march miserable, as we went through the woods and underbrush for most of the day. Our movement caused very wet branches and leaves to shed raindrops on us. The cumulative effect was as if we went through two rainstorms simultaneously. One should either be wrapped in rubber from head to toe or else go about stark naked, because there is nothing halfway about the rain in Georgia.

Cursing the weather and our ill-luck, we proceeded until the foot of the mountain was attained, where we found the 3rd Division massed up in an open field and the 1st Division then in line and skirmishing heavily with the enemy. Our division moved to the right of the 3rd and massed in the woods, where preparations were immediately made for dinner. Unfortunately, these preparations also came to naught, thanks to this wretched Georgia summer, for one of the most tremendous rain showers that I ever saw then ensued. The water literally fell in torrents for about an hour and of course extinguished all our little fires, so that we could not make our coffee. The rebels have in Mother Nature an ally which surpasses all others.

In this maddening situation, we remained until about four o'clock. At that time, we proceeded to the left about one and a half miles and took up a new position. Companies A, F and D — all with bellies rumbling angrily — were deployed as skirmish companies and pressed steadily forward in the direction a little to the right of Kenesaw Mountain.

Dirty, hungry, tired, angry, stinking — we were nearly beside ourselves. Oh, to have come upon the enemy then! However, after some distance, the line was halted and then our only task was to build heavy works, partly of logs and rails and partly of cordwood, which we found piled up nearby. There we lay until sundown, not having seen more than half a dozen rebels since about 11 o'clock.

After all the arrangements had been made for our comfort during the night ahead and some of the men had laid down to sleep, an order came to move forward instantly, towards Kenesaw Mountain. Exasperation overrode mere exhaustion and there were such voluble curses as may surely be imagined, as everyone fell in and we set out again. We had to move by means of a kind of blind road. It led around through the woods. After having gone about a mile and a half, we again went into position, this time about a mile and a half from the foot of Kenesaw Mountain, with our left resting on the railroad.

But our torture continued. We again set to work at building more fortifications, which we managed to complete in about two hours — these having been the third line of works constructed by us this day. The men were exhausted, but all felt the importance of having these works, for we wanted to be alive to greet the morning sun 'ere our bodies be covered with ten, rather than five, layers of filth. Therefore, every bit of energy was accordingly exerted. The duty was heavy, it always is, but none shrank from it and in this wise, works were soon built in each new position. Every deep trench, every log implaced, every strategic aspect anticipated — this meant that the men could rest with considerable safety and a full assurance that if attacked, we could hold this ground.

We were on the extreme left of the line of the Army of the Cumberland and joined on the right of the 16th Corps, Army of the Tennessee. With good works on our front, protection on our flanks, and utter numbness in our bodies, we felt that the whole rebel army could not dislodge us — and truthfully, *we were damn well past caring.* So we slept for the night. [8]

Against the weather the Confederates fought a losing battle as well. On the north slope of Pine Mountain, Private John S. Jackman, the 9th Kentucky's regimental clerk, had joined his old company June 10 for a tour of duty on the skirmish line. After the day's heavy showers he wrote, "my clothes [were] wringing wet. Not being allowed any fire, and being cold, I slept none during the night. Our neighbors kept up such a noise, too, bugling, rattling drums, and chopping, etc., no one could have slept in a feather bed." [9]

Captain William J. Crook of Company I, 13th Tennessee, believed that "We have been having the most displeaseable season of weather I have ever witnessed at this time of the year. Raining almost incessantly day and night. The roads are almost impassable. I have not slept in a house or tent in the last forty-five days. Some nights have passed without my closing my eyes in sleep. Such toil and such vigilance I have never known before." [10]

In his diary for June 11-13, General Samuel French compared the plight of his command in Polk's corps to the predicament faced by the Old Testament's Noah. "11th. Rain. 12th. Rain once more, and everything is drenched. 13th. Terrible rain last night and all day to-day till noon. Eleven days' rain! If it keeps on, there will be a story told like unto that in the Bible, only it will read, It rained forty days and it rained forty nights, and the ark it rested on the Kennesaw heights; For to that place we are floating, it seems to me." [11]

The deep mud placed mounted troops and artillerymen at a particular disadvantage. "The country was so boggy that it was almost impossible to move artillery or cavalry outside of the beaten roads," recalled Second Lieutenant Samuel B. Barron of Company C, 3rd Texas Cavalry. "During this long rainy spell we rarely slept two nights on the same ground and never had a dry blanket to sleep on.

There was a great deal of thunder and lightning, and artillery duels would occur either day or night, and sometimes it was difficult to distinguish between the thunder of heaven and the thunder of cannon and bursting shells." [12]

It often required 10 horses to pull a cannon or caisson through the muck, and there was scarcely an artilleryman in either army free of a mud-caked uniform. Once emplaced, however, individual guns or entire batteries let loose at visible targets. Generally positioned on higher ground, Confederate gunners had many to choose from as the Federals inched forward.

"I would rather go into a pitched battle than be situated as we are now," wrote a 2nd Massachusetts officer on June 12. "Within five hundred yards of us is a rebel battery posted on a hill, which completely enfilades our line. We have thrown up heavy traverses, which I hope will protect the men, and I shall select a good tree for myself if there is any vigorous shelling. A little while ago they tossed a shell which killed one man and wounded another in the regiment on my left. This kind of a thing you expect in a battle, but when you are lying peaceably in camp it is rather disgusting." [13]

That same day on the 16th Corps' front, Second Lieutenant George Hurlbut of the 14th Ohio Battery was able to reciprocate. "We fired some thirty shots at a squad of enemy who had built rail piles to shield their skirmishers from our infantry fire. Our shells threw their rails in every direction." Several days later, related Hurlbut to his fiancée, "I was sent out with two guns of the Battery to shell the rebel sharpshooters from an old house and barn in which they had taken shelter, and were firing from the windows and crevices, on our skirmish lines. We threw about fifty shells through and around the building, driving them off. When we advanced we found eight dead and fifteen wounded." [14]

From his Big Shanty headquarters, Sherman informed Washington on June 11 that his lines were closing on Johnston, "but it has rained so hard and the ground is so boggy that we have not developed any weak point or flank." On the other hand, construction crews had completed the Etowah River bridge a full day ahead of schedule, opening the railroad all the way to the Union skirmish line near the base of Big Kennesaw. The first loaded train chugged into Big Shanty's station at noon on the

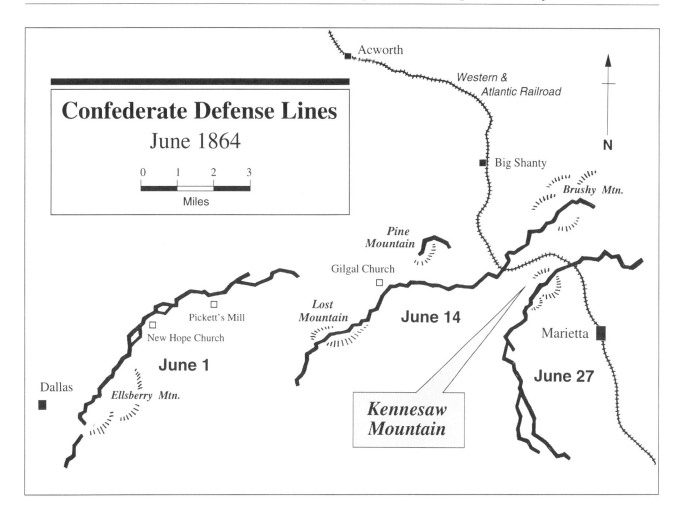

Confederate Defense Lines
June 1864

0 1 2 3
Miles

Acworth

Western &
Atlantic Railroad

N

Big Shanty

Brushy Mtn.

Pine
Mountain

Gilgal Church

Lost
Mountain

June 14

Pickett's Mill

New Hope Church

June 1

Marietta

June 27

Dallas

Ellsberry Mtn.

Kennesaw
Mountain

11th. Sherman later wrote: "The locomotive, detached, was run forward to a water-tank within the range of the enemy's guns on Kenesaw, whence the enemy opened fire on the locomotive; but the engineer was not afraid, went on to the tank, got water and returned safely to his train, answering the guns with the screams of his engine, heightened by the cheers and shouts of our men." [15]

News of this episode spread quickly through the Union camps, bolstering spirits and strengthening the rank-and-file's high opinion of their leader. "Everybody feels the utmost confidence in him," thought an Illinois officer belonging to the 15th Corps, Sherman's old command at Vicksburg. "I saw him yesterday — seems to me he is getting fleshy. He don't look as though he had anything more important than a 40-acre farm to attend to." [16]

Never a stay-in-the-rear general, Sherman made frequent trips along the Federal line to personally ascertain his troops' progress. After one stop behind

the main works of Brigadier General Jefferson C. Davis' division, 14th Corps, Sherman was assessed by an officer belonging to the 121st Ohio:

Sherman visited our works and as usual with him when his plans were working smoothly, indulged in pleasant remarks addressed to soldiers who happened to be near him, without regard to their rank.

"We are getting all right, boys, keep yourselves in good trim for tomorrow. I may need you," he told us.

It was noticeable that men from the ranks always clustered around his horse whenever he stopped along the line without fear of being frowned down, and if one happened to call him "Uncle Billy," he looked pleased rather than offended. On such occasions his manner was frank and open with his soldiers, and he did not hesitate to give them hints of what he expected to do, and yet he was a terror to newspaper correspondents, not one of whom dared show his face at his headquarters. He trusted only his men of the firing line. [17]

An Ohio artilleryman recalled:

The unaffected ease of [Sherman's] manner was wonderfully attractive, and the manner in which he expressed himself was terse and epigrammatic, and I may add, at times, a trifle profane. Swinging along the road one day in the heat and dust, tired and hungry, went a column of the Twenty-third Army Corps. They had fought in the morning, and expected to fight that afternoon, on very short rations, consequently they were inclined to growl. Gen. Sherman had dismounted near the head of the column, and was lying down on the grass in the fence corner. As a portion of the command passed him, a soldier exclaimed: "There's the old man, drunk, by thunder!"

"Not drunk," said the General, who had overheard the remark, as he arose and put his foot in the stirrup, "not drunk, but damned tired, boys." The cheer that went up convinced him that the men believed in him, drunk or sober. [18]

By morning of June 14 the rain had ceased falling, though the skies were overcast and gray. Sherman was in the saddle early, intent on examining the Pine Mountain front which the inclement weather had prevented him from doing a day or two earlier. Pine Mountain and its defenses jutted out from the Confederate main line by more than a mile, and were occupied by Kentucky, Tennessee, Florida and Georgia troops of Bate's division, Hardee's corps. Hardee was deeply concerned that Bate's three brigades and four batteries were too isolated and vulnerable to envelopment. Already the 4th and 14th corps had worked their way around the conical-shaped mountain's eastern base. Near dark on June 13, Hardee requested Johnston to visit the outpost and decide if it should be maintained. The next morning the Confederate commander, Hardee, an entourage of staff officers and General Polk rode to the mountain to investigate. Polk, whose corps held the line to Hardee's right, wanted to use the 300-foot-high mountain as a vantage point to study the ground fronting his own troops. [19]

Meanwhile, Sherman had conferred with General Thomas, who was instructed to push forward the 4th and 14th corps between Pine and Kennesaw mountains. Sherman lingered to reconnoiter. "When abreast of Pine Mountain," he wrote, "I noticed a rebel battery on its crest, with a continuous line of fresh rifle-trench about half-way down the hill. Our skirmishers were at the time engaged in the woods about the base of this hill between the lines, and I estimated the distance to the battery on the crest at about eight hundred yards. Near it, in plain view, stood a group of the enemy, evidently observing us with glasses." Sherman pointed out the knot of distant soldiers to General Howard, the 4th Corps commander, ordering him "to compel it

L.M. Strayer

Major General William B. Bate

to keep behind its cover." Howard at first demurred, answering that Thomas wanted artillery ammunition spared. "This was right, according to the general policy," Sherman replied, "but I explained to [Howard] that we must keep up the *morale* of a bold offensive ... and ordered him to cause a battery close by to fire three volleys." [20]

The nearest guns at hand were the 5th Indiana Battery's six 3-inch ordnance rifles, commanded by First Lieutenant Alfred Morrison. After quick adjustments to the tubes' elevating screws, Morrison told the 1st Section to open fire at the Confederates just below Pine Mountain's summit. He little realized his target included the Rebel commanding general and two corps commanders. General Johnston

Alabama Department of Archives and History

Lieutenant General Leonidas Polk

Captain William Gale, volunteer aide-de-camp on Polk's staff, witnessed his father-in-law's death.

Vann R. Martin

recalled: "Just when we had concluded our examination, and the abandonment of the hill had been decided upon, a party of soldiers, that had gathered behind us from mere curiosity, apparently tempted an artillery officer whose battery was in front, six or seven hundred yards from us, to open his fire upon them." [21]

Less than 100 yards right of where Johnston, Hardee and Polk were observing, Private John Jackman and Captain John W. Gillum of Company A, 9th Kentucky, sat conversing by a campfire. "For two days not a shell had been thrown at our position," Jackman wrote, "and when a shell came shrieking over the mountain to our left, I remarked to the captain, that some General and his staff, no doubt, had ridden up to the crest of the hill, and the Federal batteries were throwing shells at them. 'Yes,' said the captain, 'and I hope some of them will get shot. A general can't ride around the lines without a regiment of staff at his heels.' " [22]

Below, the Hoosier battery's center section under Second Lieutenant Jacob F. Ellison prepared to fire a second salvo. Corporal Benjamin F. McCallum sighted one of the pieces, and Private Charles Miller pulled the lanyard. Moments after their shell exploded, remembered Ezra Ricketts, a 90th Ohio private who was watching from the skirmish line, "I could see a running to and fro of the rebels for a few minutes, and then they all disappeared from that place." [23]

The shell instantly killed General Polk, passing through both arms and eviscerating his chest before exploding against a nearby tree. Captain William D. Gale, the general's son-in-law and aide on his staff, afterward described Polk's death amid the hail of shellfire:

The officers separated, each seeking some place of greater safety. General Johnston and General Polk moved together to the left, and stood for a few moments in earnest conversation behind a parapet. Several shots now passed together just above the parapet and touched the crest of the hill. Generals Johnston and Polk, having apparently completed their observations, began to retrace their steps. General Johnston fell a few paces behind, and diverged to the right; General Polk walked to the crest of the hill, and, entirely exposed, turned himself around, as if to take a farewell view. Folding his arms across his breast, he stood intently gazing on the scene below. While he thus stood, a cannon-shot crashed through his breast .... His faithful escort gathered up the body and bore it to the foot of the hill. There, in a sheltered ravine, his sorrow-stricken comrades, silent and in tears, gathered around his mangled

• *Captain Peter Simonson, standing at center, commanded the 5th Indiana Battery prior to being named artillery chief of the 1st Division, 4th Corps. On June 16, just two days after his former batterymen felled General Polk, Simonson himself was killed by a Confederate sharpshooter. His death, wrote Major General David S. Stanley, "was an irreparable loss to the division. I have not in my military experience met with an officer who was the equal of this one in energy, efficiency, and ingenuity in the handling of artillery. He never missed an opportunity and allowed no difficulties to deter him from putting in his batteries in every position that he could prove annoying or destructive to the enemy."*

The Bulletin, Whitley County Historical Society, Columbia City, Ind., October 1965

corpse. Hardee, bending over the lifeless form, said to Johnston, "General, this has been a dear visit. We have lost a brave man, whose death leaves a vacancy not easily filled." Then, kneeling by the side of the dead body, he exclaimed: "My dear, dear friend, little did I think this morning that I should be called upon to witness this." Johnston, with tears in his eyes, knelt and laid his hand upon the cold brow of the fallen hero, saying, "We have lost much! I would rather anything but this." [24]

Two other batteries by now were firing at Pine Mountain's summit. "We were sitting around with shells bursting over us when it was evident from the sound that one piece of a shell was coming close to us," recalled Sergeant Major John W. Green of the 9th Kentucky. "Every fellow was holding his breath wondering if that piece would strike him when suddenly it struck John Jackman ... on the head & turned him a complete sommersault. We thought he was killed." At first, Jackman believed "that my head was gone & I put my hand up to ascertain whether it was still on my shoulders. I did not hear the piece of shell coming, and it was such a quick

sharp lick, I did not feel it strike. After glancing off my head, it struck against a rock, then bounced and struck Col. C. [John W. Caldwell] on the leg, but did not hurt him severely." After having his wound dressed, Jackman rode a horse to the Confederate distributing hospital in Marietta. That night he took the train for Atlanta. The same train carried away General Polk's remains. Major General William W. Loring, Polk's senior division commander, was named to temporarily replace him. [25]

Lieutenant Morrison's gunners caused at least one other fatal casualty that morning — Private Charles Henderson of Company K, 31st Indiana. In a freak accident, the wooden sabot strapped to a fired shell struck and killed Henderson, a three-year veteran from Terre Haute, Indiana. According to an Illinois pioneer officer who witnessed the mishap:

The works occupied [by the 31st Indiana] had been built too near in front of the battery against the protest of the Battery officers, and the Battery lieutenant told the colonel [John T. Smith] to move his men before he opened fire, but the colonel declined to do it. About as mean and scarey a thing in the way of a missile as one man can find, are these same chunks of wood. They are concave on one end to fit the round shot or shell and square on the other so as to receive the full force of the explosion of the powder. The small tin straps that bind the wood to the shell are broken by the discharge and that infernal chunk of wood, from its irregular shape, makes the most unearthly shriek as it hurdles through the air and over one's head. There is no telling where it will light or how far it will go, and in this instance it didn't go over 30 yards from the muzzle of the cannon. Infantry frequently have to lie on the ground in front of a battery firing over them, to support it, but men are rarely hit by these chunks of wood. Still the shriek of these wooden pieces is not of a sedative nature.[26]

With Johnston's decision made to vacate Pine Mountain, Bate's troops silently withdrew to the main line after dark on June 14. Early the next morning 4th Corps' pickets discovered the enemy gone and Sherman, back at Big Shanty, was advised. Buoyed with the false hope that Johnston was about to pull back along the entire front, he or-

dered all Federal forces forward. McPherson was to threaten a turning movement at Kennesaw on the left; Schofield was to capture Gilgal Church and threaten Lost Mountain; and Thomas was to press between Pine Mountain and Kennesaw, breaking the Rebel center.[27]

By 3 p.m. Thomas arrayed all nine brigades of Howard's 4th Corps for the effort. Brigadier General George D. Wagner's brigade of the 2nd Division was chosen to spearhead the assault. In the 57th Indiana, Sergeant Asbury L. Kerwood of Company F later wrote:

[Wagner's] brigade was massed in double column. Regiments formed in columns by division, with the 57th on the left and the 100th Illinois on the right. In the rear of us the other regiments of the brigade were formed in similar manner; and also the whole corps, consisting of nine brigades, were to support our assault. We were ordered to leave every thing behind, except accoutrements and canteens.

At 4 o'clock Gen. Wagner held a consultation with his regi-

Craig Dunn

Brigadier General George D. Wagner

Mass. MOLLUS, USAMHI

Major General Oliver O. Howard

mental commanders, and delivered to them his final instructions concerning the movement. Upon returning to the regiment, Major [Willis] Blanch called up the company commanders and informed them of the important duty devolving upon them. Up to this moment no orders were given direct to the regiment, but as soon as Major Blanch dismissed the council, he turned to the 57th and said: "Men of the 57th, we are directed, by order of Gen. Sherman, to attack the enemy in their works, and drive them out with the bayonet. No man is to fire a gun as we advance upon the works. I have the assurance from Gen. Sherman that our assault will be supported, and that the works will be carried."

At 5 o'clock the bugle sounded the advance, and a single line of battle in our front commenced driving back the outposts of the enemy, who stubbornly resisted, and made a stand behind a high barricade, several hundred yards in front of the main works. The line of battle charged them, capturing some prisoners, from whom they ascertained that the position of the rebel forces was such that the assault would undoubtedly prove a failure, when it was abandoned and a line of works thrown up during the night, on the ground we occupied. [28]

The Confederates' stiff resistance convinced Thomas that the enemy was not on the verge of leaving. Further evidence also was provided on the right of his front at Gilgal Church, where the Army of Tennessee's best division commander, Pat Cleburne, was strongly entrenched.

The 20th Corps' 3rd Division, under Major General Daniel Butterfield, was dispatched down the Sandtown Road late in the afternoon to conduct a reconnaissance in force. Nearing Gilgal Church, Butterfield's two leading brigades drove in Cleburne's skirmishers but then halted in their tracks. Immediately behind the church the artillerymen of Captain Richard W. Goldthwaite's Alabama battery rushed over to the log-hewn structure. Nearby, one of Cleburne's Texas company commanders observed: "All go to work and tear that church down level with the ground in

Confederate Veteran

Major General Patrick R. Cleburne

Mass. MOLLUS, USAMHI

Major General Daniel Butterfield

about 15 minutes. Not one log left on another, even knocked the blocks, and just as the Yanks come in sight about 300 yds away they open on them with grape shot, and canister." [29]

Gunfire erupted along Cleburne's breastworks, "a burst of musketry that I had never heard equalled," thought Private Harvey Reid of Company A, 22nd Wisconsin. "It was just a roar of uninterrupted sound for at least five minutes, mingled with the rapid, deafening roars of cannon and bursting shell. The line had advanced so far beyond our batteries that they could not be used at all, and the boys had to lie down and dodge the shells the best they could. The advance line lost pretty heavily." [30]

One of the first Federals to fall mortally wounded was Major Eli A. Griffin, commanding the understrength 19th Michigan. Company E, led by Sergeant Hamlin Coe, took only 13 men into the fight and quickly lost one killed and two wounded. "It was dreadful for a few hours," Coe wrote in his journal. "Many a poor fellow fell, and we gained nothing but a little ground." [31]

It was even worse for the 70th Indiana of Butterfield's 1st Brigade. Commanded by Colonel Benjamin Harrison — future president of the United States — the 70th lost 49 killed and wounded, according to Major Zachariah S. Ragan, when the regiment "was thrown across the Sandtown road in an exposed situation in front of the enemy's masked artillery. Cleburne's division fired 135 rounds of shot, shell, and canister at our line during the hour and forty-five minutes that the regiment lay in its perilous position." [32]

Goldthwaite's four brass 12-pounder Napoleons were joined by an equal number belonging to Captain Thomas J. Key's Arkansas battery. Their combined firepower made Hoosier John L. Ketcham wonder "how we ever got out again." Ketcham, a private in the 70th's Company K, recounted that "the shot and shell were terrible, but only some forty were wounded and a few torn all to pieces. Some had very narrow escapes. A bullet struck a spyglass in Major Ragan's pocket and afterward a cannon-ball cut his belt in two, and only bruised him. One man had his haversack torn all to pieces, another his gun bent like a hoop." [33]

Second Lieutenant Charles H. Cox, the regiment's acting adjutant, believed that "never was a body of men in such a *hot* place as was the 70th on that terrible day." Writing to his sister five days

Mass. MOLLUS, USAMHI

• *Twenty-five years after the fighting at Kennesaw, Colonel Benjamin Harrison, left, 70th Indiana, became the nation's 23rd president. A native of Ohio, Harrison was promoted to brigade command later in the Atlanta Campaign, but not before suffering from the effects of poison ivy. While recuperating at a division hospital in late June, he was succeeded in command of the 70th by Lieutenant Colonel Samuel Merrill, an Indianapolis bookstore owner. Wrote Merrill to his wife: "Since the 8th of May ... our regiment has lost more than one third of its number killed and wounded, beside a large number who have fallen by the way utterly exhausted by fatigue, want of proper food and loss of sleep. You have no idea of how terrible a thing it is to advance upon a concealed foe who is pouring death into the ranks without in the least exposing himself. War is simply assassination ...."*

USAMHI

Adjutant Stephen Pierson, 33rd New Jersey

USAMHI

Lieutenant Colonel Enos Fourat, 33rd New Jersey

after the ordeal, Cox described how the regiment "pushed towards the rebel works over a troublesome abattis, but woe unto us. It was too hot a nest for Yankees at that time, for when within 200 yards of the rebel works two Batteries — 8 12-pd guns — opened on us, making a further advance *impossible* as we had no support and not a dozen men would have been left to tell the tale had we continued the charge .... For 3 hours 8 cannon flung shot, shell, grape & cannister at us and sad was the sight of the many killed & wounded around us. Several men had their heads shot off close to their shoulders, and men with arms and legs taken off was quite common. Oak trees several feet in thickness were cut square into immediately amongst us, and many trees were shattered into splinters from base to top. More than 50 shells exploded within 25 feet of me and I was almost deaf when the battle was over. Our regt expended 10000 rounds of ammunition in less than 3 hours." [34]

Closer to Pine Mountain in Brigadier General

John W. Geary's 2nd Division of the 20th Corps, Lieutenant Colonel Enos Fourat's 33rd New Jersey also ran into the Confederate wall of fire, suffering 59 casualties. One of them, Adjutant Stephen Pierson, remembered:

The rain had stopped for a time on the afternoon of June 15th, as the 33rd moved out to take its place on the line of assault. It was a repetition of Dallas or New Hope Church; the same heavy Rebel skirmish line, equal to a thin line of battle, stubbornly resisting our advance, but falling back to the cover of the same old red breastworks. We lost many as we went up.

Night came and we were told that our position was to be changed; so, for the first and only time when in the enemy's presence, we failed to throw up temporary protection. It was here that I had a very grewsome experience. In expectation of the move referred to, I was ordered by the Colonel [Fourat] to rouse the Regiment. Tired and worn by the fight and exertions of the afternoon, all the men, save the sentinels, had dropped asleep as they lay, rifles in hand, ready for any call, no matter how sudden. Passing from Company to Company along the line I wakened them. Just behind the center I came upon a row of men, stretched out with singular regularity. Passing along I shook them one after another, but got no response. Then something flashed upon me. Gently I pulled the blanket from the face of one, he was dead — they were all dead! They had been gathered there by their comrades for burial when the battle should be over.

The hours passed, but the expected orders for change of position never came, and we were caught unprotected. The Rebel fire was terribly accurate and demoralizing, but stay there we had to do. Flattening ourselves upon the ground behind any little protection we could find, we remained. Our losses became heavier and heavier as the day wore on; towards afternoon there began to develop a cross-fire from our right flank. The Brigade Commander ordered out two Companies from our Regiment to stop it, and the Colonel sent me with them. Soon after he came out himself and soon the Brigade Commander followed. They were anxious about that flank. The firing had then practically ceased, and, rather foolishly, I stood up to indicate to them the position of the men. Some fellow on the other side took a shot at the group, and his bullet struck me. I remember quite well the stinging, sickening sensation as I fell to the ground.

The old Colonel (he was perhaps 40 years old, which seemed very old to us) stooped down, picked me up and placed me with my back against a tree for protection. I am sure it was a real grief to him, for he was fond of me. I was the youngest officer in the Regiment and his affectionate name for me was "Bub." There was a hole in the lapel of my coat in front over my breast, where the bullet had gone in, and another hole in the back where it came out. He stood looking at me for a few moments, and then a look of relief seemed to pass over his face. He told me afterwards that he feared the bullet had passed through my lung and he expected to see the blood pour out of my mouth. Fortunately for me the lung was not wounded. The men that had been posted stopped the cross-fire, and the Regiment held its ground. This was the bloodiest fight, except for Peach Tree Creek later on, in which the Regiment was engaged.

But my part in the action was over. I was helped back to the rear, and soon met faithful James Polk, my servant then. Jim had my horse. I was helped up and he led me back to the field hospital. I suppose I looked pretty white from loss of blood, etc., so Dr. Reilly [James Reiley], our surgeon, poured me out a big drink of whiskey. I had never tasted whiskey before, and, by the time they had found out that my wound was not so very serious and had dressed it, the stuff had gone to my head. I was fighting mad, and they tell me my one desire was to get out and kill the fellow who had shot me, and they had to detail a man to

• *A Theodore R. Davis field sketch was the basis for the* Harper's Weekly *engraving below, depicting part of General John W. Geary's division in action near Pine Mountain. Enfilading fire from less than 250 yards away exacted a large toll in the 33rd New Jersey and 119th New York, the latter regiment losing nearly 30 percent of its effective strength on June 15 and 16.*

keep me from going out to do it. They knew but little about antiseptics and cleanliness in those days. The hospitals were full of gangrene, so, by the surgeon's advice, I rejoined the Regiment, remaining upon light duty only, while he dressed the wound for me daily. [35]

Although Butterfield was stymied at Gilgal Church, the 23rd Corps to his right captured a Confederate advance line and gained a mile of ground. On June 16, with batteries brought forward on the 4th, 20th and 23rd corps' fronts, the Yankees blanketed their opponents with shells, smothering Cleburne's defenses with enfilade and cross fire.

The biggest Federal success of June 15 was achieved on McPherson's end of the line near Brushy Mountain. General William Harrow's division of the 15th Corps was shifted at midday past the 17th Corps and placed at the army's extreme left on the west side of Noonday Creek. Harrow's mission was to "demonstrate" against the Confederate army's right flank, then supposed to be resting on the wooded ridge of Brushy Mountain. With two of his brigades and a few detachments from the 17th Corps in support, Harrow selected Colonel Charles C. Walcutt's brigade, partially armed with seven-shot Spencer rifles, for the assaulting column. Walcutt, a 26-year-old Ohio surveyor who still carried a Rebel bullet from Shiloh in his left shoulder, formed his command, from left to right, as follows: 40th Illinois, 46th Ohio, 6th Iowa and 103rd Illinois. The 97th Indiana deployed as skirmishers, one-third of a mile from the ridge's base. [36]

The skirmish line barely stepped forward, wrote Captain John D. Alexander of the 97th's Company D, "when the Rebel skirmishers opened upon us in lively style. They were in rail pens just beyond Noonday Creek. We were ordered to charge ...." Corporal Henry H. Wright of Company D, 6th Iowa, recalled: "The bugles sounded the advance and the men struggled forward through a thicket of tangled undergrowth, briars, and vines to an open field which lay sloping down to Noonday Creek, when the enemy opened fire from his rifle-pits along the creek and also from the fortified position on the heights beyond. The crackling fire of musketry, the crashing volleys of artillery, and loud cheering by the men in the assaulting lines, responded to with volleys and defiant yells by the enemy posted in his pits and breastworks, soon rose to the dignity of a battle." [37]

Karl Sundstrom

• *First Lieutenant William H. Cochrane, Company K, 33rd New Jersey, was instantly killed the night of June 15 while directing a regimental work party. Earlier promoted to captain, Cochrane's commission arrived on the day of his burial.*

His comrades' shouts also impressed Captain Charles Wills of the 103rd Illinois. "We went down on them [in] regular storm fashion. A hundred yards before we got to the hill we ran into a strong line of rifle pits swarming with Johnnies. They caved and commenced begging. The pit I came to had about 20

• *Less than seven weeks after his brigade's successful assault at Noonday Creek, Charles C. Walcutt, right, was promoted from colonel of the 46th Ohio to brigadier general. His division commander in June 1864, William Harrow, below, was a native Kentuckian and friend of President Abraham Lincoln. Harrow commanded an Indiana regiment during severe fighting at Antietam, and a 2nd Corps brigade and division at Gettysburg.*

Mass. MOLLUS, USAMHI

L.M. Strayer

in it. They were scared until some of them were blue, and if you ever heard begging for life it was then. Somebody yelled out 'Let's take the hill,' and we left the prisoners and broke. One captain offered me his sword, but I hadn't time to stop. We wanted that hill, then. At the foot of the hill we came to a muddy rapid stream, from 10 to 15 feet wide and no crossing, so we plunged in. I got wet to my middle, and many did to their breasts. The banks were steep and slippery and muddy. Though we all expected a serious fight on the hill, up we went every man for himself, and through to an open field, over which some 200 straggling sandy looking Johnnies were trying to get away, which most of them accomplished, as we were just too tired to continue the pursuit fast enough to overtake them. However, the boys shot a lot of them. Well, they call it a gallant thing." [38]

As many as 300 Confederates from Hood's corps were captured, 152 of them belonging to the 31st Alabama, which had been on picket duty in front of Major General Carter L. Stevenson's division. Among those taken prisoner was the regiment's colonel, Daniel R. Hundley, a Huntsville native and one-time resident of Chicago, who penned a vivid account eight years after the war:

As a matter of course, after fifty days of marching, fighting, bivouacking, and constant exposure to wind and weather, we were all dirty, more or less ragged, bronzed and blackened, but in the main in good spirits and health, hopeful of the future, and confident of victory over Sherman's legions. We had been considerably reduced, however, in numbers, by losses in battle and from other causes, and, on the fifteenth day of June, numbered less than four hundred men for duty ....

There had been some pretty sharp skirmishing on this line the day before, and we felt assured we should have some warm work before night. I so informed both my brigade and division commanders, who visited me early in the morning, and to whom I pointed out the unfortunate position of our line. Even before these officers left, the enemy began to shell us, and, as the day advanced, getting new batteries into position, filled the air with spherical case, round shot, grape, canister, and all the other screaming and death-dealing missiles known to the artillery arm of the service. These tore up the ground all around us, covering us oftentimes with dirt and gravel, battered what few trees were near us, and sent many a fence-rail splintered and hurtling about our heads, but otherwise did very little damage.

Meanwhile the Yankees were massing their troops in our immediate front in two lines of battle, with a heavy skirmish line in advance; and every indication seemed to evince a fixed determination on their part to charge us pretty soon. I so informed my division commander by a courier, and immediately hastened with the reserves to the right of the picket line, the captain in command there having sent me word that he was being hard pressed. But before reaching him, I heard the Federals huzzahing to the charge against the left of my line, which was the weakest and most exposed; whereupon I changed front and double-quicked the reserves in that direction.

Unfortunately, there was a wood intervening between us and the pickets on this portion of the line — a mere patch of woodland, it is true, but filled with a dense undergrowth of bushes and saplings which prevented us from seeing twenty steps ahead in some places. The men dashed through these in gallant style, with orders to advance until they should come up with our pickets, who had received instructions to fall back slowly, fighting in retreat, in case they should be attacked by any large force; but we soon perceived that we were too late, the enemy having already captured the regiment on my left, picketing in front of General [Alexander P.] Stewart's division, as well as the left in front of my own line, having charged on them impetuously with lines of battle, and captured them before they could get out of the rifle-pits.

Perceiving the danger of my position, with my whole left for the distance of half a mile entirely unprotected, I gave orders to fall back; but just as we emerged from the wood into the open field, a courier arrived with instructions for me to hold my position at all hazards, as General Hood intended to retake the line in front of General Stewart which had just been seized by the enemy. I felt convinced the struggle would be hopeless, unless reinforcements came up right speedily; but it is the soldier's duty to obey, and I unhesitatingly gave the command to advance once more. The men dashed forward with a yell — that soul-stirring yell so peculiar to the Southern soldier; but in the wood we ran right upon the enemy, a whole brigade of them, cheering and huzzahing like so many devils.

At this critical juncture, my acting adjutant informed me that no supports were anywhere in sight, that both my flanks had been turned, and that, unless a retreat was ordered immediately, I would inevitably be forced to sacrifice my whole command. As I had instructed him to make the necessary observations and report the facts of the situation to me, I felt that I must for once take the responsibility of giving to "all hazards" a very broad construction. Once more, the men were told to fall back, which they did in good order, until they got out of the brush and into

Howard Norton

Major General Alexander P. Stewart

the open field, when perceiving that they were nearly surrounded, some little demoralization was manifested, and they began to scatter in confusion, which was not helped by the Yankees dashing in amongst them, shooting right and left, and bawling out to them to surrender. *Sauve qui pent* was now the watchword, and in reply to the demands to surrender, the poor fellows made the best of their way to the rear.

Numbers of them were shot down as they ran; one gallant soldier, just at my elbow, receiving in his head the ball which was intended for his colonel from a Yankee not thirty steps distant. I heard the well-known thud as the leaden messenger struck him, and would have had him borne from the field had it been possible; but the litter-bearers had already been surrounded as they were bearing off a wounded man, one of them killed, one of them knocked down with the butt of a musket, and the rest captured. It was with a melancholy heartache I left him weltering in his blood and groaning in his death-agony.

We ran across an open field for three hundred yards, exposed to the deadly fire of the enemy's Spencer rifles, until we reached a little brook, bordered with thick growth of weeds, briars, brush and trees. Here I managed to get a portion of the

Miller's *Photographic History of the Civil War*

Major General William H.T. Walker

command partially re-formed; but it was too late. The enemy dashed in upon us from all sides in overwhelming numbers, and captured in squads of two to a dozen, all who had not already effected their escape, or had not been either killed or wounded.[39]

Hundley was fed dinner that night at the 15th Corps headquarters of Major General John A. Logan, before being sent to prison at Johnson's Island near Sandusky, Ohio. He escaped January 2, 1865, was recaptured four days later and finally was released that July. The 31st Alabama's enlisted men were shipped to Rock Island, Illinois, where eight of them died in captivity.[40]

With Union pressure mounting, especially along his left flank between Gilgal Church and Lost Mountain, Johnston ordered Hardee to withdraw during the night of June 16 and change front on high ground east of Mud Creek, facing west. Punishing,

enfilading Federal artillery fire hastened the decision. Major General William H.T. Walker, one of Hardee's division commanders, was shelled out of his headquarters. Even Hardee was not immune. "Many cannon shots passed over and through our Headquarters camp," wrote staff orderly William Trask. "One took the back out of a coat of a man sitting under a tree playing cards — that game ceased at once. Another shot killed one of our horses. A courier was killed while passing our quarters and several men have been wounded near us."[41]

Virtually undetected, Hardee's left wing was drawn back about two miles under cover of darkness. First Lieutenant Hamilton M. Branch of Company F, 54th Georgia, thought "the enemy could have done us a great deal of damage ... for it was a very still night and their sharpshooters were only 50 and 100 yds from our breastworks in some places. If they had notified their General and he had opened on us with his artillery which he had in position he could have hurt us greatly for we [were] in range of his guns for an hour after we left the breastworks."[42]

These, the Federals discovered early next morning, "were of the most formidable character." Jacob Cox's division of the 23rd Corps marched on, and by late afternoon approached the Rebels' left flank. His artillerymen, following close on the heels of the advance infantry, quickly dropped their guns' trails and resumed firing.[43]

"We commenced fortifying our new position immediately," wrote Captain Mumford H. Dixon, 3rd Confederate Infantry, whose regiment had covered Cleburne's withdrawal. "The Yankees, no doubt thinking that we were retreating, soon followed us and very soon found us. They pushed their artillery up and commenced shelling us quite fiercely. They wounded some of our men, but killed none."[44]

Private William Norrell of the 63rd Georgia was rudely welcomed to the fresh-dug trenches after spending a week sick at Walker's division infirmary. "Such firing of small arms during so long a time I had never heard. The shelling was terribly severe. During the day I had two narrow escapes. A young man next to me on my left was struck on the head and bruised considerably, while the dirt was thrown all over me by the piece of shell, bespattering my face, hat [and] clothes considerably. Afterward ... my head and the head of the man on my right was placed together (lying down) by the side

Mass. MOLLUS, USAMHI

Major General Joseph Hooker

Johnston.[46] Such unequal odds, if only temporary, produced an incident on June 17 that 20th Corps' division commander Alpheus Williams found outrageously comical:

We followed through the woods, my division being on the left, with orders to connect with the 4th Corps. I had a hard task through the underbrush, up hill and down vale. I finally found Gen. Hazen commanding the [4th Corps'] right brigade. Returning towards the center to find Gen. Hooker [commanding the 20th Corps], I saw him ascending an open hill in front and followed with Gen. Knipe [commanding Williams' 1st Brigade]. Hooker had his escort deployed as skirmishers and was vigorously at work at the Rebel cavalry down in the valley in front. The Rebs had a battery on a small hill to our right and front and were firing it over our hill pretty energetically. We at length got up a rifled battery and some infantry and were making pretty rapid work with what was in our front.

Suddenly we saw, half a mile or more on our right, a great cloud of Rebel cavalry flying in disorder to the rear. There must have been a brigade of them and every man was kicking and spurring for dear life. Many horses were riderless. We opened on them with artillery, which greatly increased the disorder. It was laughable to see Hooker's excitement. "Williams," he would cry out, "see them run. They are thicker than flies on a Mexican ranch. See them go," and we all shouted, to the astonishment of our troops who had not got up. In truth our line of skirmishers that morning had one major general, two brigadier generals, and about fifteen poorly armed cavalry! We found the Rebel works a short distance in advance and took up a new line. The rain came down in torrents all the afternoon and night, and the mud seemed too deep to ever dry up.[47]

The Confederates' stay along Mud Creek was short-lived, however. Johnston discovered that "this disposition made an angle where Hardee's right joined Loring's left, which was soon found to be a great defect, for it exposed the troops near it to annoyance from enfilade, which should have been foreseen." Accordingly, Johnston ordered another retrograde move to new positions at Kennesaw Mountain. By morning of June 19, the Confederate defense line took the shape of a six-mile arc. Hood's corps remained massed on the right fronting Noonday Creek east of the railroad. Loring's corps of three divisions extended from the railroad over Big and Little Kennesaw mountains. Hardee's corps connected with Loring at Pigeon Hill, deploying on high ground running due south across the Dallas Road, with John Ward Creek, badly swollen by resumption of heavy rain, at its left flank. Wheeler's cavalry continued screening the army's right flank while Jackson's jaded troopers protected Hardee's left.[48]

of a stump, when a bullet came and buried itself in the ground going through a small stone between our heads, missing him about 3 inches and myself perhaps 6 inches. I put it in my pocket all bruised and battered by its contact with the stone. Commenced to rain Friday night [June 17] and all day Saturday it rained incessantly, and during that time we were under the most furious shelling I ever saw — got wet through to the skin lying sometimes in the water as it puddled under us, shoes, socks, clothes and all, which made me very cold."[45]

While Hardee's troops strengthened their Mud Creek line, Brigadier General William H. Jackson's cavalry division tried to retard the approaching 20th and 23rd corps "as well as twenty-five hundred men can contend with twenty-five thousand," wrote

Wounded in action

Throughout June 1864, the Atlanta Southern Confederacy published names of Army of Tennessee casualties on its front page. This one listed wounded soldiers brought to Marietta's Receiving and Distributing Hospital on just a single day, June 17.

R McCardle, co H, 29th Georgia, left thigh; M Sikes, co F, 1st Georgia, left hip; T D Trail, co F, 16th Alabama, right leg; W T Lennox, co F, 1st Confederate, both thighs; Corp J M Pierce, Jackson's Escort, left hip and arm; S F Martin, co A, 30th Tennessee, right breast; A B Leed, co H, 16th Alabama, right thigh; Corp W J Ray, co G, 1st Georgia, right leg; J A Hoard, co A, 30th Georgia, right arm amputated; Corp W J Bailey, co C, 1st Georgia, left arm and hip; D L Cole, co D, 1st Georgia, right leg; I J Robinson, co I, 5th Arkansas, left thigh; G W Gross, co K, 25th Georgia, left thigh; Capt G Y Barch, co I, 29th Georgia, both knees; H Hester, co G, 29th Georgia, right thigh; W B White, co K, 16th Alabama, left side; Lt R D Morgan, co B, 45th Mississippi, left knee; J A Hicks, co D, 33rd Alabama, left leg amputated; W H Clayton, co G, 1st Arkansas, left arm and breast.

Lt W V McCardle, co F, 29th Georgia, both thighs; J R Cheatham, co F, 16th Alabama, left leg; J B Holland, co F, 29th Georgia, left leg amputated; S J Carter, co G, 1st Georgia, left shoulder; G W Michael, co C, 32nd Mississippi, contusion; S W Moore, same, right hand; R D Mobley (musician), co I, 25th Georgia, left arm; A F Love, co D, 25th Georgia, left hand; W Powell, co D, 32nd Mississippi, left shoulder; Sergt W Q Anthony, co E, 30th Georgia, contusion.

D Fog, co H, 7th Florida, head; R H Durham, co E, 4th Tennessee, contusion; B Redman, co K, 50th Tennessee, left knee; W Wyatt, co G, 27th Tennessee, left arm; Sergt J S Green, co A, 1st Georgia, right arm; O H Wood, co K, 17th Texas, left thigh; A Johnson, co D, 37th Mississippi, left leg; J Etheridge, co F, 30th Tennessee, right leg; S B Hewitt, co G, 28th Tennessee, right thigh; W T Lewis, co I, 29th Georgia, left thigh; J W Armor, co G, 1st Georgia Sharpshooters, right thigh; P Darley, Cobb's Battery, face; J H Rollins, co K, 9th Texas, head; L T Bowers, co F, 46th Georgia, left hand; Corp A Lawless, co F, 1st Georgia, right thigh; Lt J Warren, co E, 24th South Carolina, left knee; H Johnson, co D, 8th Mississippi, left leg; W A Osborn, co B, 20th Alabama, left foot.

J S Call, co H, 7th Mississippi, right foot; Corp J Oneal, co E, 10th Tennessee, left leg; Sergt M Roach, co I, 10th Tennessee, right hip; C Holland, co K, 11th Texas Cavalry, left leg; Asst Surg Simmons, 31st Mississippi, right leg; J A Dickerson, co F, 1st Georgia, right thigh fractured; J Littleton, co D, 29th Alabama, hip and elbow; L H Moore, co K, 25th Georgia, right leg amputated; W L Thomas, co K, 1st Georgia Sharpshooters, left foot; Lt A Dozier, co K, 46th Georgia, head; D G Grantham, co F, 46th Mississippi, bowels; J W Parnell, co E, 29th Georgia, left shoulder; Corp R Grady, Key's Battery, left forefinger.

A B Summers, co F, 3rd Texas Cavalry, left side; J McAllister, Anderson's Battery, head severe; Corp R Hart, co K, 9th Kentucky, right wrist; H C Tanner, co I, 2nd and 6th Missouri, stomach; Lt I Lightner, Barret's Battery, both legs amputated; O S Morton, co I, 46th Georgia, arm; R H Wells, co I, 63rd Georgia, right shoulder; J Parchman, co E, 9th Texas Cav, both thighs; W S Sherman, co F, 2nd Mississippi Cavalry, left arm and side; Capt G W Summerville, Gen Jackson's Staff, leg severe; R L Carmichael, co F, 3rd Texas Cav, stomach; G Stacey, Barret's Battery, head; K Edwards, co K, 29th North Carolina, left hip; W A Walker, co F, 26th Tennessee, leg amputated; Lt L B Carter, co G, 1st Georgia, died from wounds.

The twin peaks of Kennesaw provided the Rebels with a natural citadel. "The lines of both armies can be seen plainly from the Mountain," observed Private Alexander Q. Porter of the 22nd Mississippi. "The scenery from the peak is magnificent beyond describing. It gives one an exalted idea of that supreme being who created all things." After being detailed as a signal station guard on Big Kennesaw, Corporal Zachariah J. Armistead of Company H, 42nd Georgia, informed a wounded brother back home: "It is a beautiful place to see everything. We see both lines of Battle from one end to the other. The yankees are fortifying their position, it looks as if they entend to stay over there. I can see them relieving their fatigue parties. Comeing and going they keep the step as if they were on a drill. Sharp shooting has become general along the lines. I am out of danger up here though." [49]

In spite of foul weather the Confederates transformed Kennesaw's crest, slopes and projecting spurs into a virtual fortress — impregnable, many of them believed, to direct assault. Rifle pits and forward trenches helped secure each corps' front. Hardee's artillery was placed to provide interlocking fields of fire against any advance debouching from the low areas. From the heights, wrote Captain William W. McMillan of the 17th Alabama, "We are well entrenched now ... and I think it would take more Yankees than you could pack into a fifty acre field to move us from our position." [50]

CHAPTER 4

The whole country is one vast fort

By the third week of June, the nature of fighting along the Kennesaw line had been well established. Although transpiring in the midst of a timbered wilderness, it presaged the kind of war waged five decades later in Europe when trenches, traverses, parapets and storming parties also were part of a soldier's vocabulary. Casualties occurred hourly every day and night, even without a pitched battle. "Indian fighting," a frustrated Sherman called the style of campaign he was being forced to conduct. "The whole country is one vast fort," he wired the War Department in Washington, "and Johnston must have full fifty miles of connected trenches, with abatis and finished batteries. Our lines are now in close contact and the fighting incessant, with a good deal of artillery. As fast as we gain one position the enemy has another all ready, but I think he will soon have to let go Kenesaw, which is the key to the whole country." [1]

In the meantime, gunfire continued to echo through the Georgia hills.

Private William M. McLain
Company B, 32nd Ohio
3rd Division, 17th Corps

Almost all our digging has to be done at night, to avoid the rebel sharp-shooters; and as the men work by reliefs, and I attend each relief and each working party, it keeps me from getting much sleep except in the daytime, when it is entirely too hot to sleep. Then, too, the moonlight nights of a week or two back, gave the rebels an excellent opportunity of supervising our work almost as closely as I did; and their supervision was not of as gentle a style as mine, since, where any thing in the shape of a trench went wrong (which means rebelward), they expressed their disapprobation loudly, and using harder metal than is put in *lead* pencils.

Musket firing at night, however, is not a scary thing when one gets used to it; and they have hitherto hurt but few out of our working parties. Thus the loss of sleep is the worst thing about the present position; but this is amply repaid to my mind by the excellent opportunities afforded me (being on our foremost line) of seeing every thing that is going on, and watching all their maneuvers, as well as frequently having an opportunity of trying my horse's

Mass. MOLLUS, USAMHI

speed rearward.

I may very appropriately date my letters from the trenches since I have not been out of them since the middle of this month. I'm so used to ditches and ditching, to scarps and counterscarps, lunettes, salients, re-entrant angles, bastions and lines of crests, that I expect when the war is over, I'll have to employ three hundred Irishmen (about the number of a night fatigue-party on our lines), and go about ditching farms by the wholesale! But I can hardly see my lines, and must postpone further scratching to-night, since to light a candle would be to draw on me a shower of rebel shell, as well as anathemas from the boys who are completing this work, which is a redoubt pierced for four guns, which we are throwing up in a thicket on the crest of a hill; it being nearly done, we shall unmask by cutting away the timber as soon as it is dark, and then — woe to the rebellious rifle-pits in front of us to-morrow, at daybreak! We shall have a band of brass 12-pounders to play reveille for the Johnnies, and they'll like it less than "Federal Doodle Dandy." [2]

Musician Fenwick Y. Hedley
Company C, 32nd Illinois
4th Division, 17th Corps

A line was generally entrenched almost as soon as it was established, some of the men carrying spades, and others rails, against which they threw a

• *Looking southwest past the remaining stalks of a trampled cornfield, Big Kennesaw looms over the Georgia countryside northwest of Marietta, with Little Kennesaw visible at left. This view of the twin peaks was afforded to many soldiers on the Federal left flank. Wrote Private Alonzo Miller of the 12th Wisconsin on June 14: "The Rebs have [Kennesaw] well fortified as they lay on the side of the mountain, and on the mountain they have some large guns we can see. Sherman has driven Johnston out of some strong works by flanking him. Maybe he will drive him still by trying to flank him off of the mountain."*

little dirt. On level ground they sometimes dug a hole, in which to kneel down or stand up, so that they might peer over at their enemy. The best work in constructing these slight but valuable fortifications was often done by night, and the morning nearly always found the skirmish-line better prepared to inflict injury upon the enemy than it had been the night before. Frequently two or three men would occupy the same hole, and then all sorts of devices were used to circumvent the enemy. One would raise his cap on a ramrod to draw his fire, while a comrade took the opportune moment to spot the Gray who took the bait. Often the skirmishers were obliged to leave shelter before they had

Mass. MOLLUS, USAMHI

• *Federal skirmishers fire at concealed opponents near the base of Kennesaw Mountain in this Alfred R. Waud drawing. They occupy shallow earthen pits, universally termed "gopher holes."*

"warmed their holes," as they expressed it, to make a sudden dash upon the enemy.

If the Blue line made itself particularly annoying to the Gray, and being the assailant, it generally did this daily, the enemy would sweep the ground with grape, canister and shell, provoking a warm return fire from the federal artillery. This usually quieted both skirmish lines, and the occupants of the rival rifle-pits would remain under cover until the artillery duel was over, when they would blaze away at each other with more spirit than before. A storm had the same effect. No matter how severe the skirmish-

ing might be, it would speedily die away under the effects of a rain; and as soon as the sun shone out again, the firing would recommence with redoubled vigor, regardless of provocation or possible result.

A figure on the skirmish line was a vagabondish fellow. He conducted his part of the campaign entirely after his own fashion. Armed with a rifle [sometimes] having telescopic sights, and laden with a spade, a couple of haversacks of provisions, and a brace of canteens, he would find an eligible location, dig a hole, and stay there until his rations or ammunition were exhausted, when he would go to the rear for a fresh supply, only to return and resume his murderous work. He was a dead shot, and the terror of the enemy's artillerists, whose guns he had frequently silenced.

The line of battle was habitually from one to five hundred yards in rear of the skirmish line, the distance depending greatly upon the conformation of the ground, and always strongly entrenched. The men were as expert in the use of the spade and the ax as with the rifle, and two hours' work made a very fair protection. Earth was thrown up to the height of two or three feet, sometimes higher. Frequently head-logs were placed upon the parapet, the ends resting upon skids leaning inwardly, and to the ground. The space between the head-log and the parapet permitted the troops to aim their rifles at the enemy with little exposure of themselves, while the skids provided a way for the head-log to reach the ground without doing injury to the men, in the event of its being dislodged by a cannon ball. Immediately behind these works the troops erected their shelter tents. They were not allowed to leave their quarters, but were kept continually on the ground, ready to move forward at any moment to support the skirmish line, make an onslaught upon the enemy, or to resist an attack. No music was permitted, and frequently fires were forbidden. The latter regulation was, however, a dead letter, except in very rare cases, where the men themselves could actually see its necessity by immediate danger. Coffee was their staff of life, and they must have it, no matter what risk attended. The most disheartening event that could happen to a soldier was to be called into line just as his coffee pot was about to bubble.

It is highly suggestive of the unbounded self-confidence of this army, that there was never bad news from any part of itself. It would not affect the general result, and the corps which had come to grief, would make up for it to-morrow or the day after. But after every story, probable and improbable, had been told and commented upon, and after the men had exhausted their ideas with reference to the immediate future, all would agree that nobody knew anything about it, except "Uncle Billy," and that he was a "long-headed cuss" who "would work it out all right." Fertile subjects for discussion at these veritable camp-fires were the occurrences on the skirmish line, the men who had just come in, leading off, narrating with remarkable vividness and vigor of expression every incident of the day.

"Between deals" the good and the bad traits of those who had "turned up their toes," as the boys expressed it, were discussed with remarkable freedom, and the old adage *de mortuis nil nisi bonum* was set at utter defiance. If, as sometimes happened, a soldier had been killed near the skirmish line while looking on, it was unanimously voted that he

Sergeant Major John W. Green, 9th Kentucky

was "a damned fool," and "it served him right" — there were opportunities enough for a man to be killed while in the strict line of duty, without poking around where he had no business. Not that these men were heartless, but they regarded death as a necessary and familiar incident to soldiering, and they had grown into the habit of putting the best face upon their surroundings. It would have been a spiritless army if the troops had gone into mourning over every comrade lost. [3]

Sergeant Major John W. Green
9th Kentucky Infantry, CSA
Bate's Division, Hardee's Corps

June 20th, 1864. Fighting & entrenching all day. Late in the evening the yanks made quite a determined assault which we repulsed. We drove them back far enough to be able to put out picketts in front of our regular line. The pickets have built defenses with rails known as rail pens. They help a good deal in a fight with infantry but if they bring up the artillery to play upon them they are worse than nothing; if a cannon ball dont hit you, it is almost sure to hit the pen & the pieces of rails will knock you out. That night entrenching tools were sent out to the pickets & they worked for dear life digging rifle pits to protect those on duty for they knew there would be great need of them when day light came. The enemy opened the artillery on us trying to prevent our entrenching but our boys worked hard & had good pits by day light.

The enemy have moved up in force & entrenched in point blank range so that there is constant firing both from our trenches & from theirs. Any one who shows his head above the trenches is sure to have two or three minnie balls come singing around his ears, but we soon got so accustomed to it that the boys grew very careless. I had to pass along the line to give orders for the pickets to be ready to go out after dark to relieve those who had been on duty all day. I noticed Tom Wimms laying on the ground outside of the trenches, [and] I said, "Tom dont lay out there; that ball that struck that tree did not miss you six inches."

His reply was, "I am sleepy for I was out there on picket all last night & I am going to have a good stretched out sleep if they kill me for it." I passed on down the line & came back within ten minutes & poor Tom had received his death wound; a yankee bullet had passed clear through him. [4]

Captain Oscar L. Jackson
Company H, 63rd Ohio
4th Division, 16th Corps

June 16th. I am sent on the skirmish line with my own company and Company C of our regiment. *Noon.* We are having spirited fighting. We have rifle pits and logs for protection. The enemy have the same about 70 yards distant and the least exposure of a man brings a shower of balls. The general commanding informs me he thinks it probable our lines will be assaulted soon and cautions me to be on my guard. *Later.* Nary an assault. A company of the 27th Ohio on my left is suffering severely. One officer of that company [First Lieutenant James F. Day, Company K] was killed and another wounded. *Sunset.* We are relieved. Have had one man killed in Company C and several slight wounds in the two companies.

I have expended some 6,000 rounds of ammunition and my men did not fire without seeing an enemy. Our boys would raise a hat on a ramrod and it would bring a half dozen balls. With a glass I detected the rebels at the same game. But we have seen them bearing off killed or wounded to such an extent that I feel confident we have punished them severely for what we have suffered. At one time we hung a blanket tightly rolled on the corner of a log building nearby us and a rebel shot a bullet into it. On examining it I found the ball in the blanket, though it had passed through 16 thicknesses of a wool blanket.

Gen. [John W.] Fuller, commanding 2nd Brigade of our division, came to my lines and spoke a little short about my not conforming to the direction of his skirmish line and also about us shooting too much when no enemy was near enough to make it effective. I was well acquainted with him, and I told him I thought his men on his skirmish line were in a poor position and all the entrenching they had done was at least useless, and our boys had great sport at seeing him, half an hour after leaving us, move his skirmish line to conform in direction with ours.

About the time he was ready to leave me he looked to the front through a crack in the log building behind which we were sheltered, and asked me what rifle pits those were which he saw just a few yards in my front. I told him they were the enemy's and just then some sharpshooters rose out of them and fired, which was the signal for the enemy to open briskly on my entire line, dropping balls thickly all around us. The general found the enemy plenty close for shooting and asked me which way I thought the safest for him to get out of that. I showed him and he started on the run. The incident rather gratified me for the short remark he had made about my men firing at "no enemy" as he had expressed himself at first. On our return to camp when we were relieved in the evening we found that our regiment had constructed deep rifle pits and regular gopher holes for shelter of the officers.

June 17th. The usual skirmishing commenced at daylight. We were aroused once last night by an attack on the skirmish line. We lay in position in and near our rifle pits. The enemy's skirmishers' bullets flew over us. We had men killed and wounded right among us during the day.

Michael G. Kraus

Captain Oscar L. Jackson, Company H, 63rd Ohio

June 18th, 1864. Raining, raining and the men have no shelter. Skirmish firing goes on as usual. The Army of the Cumberland on our right has had considerable of a fight this forenoon and appears to have advanced its lines considerably.

4:30 p.m. Benjamin McCarter of my company severely wounded by a musket ball in the groin, said by the surgeon to be mortal. I have my tent fly up a short distance in rear of the rifle pits and a few minutes ago a rifle ball went through one of the pins holding it, not more than a foot and a half from the ground and passed on, fortunately hurting no one.

Later. The surgeon now thinks McCarter's wound not so serious and that he may recover. *Dusk.* My company goes out on the skirmish line. *8:00 p.m.* The rebs are very talkative and our boys and they have great sport joking one another as our

rifle pits are in good talking distance. The rebs propose that we do not fire during the night, to which our boys agree and a truce is thus made without the officers saying a word. *Later.* The boys keep up conversation till near midnight and nary a shot fired by either party along our line, although firing continues to the right and left of us.

June 19th, 1864. Break of day. Can get no word of the enemy. There is no firing and they will not talk. We are now doubtful whether they are in their rifle pits or not. We fire on their works and get no reply. I guess they are gone. *Daylight.* We find that the enemy has evacuated his first line of works. My company is relieved as skirmishers. I examine the ground we have been fighting over on the skirmish line for the last few days and the effects of the shot exceed anything I have ever seen. I do not see how the rebels stayed in their gopher holes at all. The advance of the Army of the Cumberland on our right yesterday, although with severe fighting, has been the cause of the enemy's falling back, as their works in our front, although very formidable, are now untenable.

1:00 p.m. We have advanced our line and find that the enemy has only left his advance, or first series of works, and still holds Kennesaw Mountain and a contiguous line of heavy fortifications. We pass over ground strongly fortified by breastworks and rifle pits and protected by abatis of felled trees on a ground densely crowded with underbrush, chinkapin, etc. I feel well satisfied that the long lines of heavy works we are passing are not occupied by the enemy and that as we are picking our way through tangled brush no shriek of shot or shell is around us.

3:00 p.m. Our skirmishers and artillery are feeling the enemy and there is heavy fighting near by our right. *Sunset.* Our skirmish line has reached the base of Kennesaw Mountain and is having brisk work. The mountain is very high and rugged, surpassing Lookout Mountain in these respects. Its top is frequently among the clouds. *Later.* We are making a temporary breastwork of logs and stone. There has been considerable fighting both right and left of us. The railroad runs between our present position and the base of the mountain and just now our men run a locomotive down the track to get water in plain view of the enemy, in fact nearer them than our main line. Our men cheered like they were

• Reserve picket posts, like this Federal one photographed near Atlanta during late summer of 1864, were commonly found along both armies' lines. Of the nine soldiers pictured here, two are officers. The building at left was stripped of boards to aid in construction of a rude breastwork.

Blue Acorn Press

wild, which, with the impudence of the trick, caused the rebels to try to bring their artillery to bear on the locomotive. The distance was short, but the mountain was so high they could not depress their guns enough and the shot and shell flew away over, but some dropped close enough to alarm us for our safety as we thought they could not possibly shell us from the mountain. [5]

Private Jabez P. Cannon
Company C, 27th Alabama
Featherston's Division, Loring's Corps

Saturday, June 18 — Our regiment went on picket early last night and stood all night in a drenching rain. Just before day our company was moved forward about 300 yards in front of the regiment, deployed 10 paces apart, and ordered to keep a close watch, as the enemy was nearby; and, indeed, we

soon found that such was the case. As soon as it got light enough we could see their picket-line less than 100 yards from us, and saluting each other "good morning," both sides took such cover as was at hand, behind trees, logs, stumps, etc. We had a "hide and seek" game all the morning, firing every time we could get a glimpse of each other, and several of our boys got wounded, one very seriously.

About 2 p.m. a squad of 15 or 20 Yankees crawled down a ravine and got possession of a log house halfway between the lines. This exposed those of us who were on the right of the house to a cross-fire, and our trees were not large enough to cover us in front and flank at the same time. When we dodged from one we were exposed to the other, and vice versa.

It was the worst scrape I ever got into, and I had rather take my chances in a regular battle than another such. They made it so hot that something had to be done, and that very quickly. We couldn't stay there, so we sent a courier back and reported the situation to Col. [James] Jackson, who very promptly brought up a detachment from the regiment, charged the house and drove the Yankees back to their picket-line, to our great relief and delight; but it cost us several casualties.

Col. Jackson had his arm shattered above the elbow, so it will have to be amputated. The Colonel was shot through the chest at First Manassas while a private in the 4th Alabama, on account of which wound he was discharged, and afterwards assisted in raising the 27th Alabama, with which he has been connected since December 1861.

After dislodging the Yanks from the house we felt comparatively safe behind our trees, but took good care not to expose ourselves any more than necessary, and spent the remainder of the evening shooting at each other at every opportunity.[6]

Sergeant William P. Chambers
Company B, 46th Mississippi
French's Division, Loring's Corps

At 11 o'clock p.m. [June 18] we were silently withdrawn and followed the command in another retrograde movement. Great quantities of rain had fallen during the past twenty-four hours, and everything was covered with mud.

On this retreat it will be understood that the main portion of our line was not disturbed at all, only the center falling back some two or three miles. On Kennesaw Mountain was our next position where we remained just two weeks. I think I never experienced more that was unpleasant in the same length of time. Our brigade was on Little Kennesaw, and we had to do picket duty at its base. The pickets were changed after nightfall, and it was no pleasant thing to clamber up and down almost perpendicular cliffs for nearly half a mile. The first week of our stay was one of almost continuous raining. We had no fuel and consequently our clothing was wet all the time. Then the rains ceased, the weather became hot and our supply of water rapidly failed. Added to these unpleasant features was the fact that the enemy had perhaps fifty pieces of artillery bearing upon the mountain, and that almost every part of its top and sides was exposed to the fire of these pieces. For days we had seen the huge bulk of Kennesaw in

our rear, and as we marched in that direction on that Saturday night, the wish was frequently expressed that our brigade might be posted on its summit, and sure enough, we were.

It was a dreary prospect on which we opened our eyes on Sunday morning, June 19th. In fact, we were literally enveloped in the clouds. Nothing could be seen save a lead-colored mist that saturated one's clothing almost as quickly as a rain. Presently the mist began to gather into vast billows, between which rifts appeared. As these rifts grew wider we caught glimpses of the country below. Gradually as the sun arose, the clouds were lifted higher and I could soon distinguish the position we had occupied the previous day. I saw the enemy make a gallant charge upon our deserted works and he doubtless carried them without the loss of a man. I saw his brigades and divisions debouching on the great plain below. First came a line of skirmishers to be closely followed by heavy lines of infantry and sections of artillery. A small detachment of our cavalry was in the enemy's front. Frequently they halted, where I suppose the ground was favorable, and as the Federal skirmishers came in sight they would fire a volley at them. This would always cause confusion, but quickly rallying they would boldly advance to find our troops had retreated to another position. This was so often repeated that it became a source of diversion to us who were merely lookers-on.

For miles in the enemy's rear the country was spread out like a map. His wagon trains were parked on a hundred open fields, and thousands of tents that sheltered his soldiers were visible from where we stood. By 10 o'clock a.m. his skirmishers had approached near enough to engage ours. Close behind them came his artillery. One reason why we had desired to be posted on the mountain was because we thought the position too elevated for cannon shot to reach us. We saw directly in front of us a battery placed in position in an open field. We had formed our line across the side of the mountain some fifty feet below its crest, feeling perfectly secure without any breastworks at all.

The first shot from the battery in our front fell at the base of the mountain, and we cheered derisively. The next shot came half way up the side, and the cheering was much fainter than before. The third shot struck the rocky cliff above our heads and instead of cheers, there was anxious looking for spots that would afford some protection. The third shot was instantly followed by a fourth, which cut a member of Company A in two. Our line was then placed on the crest of the ridge, where in some places ledges of rock formed a safe retreat from a direct fire.

During the afternoon a very heavy shower came up, and as I stood partially protected by my dripping blanket I had a worse fit of the "blues" — felt more despondent, in fact, than at any other time during the whole campaign.[7]

Private Chauncey H. Cooke
Company G, 25th Wisconsin
4th Division, 16th Corps

Dear Parents: Had just nicely finished my notes for yesterday in my diary when we were ordered to fall in for picket duty on the skirmish line. There was no hesitation on the part of any of the boys. They knew well enough what it meant. It was just as if the southern army was invading Buffalo county,

not a man of them knowing a foot of the country, yet they were expected by their officers to hold their own against the native inhabitants, who knew every road and bypath and hill and valley. The rebels had their lines already made. Under cover of the night our lines were pushed close to theirs. We made a bargain with them that we would not fire on them if they would not fire on us, and they were as good as their word.

It seems too bad that we have to fight men that we like. Now these southern soldiers seem just like our own boys, only they are on the other side. They talk about their people at home, their mothers and fathers and their sweethearts, just as we do among ourselves. Both sides did a lot of talking back and forth, but there was no shooting until I came off duty in the morning. The next relief that went on kept up a constant fire all day long. It rained so hard all the forenoon the boys were in the water over their shoe tops in the trenches. This is just about the 99th time it has rained since this campaign commenced, and it's no drizzle drozzle like we have in Wisconsin, but a regular downpour.[8]

• *Confederates of Loring's corps were able to gaze for miles from the summit of Big Kennesaw, as illustrated in this view looking slightly northwest. An embankment containing tracks of the Western & Atlantic Railroad can be discerned cutting across the lower plain. Federal troops of the 16th Corps approached Big Kennesaw from the distant woods.*

Mass. MOLLUS, USAMHI

Captain James L. Burkhalter
Company F, 86th Illinois
2nd Division, 14th Corps

Sunday, June 19, 1864. The enemy has again stole off under cover of night and left the way open for us to proceed forward a short distance closer to the mountain. We moved out early just a brief way and stacked arms, then waited for other troops to move ahead. While pausing here and waiting developments on the front, the infernal Georgia sky opened and sent down the most torrential downpour imaginable. I can't imagine where all the rain comes from or just why it always seems to strike us.

Mud became so deep that it was virtually impossible to move a step. Heavy skirmishing has been going on near the foot of the mountain; occasionally heavy artillery fired from our batteries, directed on the signal station on the highest point of Kenesaw Mountain. After considerable firing from the batteries and an eternal crackling of musketry nearly until sundown, we again moved forward and took position at the foot of the mountain and on a little ridge, which was separated from the mountain by a very small stream running along our front.

As it has rained most of the day, everyone is soaking wet. The Colonel commanding thought that a little *spiritas fermenti* might be a good thing to stimulate the weary soldier after this thorough drenching and the many sleepless nights he had spent since the campaign began.

Great care was taken in issuing the liquor, but notwithstanding all the care, some of the men became beastly intoxicated and raved about the camp like mad men. More especially so in the 22nd Indiana, several of whom had to be tied to trees until they became sober, before they could be made to behave themselves. [9]

First Lieutenant Hamilton M. Branch
Company F, 54th Georgia
Walker's Division, Hardee's Corps

June 19th 1864
My Very Dear Mother

After writing to you on the 17th we were moved about 3/4 mile to the right and put into the front trenches near the Marietta road. my company was then ordered out on picket but Genl Hardee considering it dangerous for us to go out in the day ordered

Richard F. Carlile

• *First Sergeant Robert M. Buck, Company B, 86th Illinois, exemplified the determined veterans comprising a majority of Sherman's forces. Serving his entire three-year enlistment as Company B's orderly sergeant, Buck was photographed in a Nashville studio wearing a commercially produced sack coat without chevrons.*

us to wait until night fall and so we stacked our arms and eat our dinner. the enemy then commenced shelling us and shelled us very heavyly for about 1 hour. at dark we went out in front of our breastworks, that is four of our companys with mine on the right. we were then deployed on the left file of the left company and advanced to form a new line of pickets, as the pickets from Genl Cheathams division whom we were to relieve had been driven in. my company was

Atlanta History Center

*First Lieutenant Hamilton M. Branch
Company F, 54th Georgia*

the only one that herd the order and advanced. we advanced about 500 yards when we met Genl C's pickets and I relieved them and found that there was no one on my left, and I immediately went back to try and find them which I did and was bringing them up when the enemy charged my company and were driven back. I then joined my left to the right of the other companies and prepared to fortify a picket line in the rear of the pickets. we worked all night but did not finish fortifying. the enemy attempted to make another advance but faded during the night. a little before day I put my men into the pits and made ready for the enemy, it then commenced raining and rained hard until about 9 o'clock. I made my boys fire as often as they could during the rain so as to try and keep their loads dry. the pit that I was in ... became half full of water and I suppose the others were the same, and about 1/4 8 I found that not a gun in my pit would fire.

About 1/4 9 it stopped raining and the enemy advanced to my right and extended down just past the left of my company. when they arrived about 40 yds from me I gave the order to rise and fire. the men then got up and told me that the men on my right had fallen back. the men tried to fire but not a gun would fire. seeing then that the men on my right had fallen away back, I gave the order to fall back which we did, the enemy advancing with two lines of skirmishers supported by lines of battle. they advanced until within sight of our batterys, when they opened on them and the men with the stars and stripes fell back. our men, all but my company and Cos. A & C, were then ordered to advance and three Cos of the 1st Ga to assist them, they advanced and skirmished with the enemy until night. the skirmishing was very heavy.

I will now give you an account of my self. I sat in the pit until I was cramped all over and chilled. I could not stand up because the breastworks was not high enough and the enemy were fireing the whole time. when I got up I could hardly move. after getting out of the pit, I stoped to look back after my company to see if they were all right. I found that two of the men in my pit were not out. I then told them to get out which they did. I then fell back and got behind the breastworks. as soon as the enemy were driven back by our cannon I was ordered out again, and I reported that not a gun in my company would fire and [was] ordered to go and have the loads drawn. I had already ordered Lt. [Charles C.] Hunter to take what men I had with me and carry them out, which he started to do but was shot before he got over the breastworks. he was shot high up in the hip, severe but not dangerous.

In the mean time I was looking up the rest of my company who were around the fires in the brigade trying to dry themselves. Lt. [Phillip R.] Falligant then came up and informed me that Lt. H was wounded and I then told him to carry them, the men, around to the brigade ordnance train and I would meet him there. we went there and was informed that the loads could not be drawn and that I had better see Capt Harden who was a mile and a half off. I then told Lt. F to take the company back to the breastworks and that I would try and see Capt H. Lt. F did this and was shot very slightly in the calf of the leg.

I and Sam Dowse went to look after Capt H but could not find him. I then went into a house and tried to dry myself and then went to sleep and slept

The hardest day I ever seen

On June 20 along Noonday Creek northeast of Big Kennesaw, some 1,100 Confederate troopers of "Fighting Joe" Wheeler's corps clashed with half of Kenner Garrard's division in what General Johnston called "the most considerable cavalry affair of the campaign."

Garrard's 1st Brigade, commanded by Colonel Robert H.G. Minty, was scouting south of the swollen creek when its detachments were attacked at 4 p.m. by Wheeler's mounted men, wielding sabers and firing pistols. Charge was met by countercharge during four hours of fighting. Rebel trooper Russell Mann, a private in Company C, 9th Kentucky Cavalry, recalled: "When the charge was sounded, [we] dashed across an open field to the creek under a heavy fire at short range. This creek on account of heavy rains was deep. Some few of the horses bounded over the creek, and the rest of the regiment was hurriedly forwarded into line and dismounted, and under a heavy fire renewed the charge on foot, wading the creek waist-deep and forcing the enemy back in confusion ... completely routing and driving them back two miles."

Private Daniel M. Garland of Company H, 7th Pennsylvania Cavalry, informed his wife three days later of the "brisk fight with the rebs. We charged them, and they charged us. We lost a good many and so did the Rebs." It "was the hardest day I ever seen."

Minty's line was bent back in the shape of a horseshoe, with a bridge crossing Noonday Creek in his rear. "Most of our horses were still southeast of the creek," he lamented, "which [was] perfectly impassable for either man or horse except on the bridge, and even there the [creek] bottom, about half a mile in width, was in such a condition that horses were up to their girths in the mud and floating rails ...."

His three outnumbered regiments were "saved" by well-timed fire from the division's Chicago Board of Trade battery and arrival of reinforcements from the mounted Lightning Brigade, armed with Spencer rifles. Still, the outcome was in doubt, as described by Private William F. Keay of Company D, 17th Indiana: "You had better believe the Bullets flew thick like hail. Going to fight we crossed on a bridge but coming back they had us cut off and we had to wade or get taken in. In I went up to my chin and gun and everything, it was hard work. We had to run 2 miles. We were tired and thirsty and hungry but we built fires and tried cooking supper out of muddy water and slept at our Breastworks."

Both sides claimed victory. Total losses ranged from 130 to more than 200.

Blue Acorn Press

Major General Joseph Wheeler

Mass. MOLLUS, USAMHI

Brigadier General Kenner Garrard

until dusk. I then found that we were preparing to fall back and as I was barefooted thought I had better go ahead which Sam and I did. we went until we arrived in Marietta where we found that the army was not coming back that far, but was agoing to stop about 1 1/2 miles from Marietta. we then went to bed upstairs in the Marietta Hotel and slept until morning. hearing here that Lt. F was wounded I thought that I had best go back which I did but found that Lt. F did not have to go to the rear. if I had known this I would have stayed and tryed to get me a pair of shoes in Marietta. I have been barefooted two days and it is pretty hard although by the time you get this I will have received a pair. if it were not for the rocks I could get along better. [10]

Private Franklin A. Whitney
Company F, 36th Illinois
2nd Division, 4th Corps

June 20th/1864
Dear Father

It is with pleasure that I set down to answer your letter of the 10th, knowing that you was anxious to hear from me. Yesterday the 36th was on the skirmish line and we had a prity warm time of it but the rest of the regt. sufered more than Co F that only had one man wounded. A ball struck his belt buckle and brused him prity bad and he then started for the rear and stubed his toes and fell down and hurt his chin, that is as I hurd it. The balls was flying so thick that I thought it wasent best to go and see him, and I saw 8 rebs no more than ten paces from me that I wanted to punch, and you ought of seen one of them throw his gun, clap his hand to his behind and run.

We drove them till we got [to] the other side of the crick. Then the brush was so thick that we couldent see ten feet a head of us and first we knew we was all mixed up with the rebs. Then a reble major jumped up and ordered his men to fix bayonets but didn't stop to see whether they did it or not, but steped right into our lines with a drawn saber and yells out whose command is this. We replied by presenting our guns to his breast and asked him to give up his sword. He did so but it hurt his feelings very mutch.

It wasent more than ten minutes after that when a whole brigade threw themselves on to us and we

had to skedadle or be gobbled. Some of the boys was, but escaped. We fell back to some breastworks and hold them now. Meby you would like to know whare we are. Well we are at [Kennesaw] Mountain on the southwest side. The rebs are on and around the foot of it and we are so close that we can see them on the side of the mountain. [11]

Sergeant John W. Hagan
Company K, 29th Georgia
Walker's Division, Hardee's Corps

June 21st 1864
My Dear Wife

We had a fight day before yesterday. We had a close time & lost a grate many in Killed & wounded & missing. The 29th charged the yankees & drove them back near 1/2 mile. I can not give a list of the Killed & wounded in the fight. In Capt [Edwin B.] Carrolls company there was only one killed dead & sevarl wounded. Lt J.U. Roberts was Killed dead in the charge & Sergt J.L. Roberts of our company was Killed dead & Corpl Lindsey wounded. I was in the fight & never got hurt. our Regt is very much deminished. Capt Knight is in command of the Regt. Capt Knight and Capt Carroll is all there is in the Regt, the companies is all commanded by Lieuts & Sergts. I have been in command of our company 3 days. Lieut [Jonas] Tomlinson stays along but pretends to be so sick he can not go in a fight but so long as I keepe the right side up Co K will be all right. The most of the boys have lost confidence in Lt Tomlinson.

As a general thing our Regt has behaved well. I do not Know as I have Killed a yankee but I have been shooting among them. You must not be uneasy about me. We have our chances to take the Same as others & if we fall remember we fell in a noble cause & be content that we was so lotted to die, but we hope to come out all right. I have bin hit twice but it was with Spent Balls & did not hurt me much. I havent time to write much but if we can find out how many we lost on the 19th & 20th I will give a statement.

June 22 1864

I wrote to you yesterday but I was in agrate hurry & could not give you the casualties of the Regt. Up to yesterday 6 oclock p.m. we had 83 men Killed wounded & missing. This is only the casual-

Mass. MOLLUS, USAMHI

Brigadier General Walter C. Whitaker

ties since the 14th of this month & what it was in May I do not Know. I do not beleave any of Co G have writen to Jasper [Roberts] mother about his death & if you get this before She hears the correct reports you can tell her he was in the fight of the 19th & was Killed dead in a charge. he was gallantly leading & cheering his men on to Battle and was successfull in driving back the yankees. he was taken off the Battle field & was Berried as well as the nature of the case would permit.

Our Regt sufferd agrate deal on the 19th & some on the 20th. I was in the hotest of this fight & it Seemes that thousand of Balls whisled near my head, but I was protected. Heavy fighting is now &

has been going on for some time on our right & left & I beleave the bloodiest Battle of the war will come off in a short time & I feel confident that when the yankees pich in to us right we will give them a whiping, but Gen Johnston does not entend to make the attack on them.[12]

Private William L. Trask
Headquarters courier
Hardee's Corps

Sunday, June 19th — Cannonading today, heavy on both sides. Tonight the army was withdrawn two miles farther South. Roads in inexorable condition and almost impassable; rain fell nearly all night.

Monday, June 20th — At noon the enemy advanced and attacked our lines but were easily repulsed. Shelling continued heavy all day. Many fell around our quarters and a [shell] took a cavalryman's leg clean off near by us while he was in the act of feeding his horse. Another fell in the campfire a few feet from us while we were eating dinner. We changed our base suddenly. The top of Kennesaw came in for a share of the shelling and one of the signal corps was wounded. Our quarters are now within two miles of Marietta and the citizens are rapidly leaving that town expecting it soon to be inside the enemy's lines.[13]

Brigadier General Walter C. Whitaker
2nd Brigade commander
1st Division, 4th Corps

June 19, the rebels, being hard pressed, had again vacated their position and left their formidable works. We pursued along the road to Marietta. Between two and three miles the enemy were again found in force in strong earth-works. This brigade went into line with heavy skirmishing, the right of my skirmishers having to wade and stand in a swamp with the water above the knees.

June 20, advanced my front line and again threw up strong works; the enemy's position was such that he could enfilade as far as the range of his guns our lines, right and left. I was ordered to dislodge him. My skirmishers, under the command of Lieutenant-Colonel [James] Watson, were strengthened and advanced. The Twenty-first Kentucky, Colonel [Samuel W.] Price commanding, was ordered to storm the first line of works. The Fifty-first Ohio, Colonel [Richard W.] McClain, was ordered to support, while the pioneers of the brigade were held in readiness to fortify immediately any ground taken. The skirmishers having advanced, at 4 p.m. the assault was made.

It was one of the most brilliant and successful assaults of the war. So rapidly and effectively was it done that the great bulk of the rebels occupying the works were killed or taken prisoners. The officers and men of the Twenty-first charged beyond this line, and up to within a few yards of their main lines. The color-sergeant, Henry Bryant, being wounded, Sergt. William L. Lanham seized the colors, and bearing them forward was in the act of mounting the parapet of the enemy's main works when he was fatally shot. The men with him brought back their colors to the first line of works, where they firmly maintained themselves until the Fifty-first Ohio and the pioneers [arrived], making the works more tenable. They were relieved from their

position by the Ninety-ninth Ohio, which formed on the left of the Fifty-first. The Ninety-sixth Illinois was formed on my extreme right, and the Thirty-fifth Indiana on my extreme left, the Fortieth Ohio, Eighty-fourth Indiana and Twenty-first Kentucky now forming the rear line. This disposition of forces was made with celerity, but none too soon to secure the important position taken from the rebels.

Two rebel regiments were sent to recover the lost ground. They boldly advanced to within a few rods of my line and were mowed down by the deadly fire of my men. The contest was again renewed with additional forces by the enemy to regain their lost ground. Boldly they advanced, but as boldly were they repulsed. Three brigades from night-fall till 11 o'clock at night made desperate and persevering assaults to recover the lost position.

Five companies on the right of the Thirty-fifth Indiana were driven by superior numbers from their position, and the enemy gained a lodgment in my line. 'Twas dark. Friend and foe were mixed. Major [John P.] Dufficy [35th Indiana] fell rallying his men. Colonel [John E.] Cummins, with the Ninety-ninth Ohio, repelled from his left flank, while the Fifty-first Ohio and Ninety-sixth Illinois drove them from their front. It was a time of peril and great danger, but ordering forward the Fortieth Ohio, those soldiers soon drove out the rebels from their lodgment on my line in wild disorder and with heavy loss. It was a most fiercely and deadly contested battle-ground. In two instances coming under my observation the bayonets of the loyal and rebel soldiers were found in each other's person. My loss was 273 killed, wounded and missing.[14]

First Lieutenant Chesley A. Mosman
Company D, 59th Illinois
Pioneer officer, 1st Division, 4th Corps

The skirmish line, Whitaker's Brigade, charges and took a hill in our front. Our Regiment got a severe shelling but no one was hurt. Still, it rattles ones nerves somewhat to have 12 pounders lighting within 20 feet of you, or whistling overhead. The first line gained 300 yards at one point and we moved up to the first line. The 9th Ind. lose 18 in building works on the line they advanced to. Our Regiment relieves the 9th Ind. Pioneers stay back on the old line. Our Battery opens on the Johnnies

The Rough Side of War

First Lieutenant Chesley A. Mosman

Mass. MOLLUS, USAMHI

• *Field glasses in hand, Colonel P. Sidney Post, 59th Illinois, posed early in 1864 with other officers on the nose of Lookout Mountain. He was severely wounded at the battle of Nashville in December 1864, and later was awarded a Medal of Honor.*

column of Rebels had quietly come down a ravine and entered the works thus vacated and when the men of the 35th, unconscious of the presence of the Rebels, jumped down into the works the Rebels who lay on the outer slope stuck their guns over and ordered them to surrender, when the ball opened in good earnest and lasted for some 30 minutes. The Rebels got the [major] and some 40 men but were finally driven out and the works retaken by the 35th, with the aid of the 40th Ohio, the regiment that was to have relieved the 35th.

We got mixed up in this night attack for the right of our Regiment joined the left of the 35th Ind. in relieving the 9th as we had done (the 35th and our Regiment being on the same line of works). Our Col. Post went to the right of the Regiment and found that men in the works, where the 35th should have been, were shooting right down the line at his men. Post went for them, yelling "Cease firing! You are shooting your men," but he got a volley with the information emphasized by oaths and bad language. "I know who I am shooting at." This night fighting on ground you don't know is rather nervous work but quiet was soon restored by driving the Johnnies back. When the 9th Ind. got back to the reserve line my pioneers had gone to bed and the commanding officer wanted us to move out but we declined to do so. The bullets flew pretty thick while the contest over the works was going on. [15]

Sergeant Israel A. Correll
Company A, 51st Ohio
1st Division, 4th Corps

Mon. June 20

After getting out to the skirmish line we went to work and built breast works. Considerable firing all night which is kept up this morning. Worked on the breast works all day. *4 p.m.* The Brigade is preparing for a charge which they did in fine style, captur-

who reply with a vengeance. Eighteen Rebel cannon join in their reply. Enemy's guns in front of Whitaker are able to enfilade our first line and battery, but Newton's artillery comes to our Batteries and for a while the roar was continuous.

The 35th Ind. held the front line in Whitaker's Brigade and about 10 p.m., thinking the regiment that was to relieve them from picket duty had arrived, the colonel [Major Dufficy] ordered them to fall back and dress their lines, leaving the works unoccupied. Finding he had made a mistake the [major] ordered them back into the works. Meanwhile a

Sergeant Israel A. Correll, Company A, 51st Ohio, was promoted to second lieutenant in June 1865.

Brad L. Pruden

First Lieutenant Frank Shriver, Company B, 51st Ohio, died July 9 of wounds received June 20 near Kennesaw.

ing a great many prisoners. After they got fairly started we joined them and went to the top of the hill [a spur of Kennesaw Mountain] when we went to work and made breast works. About dark companies A, F and D were moved to the right and joined the balance of the regiment. Company A having no breast works we had to go to work and make some. Before we got them finished the rebs charged our lines and were repulsed. Kept up a heavy firing all night. David Stallard, corporal of Co. F and Captain [Samuel] Stephens of Co. H were killed and Captain [Lewis] Crooks was wounded. The rebs came clear up to our works on the left. [First] Sergeant Robert Hackinson of Co. F was wounded this evening.

In the charge last night of the rebels [Private] Charles R. Leslie of Co. A was wounded having my gun in his hand at the time, a minie ball striking the gun and glancing off wounding Leslie in the wrist. This was a terrific encounter with the rebels and they were determined to recover the advantage they had lost and made repeated charges for that purpose but it was all to no purpose.

Tues. June 21

In front of Kenesaw Mt. *11 a.m.* The rebs got a battery in position and commenced to shell us putting several shots through our works at the left of Company A, one of which wounded four of Co. F. We were in considerable danger from the operations of this battery as they had good range of us in our position, but thank fortune none of Co. A were injured. We were so busily engaged with the rebels that I got no sleep last night and did not get to cook any thing from yesterday morning until this evening. The rebels loss in our front was considerable in the charge they made upon our works.[16]

Private Orson Brainard
Company K, 51st Ohio
1st Division, 4th Corps

Dear Father

We have had some hard fighting since I wrote last on sunday (19th)   We advanced about one mile and our skirmishers came up to the rebs skirmishers and of course we had to stop, and in the evening Companies K, G, B were sent out to skirmish and we were on all night   Early monday morning we

Ohio Battle Flags Photograph Collection, Ohio Historical Society

L.M. Strayer

• *The 51st Ohio's color sergeant proudly displayed the regiment's new national colors in a Columbus studio portrait taken during veteran furlough in February 1864. Painted in gold on the silk flag's bottom five red stripes were the regiment's previous battle honors — Dobson's Ford [Tennessee], Stone River, Chickamauga, Lookout Mountain and Mission Ridge. Above, the flag as it appeared in the early 1960s. The stars in the blue canton (now missing) originally were arranged in a vertical oval.*

were ordered to advance the line   Lieutenant [Peter] Lowe had charge of one half of co K and Lieutenant [John H.] Purvis [Company I] had charge of the rest of the company   We were to support the advance skirmishers   About eight o'clock the advance began   We onley got about one hundred yards further up the hill   Fredrick Winsenreed sargent of our company was shot dead   Co. G lost 5 Co. B 7 men Co. K 1.   We kept up a fire on the rebs all day till about four o'clock when the 21st Kentucky regt and the 51st were ordered to charge the hill   The 21st Ky came up with fixed Bayonets and colors flying fol-

lowed closely by the 51st On up the hill they go as our regt passed   we fell in   we connected in line with the 21st   When we got about half way up the hill we [raised] the yell and up we went   Our regt lost on monday 7 killed and 61 wounded.   As soon as we got posesion of the top of the hill we went to work and put up works   We had hardley got our works up till the rebs made a charge on us and we repulsed them with a slight loss on our side but they were not so lucky   They lost heavy   We could see the dead and wounded from our works   The rebs formed again and made another charge but were re-

Bob Willey collection

Bob Willey collection

Accoutrements of battle

Private Levi Gilpin, pictured in the faded image at left, belonged to Company E, 51st Ohio, and suffered a flesh wound above the right elbow June 20 during his regiment's fight on one of Kennesaw Mountain's spurs. The unlined four-button sack coat, opposite page, was worn by Gilpin that day, and still retains a hole where the bullet struck his arm. The 21-year-old veteran soon recovered sufficiently to rejoin the 51st, was appointed corporal on October 15, 1864, and eventually received a disability discharge in June 1865.

Following the war Gilpin preserved the accoutrements of his service, including leather belt, cap and cartridge boxes, canteen and Springfield bayonet with scabbard. Above, Gilpin's forage cap, socks, rifle sling and canvas haversack are surrounded by a variety of personal items — tin cup, plate and eating utensils, testament, knives, mirror, clay smoking pipe, fold-up sewing kit, dice and toothbrush. The Y-shaped object at lower right is an Enfield gun tool. Most of these items were carried at Kennesaw.

Bob Willey

• *A group of 51st Ohio soldiers, purportedly belonging to Company E, bivouacks on a hillside in this photograph likely taken in Tennessee during 1863. Note the enlisted man making coffee in front of the shelter tent at left.*

pulsed again   They tried it twice more within an hour but they could not make it   We worked all night and threw up the dirt   About midnight the rebs made another charge but were drove back again   Tuesday we done but little   A shell went through the works and wounded five men in Co. G   On wednesday nothing done but strengthning the works   In the morning as Lieut [Willis C.] Workman of Co. H was hanging his overcoat on a bush to dry a rebel sharpshooter shot him dead   The ball went in back of the ear and came [out] on the other side of the throat cutting the artiries   He was a good officer   On wednesday night we moved to the right about 3 miles and we are laying here this morning taking our ease   Well I will close for the present   Write soon

Just as I now finish writing [Musician] Reason Poole of our company was shot dead   The ball went in at the right shoulder and went to the heart causing instant death. [17]

Private Adam Hogle
Company H, 97th Ohio
2nd Division, 4th Corps

On the 22d day of June, 1864, we were lying in front of Kenesaw Mountain. Our regiment was on the front and was therefore the picket line. We had long since learned while we were with Gen. Sherman to dig ourselves under as soon as [we] stopped for the night. We were in our pits and the rebel picket lines were in their pits, or gopher holes as we called them, and were about 150 yards in our front.

About 3 o'clock p.m. the officers of the day concluded they would straighten our line, which formed a segment of a circle. Up to this time not a man on our line had been harmed that day, but when the order came to "Forward — March," and eight companies of the 97th Ohio bounded out of their pits, it was only to meet such a shower of lead as we had not encountered since the battle of Mission Ridge. We had gone not more than two rods [between 30 and 35 feet] from our pits until many had fallen, never to rise again.

I remember so well of one, a timid boy from Co. H, who remarked that he would be killed as soon as he left the pits, and he fell at the first volley from the rebs, not over 20 feet from our starting point, a bullet piercing his forehead. We advanced about 50 or 75 yards, but could get no farther, neither could we get back, and the battle raged fiercely from that time until dark, when we were able to get back to our pits again.

I remember so well the brave officers of our different companies facing death, first in one place and then in another, that they might place their men behind trees, stumps or something to protect them. The next morning after the recounting we found out of eight companies of the regiment that were engaged, there were 89 killed and wounded, and we buried the dead all in one grave on that morning of June 23. Why did the officers of the day want to straighten that line? What good did it do? There was whisky issued to the army that morning. Did that have anything to do with it? [18]

Brad L. Pruden

First Sergeant Joseph C. Hughes, Company A, 97th Ohio, was among the regiment's wounded on June 22 and later transferred to the Veteran Reserve Corps.

First Sergeant John W. Marshall
Company K, 97th Ohio
2nd Division, 4th Corps

Wednesday, June 22

Cleared off during the night. At 2 o'clock a.m. receive orders to move. At 6, as the regiment moves out I go to the division train to turn over some ordnance Stores. At 8 a.m. return and find the regiment on the skirmish line. Here we examine and replenish our ammunition. Considerable skirmishing is going on in our front but by keeping themselves under cover of their works our men are not losing any. About noon the artillery is quite heavy on our right, with signs of an advance. At noon a few of the skirmishers on the right of our brigade advance a short distance to reconnoiter, and are driven back by the

enemy, who, thinking they have achieved a success, become very jubilant, screaming, hollering, cheering, and firing their guns by volleys. Thinking they might attempt an advance, two companies are sent out to strengthen our skirmish line.

At 3 p.m. the whole right wing of the army is ordered to move. Swinging to the right from the position which our regiment occupies, we will form the pivot; consequently our left will not move. Soon the move commences and firing increases from an occasional firing to a constant roar of musketry, mingled with artillery. Soon our regiment is hotly engaged, the reserves are brought up and another company is sent to the left. Soon wounded begin to come in and the engagement increases on our right where it has become general. Our skirmishers have now gained the position but are exposed to an enfilading fire from the enemy which is fast thinning their ranks — yet they falter not. Men are detailed from other regiments to carry off the wounded, and fresh ammunition is taken to the boys. Every man seems to be at work, none are idle, the balls rattle and whistle everywhere. To fall back is impossible without endangering the whole line yet if this carnage continues we will have but few men left in our regiment. Will the sun never go down? This is our only hope. If a further advance is made, we will be in range of the enemy's main line.

Night at length comes and with it a lull in the firing. The pioneers are now ordered out to build works under cover of the night, and soon the sound of the pick and shovel takes the place of musketry. By midnight we are protected by works and all our dead and wounded are off the field, with the exception of two who lie so close to the enemy's lines that it is certain death to attempt their recovery. This closes a day of horror and butchery without parallel in the history of our regiment.

Thursday, June 23

At 3 o'clock this morning our regiment is relieved by the 57th Indiana regiment, and by daylight what is left of our regiment is safe in camp and we have time to ascertain our losses which amount to 11 killed and 78 wounded — many of them mortally. No wonder a feeling of gloom and sadness pervades the regiment, and it is quite common to see men who have never quailed amid the strife of contest weeping like children. Breakfast is gotten but little is eaten — the boys all seem anxious to go to the hospital to see their wounded comrades. Permission is easily gotten and after making out some reports I go over. What a mournful sight — boys who a few hours since were full of health now lying wounded and maimed in every conceivable way. Some have lost a leg, others an arm, some are slowly sinking in death, but all cheerful and patient. At noon having seen all the boys, I return to camp. At

1 p.m. ten of our boys who were killed are buried and a short and feeling address is delivered by the chaplain. This last duty performed, again the same unusual quiet reigns throughout the regiment. No one seems inclined to mingle in the usual joys of camp. [19]

Assistant Surgeon William F. King
124th Indiana
1st Division, 23rd Corps

June 23 1864
Dear Wife

We have had hard fighting since [June 17]. For three successive days there has been very hard cannonading and musketry on our left. We have not heard the result yet but suppose we have been driving [the Confederates] but they contest every foot of ground and fight with an obstinacy almost unprecedented. You probably have before this time had newspaper accounts of our doings. The rebel prisoners that I have seen are all large fine looking and healthy men. They don't look much like being starved. I think what starving is done is on our side. Our boys are nearly all the time on short rations and they would give any thing almost for sow belly, as they call it, as they draw none of it but get fresh beef instead. I do not eat the beef as it is poor and badly butchered. The officers can buy pork of the commissary and I keep myself in meat that way.

My health is a good deal better than it was and I am on duty with the Regiment. We had quite a gloom cast over our Regiment this morning. A young man in Co. A was cleaning his gun and it accidently exploded. The ball passed thru the brain of a young man by the name of [James T.] McIntosh, son of a lawyer in Connersville and wounded two others. The fact of it being accidental caused the gloom. Had it been done in battle little would have been thought of it, so accustomed have we all become to it. [20]

Major George S. Storrs could not understand the general's pessimistic point of view. Little Kennesaw mountain was a magnificent position for artillery, Storrs argued, but the Confederate army's artillery chief, Brigadier General Francis A. Shoup, was unmoved. The report of an inspection previously made by Johnston's engineers clearly advised against placing guns on Little Kennesaw. They reasoned that a rough road leading to the crest was too steep, that the hilltop was too exposed to enemy fire, and that in the event of a retreat field pieces could not be withdrawn without great hazard. No, Shoup replied to the major's entreaties. The engineers did not value Little Kennesaw highly for artillery and he would not authorize sending any more guns there.

Storrs, an artillery battalion commander in Loring's corps, was convinced the engineers and Shoup were wrong. He had inspected the mountain himself on June 20 and discovered a route on the southeastern side whereby cannons *could be* dragged by ropes. An experiment ordered by General French, Storrs' division commander, proved the method was feasible. Additionally, the major believed the timberless crest held room for 20 guns.

French, a West Point graduate twice brevetted as an artillery officer during the Mexican War, was "provoked" when told of Shoup's refusal. He ordered Storrs to take eight Napoleon 12-pounders — Captain Henry Guibor's Missouri and Captain John J. Ward's Alabama batteries — and emplace them near the crest during the night of June 21. Two other Napoleons and two 10-pounder Parrott rifles belonging to Captain James A. Hoskins' Mississippi battery already were in position on French's left flank. Infantry was detailed to help the cannoneers build protective works and carry projectiles up the mountain by hand.[1]

June 22 dawned clear and free of rain. French was in the saddle early and rode to the top of Little Kennesaw. "During the night," he wrote, "the enemy had moved a camp close to the base of the mountain. It was the headquarters of some general officers. Tent walls were raised, officers sitting around on camp stools, orderlies coming and going, wagons parked, soldiers idling about or resting in the shade of the trees, and from the cook fires arose the odors of breakfast, and all this at our very feet.

CHAPTER 5

The worst thing I fear is the blasted Bomb shell

Kennesaw Mountain
National Battlefield Park

• *This uniform coat was worn by Major General Samuel G. French, below, one of three division commanders in Loring's corps. A New Jersey native badly wounded in the right leg during the February 1847 battle of Buena Vista, French was a planter in Mississippi before the Civil War.*

Mass. MOLLUS, USAMHI

It was tantalizing, that breakfast, not to be tolerated. So I directed the powder in a number of cartridges for the guns to be reduced, so as to drop the shells into the camp below us. I left them in their fancied security — for no doubt they believed that we could not place artillery on the height above them, and they were not visible to our infantry on the mountain side by reason of the timber. How comfortable they appeared, resting in the shade and smoking! At length the gunners, impatient of delay, were permitted to open fire on them." [2]

From a prime vantage point, Storrs scanned the Federals with his field glasses. He recalled:

At daylight the guns were in position, loaded, and the artillerymen at their posts, and then began a fine display of artillery practice. The enemy's line of earthworks immediately in front was hidden by the forest, but it could be distinctly seen, first in short and then in long stretches, trending far out to the left or southwest. The smoke of camp-fires rose above the tree-tops, and this was our first target. We rained shell and spherical-case shot down upon them until satisfied that the camp-fires had been deserted. Then we turned our aim upon the encampments of quartermasters, ordnance and commissary trains of wagons, and on the tents at the headquarters of generals, colonels and staff officers.

For over two miles to the rear and far to the right and left large open fields white with wagon-covers were in plain view and within easy range. Sherman had moved all his artillery from the front of Little Kennesaw to concentrate on some other part of our line. We observed no parks of reserve artillery before us, and not a single gun replied to ours till the day was far advanced. So we ran our guns out of our works upon open ground on the brow of the mountain, and our men worked with a will to throw as many shot and shell among the wagons and teams as possible while the opportunity lasted, for the teamsters were seen to be very busy hitching up and going at full trot further to the rear. Instead of the old stereotyped command, "Fire slow but sure," I ordered the batteries to "Fire quick and true," which is a better command, because it stimulates the men to greater activity and often enables two guns to fire as many effective shots as three worked at the ordinary rate. Our solid shot were the more accurate and effective in disabling wagons, but shells were more demoralizing and did more mischief among teams and teamsters.

After the wagons had passed out of range and tents had disappeared, we turned our guns down on the enemy's line of intrenchments. We could only approximate the position of the line in front by the direction of the line entering the woods from the left and by what had been indicated to us by the smoke of camp-fires. With the greatest possible depression of our aim we overshot their line, but by reducing the charge of powder we were enabled to throw shell, spherical-case and canister exactly along what we estimated to be the enemy's position. And thus we poured these projectiles down upon their infantry from about nine a.m. till dark, only stopping occasionally to let the guns cool, and now and then engaging a battery that came up to reply to us, but as they had not yet built works for their guns we silenced them without difficulty. It was a genuine field-day for our battalion and so remarked by Generals French, Loring, Gibson, Holtzclaw, and various artillery officers and engineers who came upon the mountain during the day. I have always thought that this was the best position for offensive operations that General Johnston had while in Georgia. It is presumed that he did not fully appreciate the value of artillery on the mountains, because of the unfavorable report of his engineers heretofore mentioned.

General Shoup soon changed his view of the situation and that evening offered to furnish me more guns. I protested

Battles and Leaders of the Civil War

• *Confederate artillerymen drag a field piece up the steep, rugged slope of Kennesaw Mountain.*

against receiving them as earnestly as I had the day before pleaded to get them, because the opportunity had passed and gone. Any amount of artillery could be concentrated against the mountain-tops, while not more than thirty-five guns could be placed there. The next day I only reinforced with two guns, a section of Hoskins' battery. General Sherman brought one hundred and twenty guns to bear upon us, and a few days later one hundred and forty, thus showing that our first day's operations had demonstrated to him the high value of our artillery position. With this heavy fire converging upon us our guns were virtually silenced, and we thereafter only did a kind of picket duty, firing now and then a few rounds on exposed infantry and quickly running our guns back under cover.[3]

Few accounts by Union and Confederate soldiers fail to mention the use of artillery at Kennesaw. Its booming bark was ever-present and sometimes over-

L.M. Strayer

Major Robert P. Findley, 74th Ohio

whelming to the senses. On one occasion, Georgia artilleryman William R. Talley of Havis' battery "shot our gun so much that I was deaf for several days." John D. Broadman, a private in Battery F, 1st Illinois Light Artillery, wrote home about the noise of "volleys of artillery" directed at the mountain. "The roar of cannon and the bursting shells together with the peculiar whir of the flying pieces [make] it appear almost sublime." Corporal Charles M. Smith of Company F, 16th Wisconsin, admitted to his father that "the worst thing I fear is the blasted Bomb shell. They tear so. There was about a dozen of us that come very near being buried all up. The top [of Kennesaw Mountain] is lined with Rebel batteries that hurl their misels [*sic*] with deadly intent." An Illinois infantryman in the 20th Corps believed "Artillery was a headache to us one way or the other a lot of the time. We had to help get ours out of the mud, then defend our batteries against Rebel charges. In the meantime their artillery would

give us fits."[4]

Storrs' bombardment from Little Kennesaw on the 22nd caught the attention of Private William K. Armstrong of Company D, 52nd Ohio. Armstrong, fated to lose a leg and bleed to death five days later, wrote in his diary that "the Rebs ... kept up a fire all day [and] threw several hundred shots at our works. Fortunately but few men hurt but they keep us close to our works." Nearby in the same brigade, Second Lieutenant Leroy S. Mayfield of Company I, 22nd Indiana, noted in his own diary: "The firing was very rapid and exciting. Shells flew thick over head bursting in the woods behind. Some dropped among our tents, others bursted high in the air. This state of affairs continued near all day. Our batteries, except those far to the right, did not reply, the time being occupied in preparing works. We were annoyed considerably ...."[5]

Artillery fire on other sections of the line was not only annoying but dangerous and deadly. Major Robert P. Findley of the 74th Ohio recorded a close encounter on June 21:

We sat in works all day, in a cramped position, our feet half buried in the mud, the sun now boiling hot, and now a drowning rain falling. Our clothing was literally besmeared with the red clay with which this country abounds. We dare not get out of our works, lest a sharpshooter would try his hand on us, and the shells occasionally screamed over us.

I went back a short distance farther, and began plucking leaves and branches off a fallen tree top with which to make a bed for myself. While thus engaged a shell came along, but passed so far above me that I paid no attention to it. But almost immediately another came, passing very near me, and tearing up the ground in its course. I concluded I didn't want leaves bad enough for that and returned to the tent; threw in my leaves, saw I had not enough to make a bed, and on this account went and sat in the ditch near the breastwork.

Shortly after, a shell bursted either *in* or *above* the tent, knocking it down, blacking it with powder and tearing 44 holes in it, some as large as my hand. Had the former shell not driven me away from gathering branches when it did, I would have gotten enough and had I gotten enough, I would have had my bed made, and would have been occupying it when the latter shell came along, and if so, I would have been in a coffinless grave today, instead of as I am. That shell would have torn me to pieces.[6]

"When the enemy opened with his batteries it was really hot," recalled Illinois musician Fenwick Hedley. "The shells burst at the most awkward moments, while the solid shot whistled through the trees, tearing off huge branches, and making it generally uncomfortable. In one case an elongated shot,

First Lieutenant Wilbur F. Hinman

First Lieutenant Joseph F. Sonnanstine

I wish those fellows would let me sleep

In June 1864, Wilbur F. Hinman and Joseph F. Sonnanstine were lieutenants in the 65th Ohio and close friends. A post-war journalist and author, Hinman recalled an amusing incident involving Sonnanstine that took place near Mud Creek as their brigade inched toward Kennesaw.

The opposing lines were near each other at many points and an irregular fire was kept up almost continuously. Our "pup" tents were usually pitched directly in rear of the breastworks. One brigade of each division, by turn, was permitted to retire to the second line, out of range, several hundred yards back, twenty-four hours at a time, to rest, cook and wash. One day Lieutenant Joseph Sonnanstine of the Sixty-fifth was lying under his little shelter trying to get a nap. A stray bullet struck one of the sticks supporting his tent and broke it squarely off, the tent falling upon him.

"I wish those fellows would let me sleep," he said in his cool, inimitable way, as he crawled out from the wreck. He went a short distance into the woods and in a few minutes came back with another forked stick, and in a jiffy his tent was up again.

"There," he exclaimed as he lay down, "I don't believe they can hit that. They say lightning never strikes twice in the same place, and I don't think bullets do either!"

After sleeping soundly for a couple of hours he rolled out with a broad smile on his genial face.

"Boys," said he, "I just dreamed I was at home. I thought I pitched and tossed about half the night, but couldn't sleep a wink. Then I hired a boy to shoot at me and I was sound asleep in five minutes. I guess we will all have to do that when we get home — if we ever do."

a 'lamp-post,' as that sort of a projectile was called, struck the root of a tree in front of a staff tent belonging to General Giles A. Smith's headquarters. [At the time, Smith commanded a brigade in the 15th Corps]. The shot glanced and followed the trunk twenty feet upward, tearing off the bark, and finally cutting away a large limb which, in its fall, nearly wrecked tent and occupants as well. The next shot cut down a tree which fell upon a [tent] fly adjoining, spraining the leg of an ordnance officer, and breaking one for his orderly." [7]

Benjamin T. Smith, a 51st Illinois private serving

Janis Pahnke

Second Lieutenant Ebben Bingham was killed June 18 while commanding Company C, 65th Ohio.

Indiana State Library

First Lieutenant George H. Bowman, Company I, 36th Indiana, was fatally wounded June 19.

as orderly on Brigadier General John Newton's division staff, 4th Corps, described a harrowing experience while accompanying the general on a June 19 inspection tour of his line's breastworks: "Two of the staff officers are with us, riding along in plain view of the enemy, who take the opportunity to train one of their guns on us, and send a shell into us, as we were all bunched together; the gun was well aimed. The shell came along with its usual infernal shriek, and landed square on the side of one of our escort horses, just behind the riders right leg and passed diagonally through the animal, and out just in front of his left leg, striking the bones of the horses shoulder, exploded, sending fragments of the iron in all directions. The horse was dead in an instant, but strange to say, none of us got a scratch. The horses nearest were staggered, and Genl Newtons fat old yellow 'cob' came very near tumbling over."[8]

That same day on Big Kennesaw, Loring's troops endured the Federals' complimentary shelling and shared in some narrow escapes of their own. Sergeant Daniel P. Smith of the 1st Alabama Infantry witnessed "a notable act of bravery — during a heavy artillery fire a shrapnel shell fell in the entrenchments amidst Co. K. Sergt. [Norman] Cameron, without an instant's hesitation, seized the smoking missile and hurled it outside the works ere it exploded." Not far away Captain William McMillan, the 17th Alabama's acting surgeon, thought he was safe on the mountain's rear slope. "It was sprinkling rain and I was kindling a fire before a little Yankee tent that one of my men captured from the picket line — when a shell exploded in a few feet of me. A fragment passed through the tent and threw dirt and leaves all over me. My tent was 'dangerously' wounded and I was 'severely' frightened. A fellow of my Infirmary Corps was driving one of the tent pins in the ground when the fragment passed him. He and I adjourned to the side of a big rock — the side on which the shells didnt come — and never changed base until the Yankees quit their foolishness."[9]

First Lieutenant John I. Kendall of Company B, 4th Louisiana Infantry, later commented: "The enemy's artillery kept us, more or less all the time, in trouble. Shells fell at intervals throughout the day and the night. It was, however, only occasionally that this intermittent fire swelled into a serious

• *Photographed in Mobile, Alabama during the autumn of 1863, John I. Kendall, center, posed as second lieutenant of Company B, 4th Louisiana Infantry, with Captain Robert L. Pruyn, left, and First Lieutenant David Devall. "About the hardest task a soldier is called upon to endure [is] to take a shelling," Kendall recalled. "The summit of the mountain was the focal point of countless missiles. Shrieking, yelling, howling, hissing, gobbling or sharply cracking, the shells were like a swarm of unseen fiends, whilst the smoke of their explosions, the villianous smell they let loose, and the heavy, curtain-like vapor floating slowly up from below, made a hot and sulphurous atmosphere highly suggestive of the place where His Satanic Majesty is reputed to reside."*

Confederate Veteran

bombardment. On one of these occasions, however, I had occasion to make my way down from division headquarters to the spot where the regiment was stationed. I had a time of it. The top of the mountain could not be avoided. I had to go over it. It did not take me very long. As I ran forward, I saw a man coming toward me. Suddenly he jumped behind a big tree, and simultaneously a shell burst on the other side of it, scattering its pieces and contents all round him. What made him do that? A sort of instinct. Who can tell? That individual, somehow or other, had a feeling of peculiar and impending peril, and acted on it. Perhaps he heard the voice of that particular shell saying, 'Where are you? Where are you? Where are you?' Such, we used to declare in those days, was the voice of the shell, when we sat around the camp fires and talked of our experiences. At last that bombardment ceased. We were able, then, to take a little breath and to count up casualties." [10]

These were not inconsequential. A Georgia private recalled that one day Union shells "in front as well as an enfilading fire from several batteries just skimmed over our lines in the breastworks, and raked the ground where we were posted so that our losses for a few minutes was frightful. I saw one 6-pound solid shot kill four men in the 40th [Georgia]" — a lieutenant and three enlisted men. [11]

Sergeant William P. Chambers, 46th Mississippi, wrote of an incident occurring on the slope of Little Kennesaw: "The Federal batteries began throwing shells directly at the frail breastwork behind which,

Mass. MOLLUS, USAMHI

Brigadier General Lucius E. Polk

nonball. Recounted a comrade, "Even when thus torn and bleeding, his happy, genial nature did not forsake him. When being borne from the field he met his beloved General Cleburne, and, saluting, asked: 'General, have I not won promotion today?' " Lightner was transported to LaGrange, Georgia, where he died of his wounds.[13]

Yankee artillery fire also robbed Cleburne of one of his best brigade commanders. East of Mud Creek, a solid shot plowed into the horse ridden by Brigadier General Lucius E. Polk, badly fracturing the officer's left fibula. It was the fourth wound of the war for the 30-year-old Polk, a nephew of recently slain corps commander Leonidas Polk, and permanently incapacitated him for further field duty.[14]

* * *

At Kennesaw, Federal batteries were equipped with 3-inch wrought-iron guns (dubbed Rodmans), 10- and 20-pounder Parrotts, and 12-pounder Napoleon smoothbores. The first three were rifled pieces, relied upon for accuracy and range. The Napoleon was the weapon of choice on the battle line, where its facility of service and effectiveness firing solid shot, spherical case and canister were most required.[15] Working these guns, wrote Private Robert H. Strong of Company B, 105th Illinois, was a dangerous undertaking:

> Our artillerymen were stripped to the waist. It was a sight to watch them firing those cannons. Each man at the cannon is numbered, and each number has just certain things to do. He does this with the regularity of clock work, and does nothing else. The caisson holding the ammunition is brought up to a few feet in rear of the cannon, the horses are unhitched and taken a short distance to the rear and hidden if possible, and firing begins.
>
> One man brings the powder cartridge from the caisson. Another man shoves it into the cannon muzzle. Another one rams it down. By this time, the first man has returned from the caisson with a shot or a shell. If it is a shell and the fuse is already cut to the required length, the shell is passed on to the cannon, inserted and rammed home. If not properly fused, the fuse is adjusted first. Then the priming is inserted in the touch hole and the string that fires the cannon is pulled. After the shell screams out and the cannon recoils, the cannon is run back into position. Then one man puts his finger over the touch hole to keep out air. Another with a swab or sponge on a pole wipes out the cannon. Another shell is inserted and fired. As this is done two or three times in a minute, everybody is on the jump. Every so often, the end of the swab is dipped in a bucket of water and the cannon thoroughly washed out. If an artilleryman is killed or

at the time, our company was crouched. One of these shells penetrated the earth at the base of the works with the fuse still burning. In a spirit of rashness I leaped upon the breastwork, ran and stood directly over where it was, believing that when it exploded the fragments would all go to the rear. Another shell from the same gun, elevated a little, came whizzing through the air, barely missing my feet as it exploded. Sergt. Jonathan H. Bass of our company had at that moment stood up in the trench directly in front of the exploding shell. I never saw a human body more horribly mutilated than his was."[12]

Second Lieutenant Isaac Lightner, a section commander in Captain Overton W. Barret's Missouri battery, had both feet carried away by a can-

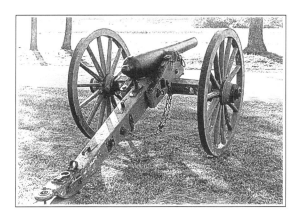

• *Members of a Federal gun crew, below, ready their M1857 12-pounder Napoleon smoothbore for firing at Stevenson, Alabama. The gun's commander, a sergeant, stands third from right. Made of brass, the muzzle-loading fieldpiece, bottom, originally was developed in the mid-1850s under the auspices of Napoleon III of France. It was most effectively employed firing canister in close support of infantry. At left, the wrought-iron 3-inch ordnance rifle was extremely accurate, "a dead shot at any distance under a mile," attested one Yankee cannoneer.*

Mass. MOLLUS, USAMHI

wounded, another stands ready to take his place. Each is trained to do the next man's job when needed.

At this time we had a good view of the enemy's guns and of their lines behind. We could see our shells burst inside their lines. One shell knocked a wheel off one of their cannon. All this time, their shells were striking and bursting among us. Some of our gunner men were just literally blown to pieces. As they were, the next one would take his place. It was a grand sight, but a horrible one.[16]

In the opinion of Federal artillery chief Brigadier General William F. Barry, a New Yorker who had organized the Army of the Potomac's artillery early

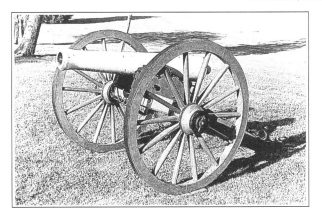

Dale Snair

• *First Lieutenant Aaron P. Baldwin, above, poses with one of the 6th Ohio Battery's 10-pounder Parrott rifles. Less effective than the 3-inch ordnance rifle, the Parrott was characterized by a thick cylindrical band of wrought-iron around the breech. At right, 19-year-old Private Albert Hersh, 6th Ohio Battery, was killed near Kennesaw Mountain on June 18.*

Brad L. Pruden

in the war, "the western life of officers and men, favorable to self-reliance, coolness, endurance, and marksmanship, seems to adapt them peculiarly for this special arm." After three years' service, the artillery of Sherman's command was "unusually reliable and effective."[17]

A Massachusetts officer, veteran of Antietam and Gettysburg, agreed. "I will give the Western army credit for their superior use of artillery. Wherever infantry goes, the batteries follow right in line, and in this way guns can be used continually at very short range, producing, of course, deadly effect. At Gettysburg, every colonel in our brigade besought the chief of artillery to put some guns in position in our line, but we were told that it couldn't be done, as the gunners would be picked off by sharpshooters. Here they have to take the same chances as an infantry man." [18]

Several artillery officers were so successful plying their craft that they gained army-wide reputations. Captain Andrew Hickenlooper, 5th Ohio Battery, performed the duties of McPherson's artillery chief and eventually received a brigadier general's brevet. As the 23-year-old commander of Battery H, 1st Illinois Light Artillery, Captain Francis DeGress used his four 20-pounder Parrott rifles with such effect that one prominent general called the native Prussian the best artillerist in the Western armies. [19]

Perhaps the most well known Union artilleryman was another German. Captain Hubert Dilger was on extended leave from the Grand Duchy of Baden's army when he commanded Battery I, 1st Ohio Light Artillery. A veteran of Gettysburg and Chancellorsville (where he earned the Medal of Honor), Dilger acquired the nicknames "Old Buckskin," "Leather Breeches" and "Jack of Clubs" after his six-gun battery's transfer to the West. His marksmanship was extraordinary and he often fired Battery I's brass smoothbores in volleys, an unusual practice for artillery at the time. [20] Officially attached to the 1st Division, 14th Corps, Dilger and his cannoneers caught the attention of privates and generals alike throughout the army.

Colonel Benjamin F. Scribner
3rd Brigade commander
1st Division, 14th Corps

On the 18th of June ... the rain poured down. Solid shot and explosive shells fell among the overhanging branches of the trees, and, crackling and crashing, the limbs fell about us, made more visible by the bursting shells and flashes [of lightning] from the angry sky. Staff officers dashed to and fro with orders concerning the [forward] movement, and as they were orally delivered, the officers would lift their feet from their stirrups to permit the water which overflowed their boots to pour from them.

Amid all the clangor and uproar the business in hand was not lost sight of. When we reached [a] stream which we expected to find at the foot of the slope, we could see the entrenchments of the enemy, which could only be approached by us over the open space in their front. While my division commander [Brigadier General John H. King] and I were consulting together Capt. Dilger rode up. His battery

• During veteran furlough earlier in 1864, these eight enlisted men from Battery H, 1st Illinois Light Artillery, gathered for a group portrait. Seated from left: Sergeant Henry O. Olson, Wagoner Charles D. Roberts, First Sergeant Henry Meyers and Sergeant Frank K. Laha. Standing from left: Bugler Frank B. Moroney, Sergeant John McGeorge, Bugler Wentzel Maschka and Artificer Frederic Dohmeyer.

Ivan C. Peterson

had been assigned to my command. He pointed out a spot where he wished to take his battery. I objected, and said to him that the place was not in our front, and that Gen. [Absalom] Baird [commanding the 3rd Division, 14th Corps], in whose front it was, should use one of his own batteries there, if he thought it desirable. He replied, "I ask it as a favor, for Gen. Baird wanted some guns placed there, and his chief of artillery persuaded him from it, saying that a battery could not live a minute in such a place." The Captain was so earnest that I looked inquiringly to the General, who answered me aside, "Let him do it," and soon the six guns, drawn by twenty-four horses, came clattering and splashing down, and, sweeping out into the open space in front of the works of the enemy, they were unlimbered, and the horses rapidly sent to the rear for protection, while the guns were loaded and fired with a rapidity I have never seen excelled.

The men went to work to construct defenses for the guns. I intended to make a detail for this purpose, but Dilger was a great favorite with the men, and volunteers in abundance soon came forward for the work. The Captain was known by them as "Leather-breeches," and was rarely spoken of by any other name or title. When cover for a gun had been sufficiently completed to afford protection to it, it was moved by hand to its place. Their fire did not cease or slacken, but was kept up continuously and vigorously under the galling fire of the enemy, who had concentrated his batteries upon them. The rebel infantry also soon joined in the combat, and soon the battle raged along the line, and did not abate until darkness enshrouded the scene.

Captain Dilger came to me one day for permission to take two of his guns out from their defenses into the field in front of the troops on our right. He added that Gen. [Thomas J.] Wood [commanding the 3rd Division, 4th Corps] wished him to do so. I forbade it, and this time he did not insist; but after a pause he resumed, saying, "I am glad not to go there, for I would lose some horses, and I am very scarce of horses." He did not seem to consider that he would also lose some men.

Orders were frequently received to open out with the battery at a specified hour, which I suppose was to cover some movement, or to make the rebels show themselves, and thereby prove to us that they were yet in our front, or not, as usual, falling back.

Mass. MOLLUS, USAMHI

Captain Hubert Dilger, Battery I, 1st OVLA

One morning [June 22], just as Dilger had commenced to fire, in compliance with one of these orders, the enemy replied with unexpected readiness and vigor from sixteen guns. It soon became a serious matter to us. They had our range and used their guns with terrible effect.

Our battery was planted on our front line with the infantry on the right and left of it. This point was a salient. Of course, the enemy, by placing guns at certain points, could converge on us, and this they did with much precision, and we were very well satisfied when they slackened and then ceased firing. This was the first time they had succeeded in projecting a ball through one of our embrasures. Dilger frequently did so to theirs. But now they had dismounted one of our guns, had killed one of the Captain's best sergeants [Ventz Lohrer died July 24 of wounds], besides other casualties. His fortifications were so battered that they could have been shaken down with the hand, and one more direct hit would have made a breach.

The last time I ever met this gallant and efficient officer was when I called on him one day to give him some directions. It rained, as usual, that day, and had not ceased. The guns were covered [with] tarpaulins, under which the company had crawled for shelter. I called out and was promptly answered by the Captain. As he emerged bare-headed into the weather I besought him to remain where he was; that I could say to him what I had to say just as well there. But he persisted in coming out, and standing forth he saluted and said, "I cannot remain under cover while my officer stands in the rain giving me orders."[21]

First Lieutenant Alexis Cope
Adjutant, 15th Ohio
3rd Division, 4th Corps

Capt. Dilger had become quite noted as a sort of free lance in the artillery service. He wore buckskin trousers and the boys called him "Leather Breeches." It was said that he would carefully examine the location of the enemy's batteries, get permission to choose his own method of attack and then rapidly lead his battery to a new position, sometimes outside of our skirmish line, and open out on and silence the enemy's guns almost before they knew of his presence. Gen. [David S.] Stanley [commanding the 1st Division, 4th Corps] was reported as saying, in his quiet, humorously sarcastic way, that "he was going to order bayonets for Dilger's guns."[22]

Private William P. Fulton
Company F, 98th Ohio
2nd Division, 14th Corps

The evening [of June 22] at 7 o'clock Cos. F and E of the 98th were sent to [the] skirmish line, Co. E going into line, Co. F lying in reserve. Relieved them at 3 a.m. On the 23rd we had sharp practice with Johnny's pickets, but as they were high above

us and the woods was thick they always overshot us.

About 10 a.m. the Rebs artillery above us opened fire but he soon had to shut up as our friend, a young European officer whom we all know by the title of Jack of Clubs, a comic fellow who wears buckskin tights, had moved during the night and had taken position under cover of the woods so that he had a cross fire, while Capt. [Charles M.] Barnett's battery [I, 2nd Illinois Light Artillery] remained directly in front. Johnny opened fire thinking he would knock Barnett's battery to pieces as his works were not completed, but whizz, bang, bang, came Buckskins shells through the tree tops by volleys and we could hear them as they reached Johnny's works. They had to dry up and all was quiet until evening when they opened a furious cannonade which made the hill tremble.

We soon heard old Barnett's battery open in front and Jack of Clubs to the right commenced to play his hand, the shells all passing over us, cutting the tree tops over our heads and occasionally bursting prematurely, scattering pieces in our line. For a time the contest was furious, the Rebs making the most noise, but shooting wildly, while our gunners having gotten correct range struck their shot close. The Rebs shut up and Buckskin kept them that way by throwing a volley whenever they came near their guns.

Yesterday [June 24] the Rebs remained quiet but today they attempted to shell us. Barnett's battery assisted by Jack of Clubs soon silenced them. I had just stopped to get supper and the mail had been distributed, bringing me a letter from my deary, when bang, bang, came a shower of shell which made us hop into our trench like frogs. Barnett and Jack began banging in quick succession. The Rebs could only slip quietly up to their guns and load them, firing into a crowd and then running their guns back of the hill to prevent them from being knocked to pieces as we could see our shot stirring up the dirt in fine style.[23]

* * *

Artillery fire played a major role in blunting Confederate assaults by two of Hood's divisions on June 22. For three previous, rain-soaked days Schofield's 23rd Corps and Hooker's 20th Corps had pushed south, then east, in a gambit to turn the Rebel left flank. Grayclad cavalry was forced back at

Paul M. Smith

Sergeant Rice C. Bull, Company D, 123rd New York

The battle of Kolb's Farm, named after farmer Peter Kolb's log house and cornfield astride the Powder Springs Road, began with sporadic picket fire. Information gleaned from a few prisoners alerted Hooker and Schofield that Hood's troops were somewhere in their front. Both were well aware of Hood's combative demeanor. Eleven years earlier Schofield and Hood had been classmates at West Point. The Federals hastily dismantled farm fencing, some piling clods of drying mud against logs and rails for protection. Hooker's line, facing a large tract of open land drained by a marshy stream, extended north of the road with the divisions of Williams, Geary and Butterfield positioned right to left, respectively. Schofield's left division, commanded by Brigadier General Milo S. Hascall, connected with Hooker south of the road. Two regiments from Williams' and Hascall's commands — the 123rd New York and 14th Kentucky — were sent forward as skirmishers to develop the enemy.

Sergeant Rice C. Bull
Company D, 123rd New York
1st Division, 20th Corps

As we advanced through the open country the Johnnies held to every protected spot as long as they could. They clung to every hill and ravine until our men on the right and left advanced so far as to endanger their capture then they would crawl back to the next hill or ravine. While this was going on we were using every protection there was to give us cover. One looking lengthwise of our line would have seen men behind trees and stumps, others lying flat on the ground behind some hummock, and many in the little gullies and ravines.

By this time we had forced them back to the woods beyond the clearing; there we saw a line of rifle pits that were well protected from our fire. When they dropped into the pits they gave us a big yell; which was saying, "Now get us if you can." In front of their breastworks and about a hundred yards from them was a ravine running for a long distance parallel to their line. On our last rush we were ordered to take the ravine. To get there we were in the open and while we covered the ground in record time, we lost several men. It was now four in the afternoon and we were as close as we could get to the rifle pits with a skirmish line. For more than an

swollen Noyes' Creek, which Schofield crossed before linking up with Hooker's far right division (Williams') on the 21st. The move seriously threatened Johnston's Kennesaw line as part of the Federal army now was positioned to march toward Marietta along Powder Springs Road and gain its rear.

Reacting to the emergency, Johnston shifted Hood's entire 11,000-man corps from its breastworks east of Big Kennesaw to the imperiled left flank. Wheeler's cavalry and a thinly-stretched portion of Loring's corps occupied the vacated trenches. Almost four miles southwest of Marietta, Hood deployed with Major General Thomas C. Hindman's division on the right, Carter Stevenson's in the center and A.P. Stewart's, acting as a reserve, on the left. Although he had no instructions from Johnston to attack, Hood did exactly that late in the afternoon of June 22.

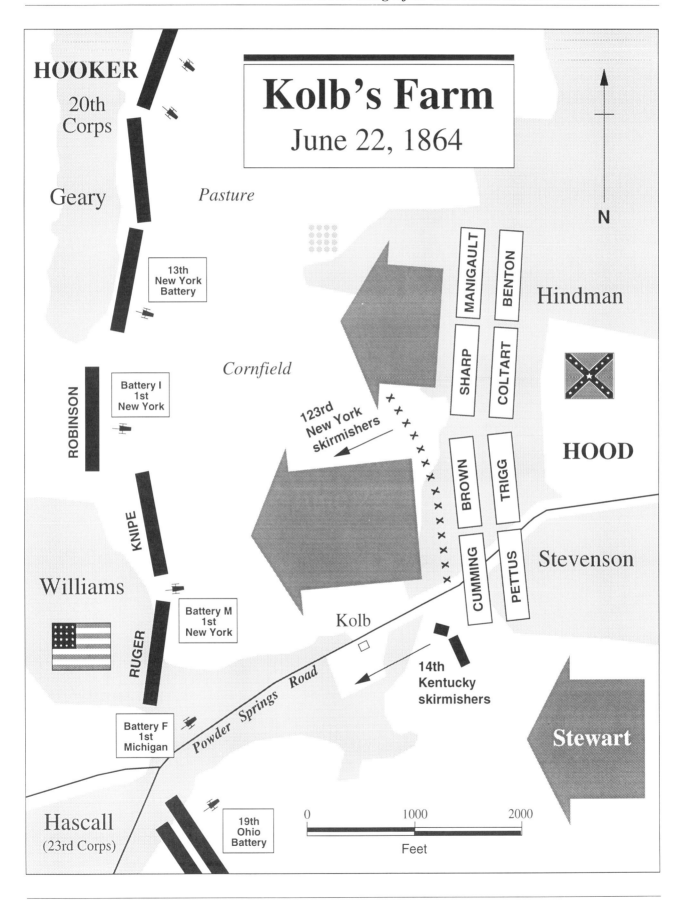

Kolb's Farm
June 22, 1864

HOOKER

20th Corps

Geary

Pasture

13th New York Battery

Cornfield

ROBINSON

Battery I 1st New York

123rd New York skirmishers

KNIPE

Williams

RUGER

Battery M 1st New York

Kolb

Battery F 1st Michigan

Powder Springs Road

14th Kentucky skirmishers

Hascall (23rd Corps)

19th Ohio Battery

MANIGAULT

BENTON

Hindman

SHARP

COLTART

HOOD

BROWN

TRIGG

CUMMING

PETTUS

Stevenson

Stewart

N

0   1000   2000

Feet

Richard W. Nee

Captain Henry O. Wiley, Company K, 123rd New York, was killed July 20 at Peachtree Creek, four weeks after the battle of Kolb's Farm.

low voice, the neighing of horses, and further back, bugle calls. There was no question what was going on in our front. The enemy was massing troops very rapidly and we could hear every movement as this went on. When the Johnnies came in we noted the warning commands of their officers, the orders to halt, front, dress, etc., orders familiar to us. The massing of a division cannot be made under any conditions in less than an hour and it was fully five o'clock before their work was completed and they were ready to advance. To us on the skirmish line who were waiting for them to move it seemed as though they would never start. Our guns were cocked and we were ready to fire at sight of them.

Shortly after five a bugle sounded "forward," then we heard low commands given by their officers, followed by the rustle of many feet, as they marched through the underbrush. They had not far to go before they reached the crest of the hill on the opposite side of the ravine where we could see them. They came without skirmishers which meant an attack in force. We fired and dropped back through the woods ... and into the open field over which we would have to retreat for nearly a half mile to reach our battle line on the hill. The men there were working with pick and shovel, as men will work whose lives depend on constructing barricades to stop bullets. Back of them we saw our batteries being wheeled into place. Everything was being done that could be for the fight that was coming.

The Rebel line advanced rapidly for they were in light marching order. We skirmishers were loaded with our full equipment, knapsacks, etc. This made it harder for us to retreat than for them to follow. When we reached the [Kolb] buildings we halted long enough to load our guns but the enemy were so close we continued to run, with them calling on us to surrender. As soon as they were in front of the buildings they commenced firing on us as we retreated. As their bullets would strike in the sand around us, little fountains of dust would rise two feet in the air. On our way back on the run we came to a knoll and halted on the crest long enough to fire our last volley; then we started for our line, every man for himself.

By this time the enemy were in view of our forces; and several of our batteries opened fire with shot and shell; we were in their line of fire and for a

hour we remained in the ravine and the firing was lively as we waited ....

The ravine was filled with trees and underbrush; and from where we were descended about seventy-five feet to a dry stream in the bottom and then up the other side to the same level we were on. Our advance was so quiet that the enemy on the other side, not more than two hundred feet from us, did not know we were there. At first it was very still but soon we heard voices beyond the opposite hill. As we silently waited the noise increased in volume. I could hear men marching, the giving of orders in a time in as much danger from them as the enemy, so we tried to file off to the right and left out of range. Winded, we made a last effort and struggled through our lines. Everyone fell to the ground exhausted, and many were in a dead faint. Four were wounded in our Company, including Lieutenant [Edward P.] Quinn, whose wounds were so severe that he did not return to duty. One of our Company, Oliver Smith, was captured and spent the rest of his service in Andersonville Prison.[24]

Sergeant Henry C. Morhous
Company C, 123rd New York

The right of the skirmish line was in the woods, the left in an open field, and the right had advanced considerably more than the left, owing to their cover. Once the left undertook to straighten the line by advancing, but the Rebels opened such a terrific fire on them that they were compelled to give this up. In this effort to straighten the line J. Willard Allen of Co. C succeeded in gaining a position behind a stump far in advance, and did not fall back with the rest. The Rebels must have known there was a Yank behind that stump, for they kept pouring the minie balls into it, peeling the bark off from each side, and knocking the splinters from the top of it. Willard shrunk himself into as small a compass as he possibly could, waiting for a favorable opportunity to come back.

The enemy, after amusing themselves for awhile at Willard's expense, ceased firing, and, seizing the favorable opportunity, he made a few rapid and very lengthy jumps and landed among his comrades, and glad were they to welcome him, for he had been in a very dangerous position. The Rebels opened fire on him as soon as they saw him, but he escaped without injury. Lieut. Quinn of Co. D, in his anxiety to straighten the line, took a gun in his hands and made an advance, calling on his company to follow him. He had advanced but a few steps when he was hit in the face with a bullet, which broke his lower jaw, and he fell to the ground. In this position he lay some time. Several times he was heard to call, "Company C, c-o-o-me and t-a-a-ke me in," and as often the answer would be yelled back, "Lieu-ten-ant Quinn, g-o-o to hell!" After awhile he came in without any assistance, the Rebels seeming not to fire at him. It would have been as much as a man's

Mass. MOLLUS, USAMHI

Colonel George W. Gallup, 14th Kentucky

life was worth to have gone to his assistance, and probably this was what Co. C thought.[25]

Sergeant Lorenzo R. Coy
Company K, 123rd New York

Arriving at the outer edge of a piece of woods we found the rebels moving along the road in force, and at once opened fire upon them at a distance of not more than ten rods. We were soon driven back, rallied again, and advanced to be again driven back and again rallied. In the meantime the 1st Division had taken position on the ridge and were at work throwing up works. The rebels advanced upon us in solid column driving the 123rd before them, taking, I fear, many of them prisoners. I had today the command of the left of our Co. and before we knew that there was anything more than a skirmish line coming, the whole force was upon us. In falling back, which I did as fast as I could, I found myself at one time under the fire of the rebels and our own line of battle, and thanks be to God for His preserving care, I escaped unharmed, but do not know where the regt is and will be here in the woods to the rear tonight.[26]

Colonel George W. Gallup's 14th Kentucky managed to resist a little longer. His men were lying down south of the Powder Springs Road behind a partially constructed barricade. "The enemy approached reluctantly and in much disorder," Gallup reported, "resembling a mob more than they did soldiery. The first line came within thirty feet before we fired. At the first volley deliberately delivered, the enemy was thrown into confusion and gave way, firing a heavy volley, not a shot of which took effect." The assaulting Rebels soon pushed back the regiment's left companies, however, and enfiladed Gallup's entire line. Fighting "Indian-style" back to Hascall's defenses, the Kentuckians lost eight killed and 52 wounded while taking 36 enemy prisoners. Losses in the 123rd New York amounted to five killed, 28 wounded and 14 captured.[27]

Stevenson's and Hindman's divisions swarmed into view, formed several lines of battle and began double-quicking toward Hooker's unfinished works, yelling wildly. An instant later five well-sited Union batteries burst into action. "They came out of the woods and had to cross an opening to reach us," wrote Corporal Frederick Smith of Battery I, 1st New York Light Artillery. "But they did not get very far, as our Battery and two other batteries of our corps opened on them with shrapnel or case-shot."[28]

Captain Joseph C. Shields' 19th Ohio Battery, 23rd Corps, had barely unlimbered on a knoll southwest of the Kolb house when the Confederates appeared, hot on the heels of Gallup's Kentucky skirmishers. Artillerist Theodore Tracie witnessed the spectacle:

There was a loud, fierce yell, and out of the woods the 14th Kentucky Volunteers poured, and over a low fence on the edge of the timber, where they halted. The loud yells became fiercer, and dashing out in strong, bold front came triple lines of gray coats. The firing swelled into a loud crash, and as we saw the skirmish line fall back a few yards under the brow of the slope and return the fire of the massed lines, we heard the Captain's voice above the roar:

"Load with canister!"

There was a mighty excitement in the moment. We threw the canister into the gaping guns, and then, like a tornado, volley after volley were sent plunging and tearing through the massed

Alabama Department of Archives and History

Major General Carter L. Stevenson

lines, strewing the ground with fallen men. It was a magnificent range for canister, and the effectiveness of the gunners' aim was made terribly manifest. They trembled under the awful fire, wavered, and then retreated in confusion. As they retreated the guns were elevated, and for a mile they were followed with the fierce storm of shot and shell. All the guns of [Hascall's] Division were worked with splendid effect.

"Don't shoot those men coming over," was the order shouted down our line, and looking under the smoke we saw scores of Rebels flying across the valley with uplifted hands. As they came panting into the lines, exhausted with their hasty trip and the terror of the gauntlet they had run, they looked like dead men, so wan and ghastly were their bloodless faces.

From one of our own men, who as prisoner had been carried back with the retreating Rebel lines, and who escaped in the confusion of the unexpected repulse, we learned something of the effects of our fire. The shot and shell that poured into them, by the elevation of aim as they retreated, seemed to follow them with almost human intelligence, and the officers were powerless to rally their lines to another assault.[29]

Across the Powder Springs Road from Private Tracie's position, some members of Brigadier General Thomas H. Ruger's six regiments, Williams' division, almost were caught unprepared for the Rebel battle columns rolling toward them. Just prior to Hood's assault, wrote Private John E. West of Company G, 150th New York, "it was discovered that the field in our front contained a fine lot of blackberries, and it was but a moment before it was dotted with 'blue-coats,' filling their tin cups with berries. The men were very much engaged in their new occupation when Major [Alfred B.] Smith appeared, shouting, 'Get back you skallawags! What are you doing out there? How can we get the Johnnies out with you there?'

"We took the hint at once, and in less than the time it takes to tell the story we were again inside the works, secure from the enemy's vision. We had hardly regained our position when our skirmishers, who so gallantly a short time before had driven the enemy's skirmishers up the opposite hill and into the woods, themselves came running back as though the devil himself was after them. The cause of their hasty return was soon evidenced, Hood's Confederate Corps emerging from the woods into the open and advancing on the double-quick, forming in three lines of battle as they came on. From our concealed position the sight was an inspiring one, and our attention was much attracted by an officer riding up and down their line, mounted on a white horse.

"On they came with a rush, advancing into the valley and then up the rise of ground in our front until we could almost see the whites of their eyes, when they received such a withering fire from our line and the two batteries at our left that they wavered and finally fell back to the ravine for shelter, leaving the space thickly strewn with their dead and wounded." [30]

Nearby, Private Samuel Toombs of Company F, 13th New Jersey, praised the work of Williams' gunners. "The Artillery of the Division did splendid execution on this occasion, and the repulse of the enemy was due mainly to their rapid and unerring fire. Our lines were so formed that Geary's men enfiladed the enemy's whole line when it reached the foot of the hill on the top of which we were stationed. Before the infantry fired a shot the artillery poured a destructive fire of grape and canister into them which caused them to waver and threw them

Marcus McLemore

Private Edward W. Fairchild, 19th Ohio Battery

Marcus McLemore

Private Simon W. Killam, 19th Ohio Battery

Frank & Marie-Therese Wood Print Collections, Alexandria, Va.

• Harper's Weekly *published the above engraving of the Kolb's Farm battle in its July 23, 1864 edition. The scene originally was sketched by youthful* Harper's *artist and correspondent Theodore R. Davis, right, whose talent caught the eye of 20th Corps' division commander Alpheus Williams. Shortly after the June 22 fight Williams wrote to his daughters in Michigan: "Dory Davis (T.R.) has been here making a sketch of the ground for* Harper's; *but he says that* Harper's *don't put in half he sends and those are bunglingly and incorrectly copied. He sketches beautifully and the pictures he has sent give a most correct idea of the field of fight, so far as landscape is concerned." Like General Sherman, Williams had little good to say about newspaper correspondents accompanying the army. "I am not indifferent to the ephemeral praise of reporters, but I cannot sell my self-respect to obtain it," he wrote home. The New York* Tribune *was especially suspect. "I don't know who writes for that paper but he hardly tells a truth and a great many lies."*

Mass. MOLLUS, USAMHI

into confusion, but they soon rallied in our front and pressed forward again impetuously ....

"They marched up within, perhaps, fifty yards of us, their colors floating defiantly almost in our faces. The order passed down the line to fix bayonets, and when they saw the determined faces in front of them and viewed the line of bristling steel which projected over the rail breastworks, they wavered and fell back. We should then have been ordered forward.

The Regiment never had a better opportunity for capturing a large number of men and several stands of colors than on this occasion, but we remained stationary, and did what execution was possible with our rifles." [31]

Another soldier in Ruger's brigade, Private Edmund R. Brown of Company C, 27th Indiana, watched the Confederate charge and later described the carnage, though his regiment took little part:

A large number of the enemy took refuge along the creek in the ravine between the lines, fearing to ascend the slope back of it, and were handled very roughly later on. They seemed to be crowded into that depression in almost a compact mass. They were partly screened from the fire of our line directly in front of them, but our men farther to the right could reach them with a damaging flank fire, while some of our batteries had an enfilading range upon them that was terrible.

The commander of one of these batteries, who could not from his position see the effect of his fire, or even tell when he had the range, rode up to the Twenty-seventh and asked the men to cheer when his shots seemed to be doing execution. After a few trials he succeeded in dropping his missiles, and exploding them, squarely in the midst of the cowering, defenseless enemy. The men of the regiment cheered, and then followed the most galling, merciless shelling of men, corralled where they could neither defend themselves or escape, that it ever fell to our lot to witness. From first to last, the enemy was severely punished in this battle. [I] quote the following from a correspondent of the New York *Herald:*

"Along the little stream ran a rail fence. The rebels had crowded behind this for protection, but were literally mowed down. The torn, bloody knapsacks, haversacks and frequent pools of blood were ghastly evidences of how they suffered. The stream was choked up with bodies and discolored with blood. In the ravine and around the house, where they had crowded for shelter, their bodies lay piled on one another."

Newspaper statements are often exaggerated, but this reference to "pools of blood," and the water in the little stream being "discolored" by it, unusual as it is, even in war, is confirmed as being literally true by conservative eye-witnesses in the Twenty-seventh. Different ones have affirmed that they had always supposed such language to be figurative only, until they passed over this fatal field. They here saw not pools of human blood only, but also places where it had run in streams over the ground for considerable distances. And the stagnant water in the brook was plainly affected by it in many places.[32]

General Stevenson reported the fire that scythed through his division "was exceedingly heavy, and the artillery of the enemy, which was massed in large force and admirably posted, was served with a rapidity and fatal precision which could not be surpassed." One of his regimental commanders in the leading wave, Major John P. McGuire, 32nd Tennessee, thought for a few minutes that "we were in the midst of one of the fiercest battles of the war." Through "a perfect torrent of lead and iron," McGuire's men struggled to the marsh-like creek separating them from their foe. It was then they discovered the troops to their left, Brigadier General Alfred Cumming's four Georgia regiments, had not kept pace. Federal fire focused on the Tennesseans. McGuire went down with a severe wound and was

Richard F. Carlile

• *First Lieutenant William J. Augustine, 29th Pennsylvania, served nearly three years as General Williams' division ordnance officer. Note metallic 20th Corps badge pinned to his coat and the distinctive Ordnance Department "bursting bomb" emblem sewn at the front of his cap.*

carried from the field. His colonel, Edmund Cook, acting as brigade commander, was shot dead. "What to do in our present condition was difficult to determine, for our loss in the charge had been immense. To pursue the attack farther would have been madness. More than half of the officers and men of the Thirty-second Tennessee Regiment were killed or wounded in this engagement."[33]

Brigadier General Arthur M. Manigault, whose five Alabama and South Carolina regiments advanced at the right-front of Hindman's division,

Generals In Gray

• *Major General Thomas C. Hindman, whose eyes were injured in a riding accident July 3, was severely criticized in the aftermath of the Kolb's Farm debacle by one of his brigade commanders, Arthur Manigault: "Hindman, who never led his division, but left it entirely to his brigadiers ... was so entirely ignorant of the ground, having made no observation of it previous to the commencement of that attack, that they, acting under his orders and directions, found themselves, soon after getting under fire, clashing with each other, and in an almost inextricable jumble."*

considered "the affair [to be] a miserable failure." Writing three years later, he flatly censured Hood. "This engagement ... was a disgrace to the officer who planned it, and showed an amount of ignorance of the enemy's position, and the difficulties to be overcome before he could be reached, for which there could be no excuse .... I formed my estimate of him on this occasion for the first time, and subsequent events only confirmed me in the opinion that

he was totally unfit for the command of a corps, altho he might have deserved the reputation he had acquired as the best division commander in the Army of Northern Virginia." [34]

In spite of the "galling fire" the Confederates were subjected to, Manigault still believed the Union rail piles could have been carried. "But no one expected to find, as two-thirds of the attacking force did, on nearing the works, that they were located on the opposite side of a creek, with a boggy, miry margin on each side. The delay caused by the difficulty in crossing gave the attacked great advantages, and produced so much confusion and disorder that the whole impetus of the charge was lost." [35]

The stream indeed impeded forward movement, but it was the combined effect of musketry and artillery fire, some of it at point-blank range, that cost Stevenson 870 and Hindman 215 casualties. A majority of these losses can be attributed to Yankee cannoneers. On Hascall's front, the 19th Ohio Battery expended 167 rounds while Battery F, 1st Michigan Light, threw 53 charges of case-shot and canister at the Rebels from a distance of 400 yards. Batteries I and M, 1st New York Light, were much closer to Stevenson's point of attack aimed at Williams' division, and together fired 949 various types of ammunition. [36] For a while, Captain John D. Woodbury's Battery M was sorely pressed, as vividly described by one of his non-commissioned officers, Sergeant Frank Elliot:

For 30 minutes the scrap was animated and everybody kept busy. I did not see a Yankee who was not doing his very best. The rebel line was much longer than ours; they overlapped our left but the batteries in the main line opened on them and they were forced back to our left front, and soon a similar movement was tried on our right — with the same result. Their whole force then moved forward under cover of the hill and the firing slackened. We distinctly heard the order "Fix bayonets!" and we were expecting them to try a rush upon us. From the beginning of our service we had never been budged from any place we tried to hold, and we had no thoughts of being driven then.

The 46th Pennsylvania occupied the space between the sections. [An] old cotton gin was about 40 rods to the front and somewhat to the right, a two-story building about 25 to 40 feet in size. The left half of the first story was open and occupied by a large horse-power engine. We had a fair view of the west end of the building; a stovepipe hole was visible a few feet below the peak.

I was at the right of my gun when a ball crashed through the top of the head of a man standing at arm's length from me. He was a young fellow about 17. He fell on his back and every

Killed at Kolb's Farm

Although Confederate casualties at Kolb's Farm exceeded their opponent's by more than five to one, the Union 20th Corps lost a number of officers, including those pictured here.

At right, Major David C. Beckett, 61st Ohio, was shot down while moving his regiment to reinforce the left center of Williams' division, and was the highest ranking Federal killed in the June 22 battle. Below, First Lieutenant Henry A. Gridley, commanding Company A, 150th New York, fell with a bullet through the heart. At lower right, Captain William Wheeler, 13th New York Battery, commanded the artillery of Geary's division. Early in the action, while directing fire of one of the 13th Battery's sections of 12-pounder Napoleons, he was struck by a musket ball and instantly killed.

Brad L. Pruden

USAMHI

USAMHI

muscle seemed strained to its utmost tension. His captain, standing near, assisted by another comrade, raised him to his feet, when he opened his eyes, seized the captain's coat collar with both hands and exclaimed: "Captain, am I killed?"

The captain laughed and replied: "You certainly don't act much like a dead man." But he was dead, and did not hear the captain's reply.

I saw a gun stuck out of the stovepipe hole mentioned, and another rifle ball shattered the stock of a soldier's musket near me. I stepped to the side of my gunner and requested him to blow a shell through that stovepipe hole. He sighted the piece and fired, but the shot went too high by several feet. Out came the rifle again, and down went Charles Hatch, my No. 5, who was coming up with a round in his leather bag. The shot penetrated his right temple and passed out at the base of the brain. He fell about 15 feet back of the gun's trail. I stepped up to him and tried to arouse him, calling him by name. His eyes were wide open, but they were sightless. I then noticed the wound. Evidently he never knew what hit him.

I then said to the gunner: "You shot too high. You must shoot lower and hit that fellow or he will kill the whole of us."

Two comrades with a stretcher were about to carry Hatch's body away. I told them he was as safe there as anywhere, but to leave the stretcher as we might have use for it.

John Dryer, my No. 1, then said to me: "We are out of water and this sponge is dry and sticky, and I am about out of wind. I wish someone would load a few times for me." I reached for the sponge staff when a ball struck him in the right breast, passing out at a point between the shoulder blade and the spine.

"Frank, I am shot," he said as I caught him under the arms.

"I know it," I replied.

The stretcher was quickly brought, and as I laid him back on it — the blood gushing out between his fingers as he held his hand over the wound — he said: "Frank, I don't care a damn for the wound if we only lick them."

I swabbed the gun and sent the charge home. As I stepped back a musket ball passed close enough to my left ear to be suggestive. My gunner had lost his head and missed again, and I said to him: "You get around here and load this gun. I can hit him," and we exchanged places.

In my two years' previous service as gunner I had fired or aimed a 10-pounder Parrott for more than 1,500 rounds, and with the old gun could have hit a man's face every time at that short range. This gun was a brass 12-pounder Napoleon, and I had not studied the ranges; consequently, my first shot was three feet too high and passed through the roof. My second shot was as much too low. It hit the main part of the engine, knocking it down and the big drive wheel with it. My next aim was correct, and as I gave the finishing turn to the [elevating] screw the fellow shot again and knocked the muzzle-sight off the piece. I gave the order to fire. The shot seemed to burst against the building, three feet below the pipe hole. For an instant the atmosphere in that vicinity was filled with smoke, splinters, clapboards and building materials. There was a hole in the end of the old gin that a mule and cart could have gone through. Some 20 long-legged rebels who were inside concluded that was a good place to make tracks from, and they started for the

Mass. MOLLUS, USAMHI

• *Brigadier General Joseph F. Knipe's four regiments at the center of Williams' division bore the brunt of Stevenson's assault. Knipe termed the battle of Kolb's Farm "as spirited a little fight as we have had during the present campaign."*

woods with much cheering from our side, emphasized by a few shots from the infantry boys.

[The sergeant] of the right gun came over and placed his hand on my shoulder and said: "Can you see those fellows in my front? They have fixed bayonets and are going to charge on us."

"Yes," I replied, "I can see them, but the gun sits too low to be brought to bear on them." He went back to his gun.

We loaded with two charges of canister, 12 pounds each. I

then [took a] bag of musket balls — over 20 pounds — and they were added to the charge in the gun, which we ran by hand a rod or so to the front and right. A slight depression in the hill led down to Hood's front lines. We forced the gun up on a small pile of rails and thence had a fine view of about 200 of the enemy. I depressed the muzzle, aiming by guess as the muzzle-sight was off, and fired. The gun backed off that rail pile, and the way the grass and gravel and jumping bullets went down that hill was a caution. The shot mowed a swath 20 feet wide through the rebel line and over 40, with guns in hand, believing there were more to follow, walked up into our lines and were received with great rejoicing as our prisoners.

At this time the enemy appeared to abandon the project of capturing the hill, and large numbers of men in squads of from 10 to 100 would break cover and make for the timber from whence they had come. The rebel line, however, remained under cover of the hill until night let down her sable curtain, when they withdrew, taking [many of] their dead and wounded with them. [37]

"The slaughter of the rebels was actually murderous," a Wisconsin soldier reflected. New York lieutenant Edwin Weller walked over the battlefield the next morning to view the debris. "Prisoners who have been captured since the fight state that they lost very heavy ... and carried off most [of] their killed. We buried some fifty in front of our lines. I think what they suffered will repay them in part for the damage they did us on the 25th [of May]." [38]

General Williams wrote home shortly after the battle, extolling his troops' conduct. "The Rebs had been badly shaken by our artillery fire before they left the woods. All the prisoners say this. Indeed, after the first half-hour [my] men considered the whole affair great sport. They would call out to the Rebels who had taken shelter in the woods and in the deep ravines in our front, 'Come up here, Johnny Reb. Here is a weak place!' 'Come up and take this battery; we are Hooker's paper collar boys!' 'We've only got two rounds of ammunition, come and take us!' 'What do you think of Joe Hooker's Iron Clads?' and the like. The fellows down in the shelters, I regret to say, generally answered with some very profane language and with firing of their guns. [The next morning] over sixty of them lay dead there .... Altogether, I have never had an engagement in which success was won so completely and with so little sacrifice of life. Considering the number of the enemy sent against my single division, the result is indeed most wonderful and gratifying." [39]

CHAPTER 6

There was no alternative but to attack

The heat and humidity of June 23 was oppressive, and the soldiers of the 125th Ohio sought comfort under the shade of oak and chestnut trees. They had been in the front line the entire previous night. With relief, the Ohioans idled away the early afternoon quietly in camp. At 3 p.m., however, their much-needed rest was rudely disturbed when shouted orders called everyone to fall in.

As part of Newton's 4th Corps' division, the 125th, known as "Opdycke's Tigers" after the regiment's stellar performance at Chickamauga in September 1863, marched south to occupy a section of Hooker's vacated trenches. The long tramp brought the Tigers to the rear of the 100th Illinois, whose one-armed colonel, Frederick A. Bartleson, was up on the skirmish line as Newton's division officer of the day. The Ohioans again plopped down and waited.

First Lieutenant Ralsa C. Rice of Company B stretched out on the ground to relax. A few minutes later one of his men named Robert F. Rice [no relation] sat down beside him. "We are going to have a battle today," the private said, "and I will be killed. I want you to notice that I go as far as anyone in our company."

The lieutenant was puzzled, and later recalled: "I saw no indications of a battle and tried to reason with him. While thus engaged we were ordered up to the reserve where, without halting, Companies K, E and B were ordered out on the skirmish line. We quickly deployed and ran out. We found [the 100th Illinois] occupying rifle pits in the edge of the woods. We were offered no accommodations with them as their pits were already crowded. We took position behind trees in front of their line and began firing."

Rice noticed no unusual enemy activity ahead, and could not fathom why his regiment's three companies were so urgently required in such an exposed location where the trees were almost useless as cover. Suddenly, the man standing next to him slumped over, shot through the head. "I then thought of Robert," the lieutenant continued. "I saw him several rods in front of everyone else and while I was looking he, too, fell dead. Our best and bravest were falling fast. It was a sorry day for the left wing. Capt. [Sterling] Manchester of Company K was mortally wounded. Our loss here was three

Mass. MOLLUS, USAMHI

• *Inured to nearly three years of hard campaigning and combat, members of Company B, 125th Ohio, above, pose for a group portrait at Nashville in June 1865. Twelve months earlier their lieutenant, Ralsa Rice, called Kennesaw Mountain the "Gibraltar of America." Private Robert Rice of Company B and Captain Sterling Manchester of Company K were killed on June 23, 1864.*

Opdycke Tigers, 125th O.V.I.

First Lieutenant Ralsa C. Rice

Private Robert F. Rice

Captain Sterling Manchester

Craig Dunn

• Eight members of Company D, 57th Indiana, gathered to be photographed on Lookout Mountain early in 1864. Standing from left: Second Lieutenant Jacob B. Swisher, Sergeant Isaac Vanuys, Corporal Anderson L. Davis, Sergeant William H. Turner, Sergeant Asher Pearce and Private Samuel Nixon. Seated: Private Jacob B. Renfrow, Private William D. George and "Tobe," the company's negro servant. Davis, married on March 17 during the regiment's veteran furlough in Indiana, was killed at Kennesaw on June 23 and his body left in Confederate hands. Turner was mortally wounded the same day and captured, dying in an Atlanta hospital on July 15. "I like soldiering better than ever I did," he once told his mother. An ardent opponent of the active Copperhead movement in southeastern Indiana, Turner wrote: "I only wish that their was enough of us to run them in to the Gulf of Mexico. I would not want one to get away to tell that their ever had been sutch a race of ignorant people."

killed and 14 wounded."[1]

Shells screamed overhead to soften up the Rebels as part of General George Wagner's brigade, Newton's division, prepared to assault the opposing rifle pits. On the brigade's left, Sergeant Asbury Kerwood of the 57th Indiana listened for the bugles to signal the infantry's advance. "In an instant the 57th was over the works and moving forward under a most galling fire from the enemy," he wrote. "They fought desperately to retain possession of their line of rifle-pits, but when the reserve line of the regiment came up they were forced to retreat behind their main line, and we took possession of their pits. Up to this time the regiment had met but a slight loss, for the first movement of the skirmishers was well supported by the reserve. In a short time the rebels came swarming out of their works, and, yelling like demons, advanced to the attack, in front and on both flanks. Then commenced bloody work. It was madness to think of resisting such a force, and the regiment was ordered by Major Blanch to retire to the line of rifle-pits from which we advanced." [2]

Some of the Hoosiers, like Captain Joseph S. Stidham of Company C and First Lieutenant Robert F. Callaway of Company E, stood their ground and were shot down. A number were left dead between the lines and others, too severely wounded to be carried away, became prisoners. Blanch, promoted to lieutenant colonel the following day, rallied his regiment at the rifle pits. Although the 57th repulsed the Confederate counterattack on its front, further losses were incurred due to a lack of sufficient protection. There simply were not enough holes for everyone. [3]

The 26th Ohio charged to the Indianans' right and likewise was forced back, suffering four killed and nine wounded, three of them mortally. It was "awful hard fighting," Company B's orderly sergeant William Jones informed friends back home. His letter told how one member of his company had a hand mangled, while another was hit in the head, the bullet entering the man's left eye and exiting at his jaw. "They shot a hole through my sock leg. I had my pants inside of my socks and they shot a part of one of my finger-nails away causing it to bleed quite freely, but I am all right now." Jones concluded plaintively: "I hope to God I may never be called to witness such sights again. Oh I loath and abhor the name of war and do wish it may be settled soon for I am very tired of this miserable way of living." [4]

The highest-ranking casualty of June 23 on this portion of the Kennesaw line was Colonel Bartleson. His regimental surgeon, Henry T. Woodruff, wrote two days later:

Illinois State Historical Library

• *Colonel Frederick A. Bartleson, 100th Illinois, lost his left arm at Shiloh. Captured at Chickamauga, he spent six months confined in Richmond's Libby Prison until exchanged in March 1864. He rejoined the regiment less than two months before his death on June 23.*

He went out as Division Officer of the Day, being in charge of the skirmish line. The forenoon was very quiet, and he came in about one o'clock to the regiment headquarters to dinner. The position of Officer of Pickets, on the skirmish line, in such times as these, is one of great danger, and we had all hoped that that day all would be quiet, but about two o'clock in the afternoon, orders were sent around which plainly indicated to us that something in the way of offensive operations was to be done. The artillery opened all along the line for several moments, and the lines were advanced, the skirmish line advancing and one brigade moving on to their support. The Colonel was killed soon after the commencement of the advance. The left of the

line did not advance as fast as the rest, and the Colonel rode out to spur them up. There was a point there which was plainly in view of the Rebel line, and they fired at everyone passing by the opening. A Rebel ball struck the Colonel on the right side, passing through the body and coming out on the left side. His death was probably almost instantaneous. The stretcher-bearers of the 57th Indiana (which regiment was on the skirmish line) saw him fall and went to him, and finding him dead, they carried the body back of a barn in the rear of the old line, and sent us word of the occurrence. We immediately sent out our own stretcher-bearers and had his body brought in ....

I have seen many officers and men killed on the field, but never saw one whose death seemed to strike such a blow to everyone as his did. Generals Newton, Wagner and Harker were nearby, and came up. The regiment passed in review by the

Blue Acorn Press

First Lieutenant Ambrose G. Bierce

Private Henry L.C. Ramage, Company C, 1st Tennessee Infantry, was killed June 23.

body, to take the last look at one they loved and honored.[5]

Elsewhere along the 4th Corps front, First Lieutenant Ambrose G. Bierce nearly lost his own life to a Confederate bullet. Bierce, whose literary skill after the war earned him international acclaim, had been sent forward to assist directing the brigade skirmish line of General William B. Hazen, on whose staff he served as topographical officer. While thus engaged he was struck in the head by a musket ball, causing a severe and painful wound. The next day Bierce celebrated his 22nd birthday lying barely conscious in a field hospital, his head swathed in bandages. An operation to remove the ball and three months' recuperation were required before he returned to duty.[6]

"The slaughter still goes on," scribbled Indiana sergeant Walter Wilson in his diary for June 24. His company commander was killed the previous afternoon, and he faced another night's labor in the trenches while "the Rebb guns on Kennesaw Ridge keep up a regular fire all the time." Between 10 and 11 a.m., Illinoisan James Burkhalter counted 400 enemy shells thrown in his brigade's direction, an occurrence repeated several times before nightfall.[7]

The cannonading was distinctly heard by Sherman, who now was even more determined to break the apparent stalemate at Kennesaw. His attempt on the 22nd to flank the Confederate left along the Powder Springs Road had been stymied by Hood's preemptive attack at Kolb's Farm. Since then, further shifts south by Schofield's troops continued to meet Rebel resistance as Johnston stretched his already thin line to block the flanking Federals. To keep moving in this direction, Sherman was convinced, meant extending his own lines beyond a secure distance from the railroad. Maintaining his supply route and communications via the Western & Atlantic tracks was critical; consequently, the alternative of flanking the Confederates on McPherson's front east of Kennesaw Mountain was given scant consideration. That left one other course of action — to attack the Southerners frontally at some vulnerable point. The Union leader consulted his three subordinate army commanders who, Sherman claimed, "all agreed that we could not with prudence stretch out any more, and therefore there was no alternative but to attack 'fortified lines,' a thing carefully avoided up to that time. I reasoned, if we

A fallen officer's sword

Captain John Eastman, Company H, 93rd Ohio

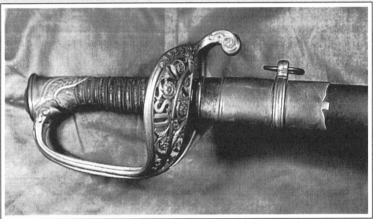

L.M. Strayer

Detail of Eastman's sword hilt.

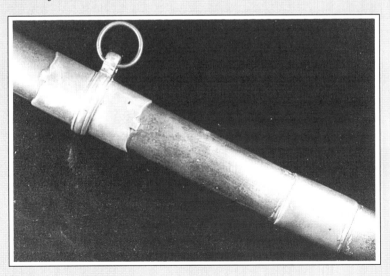

Scabbard detail, showing Lake's repair, right, and hanger mount.

On the afternoon of June 23, 4th Corps' skirmishers started toward the Confederate works, advancing about 75 yards before the men fell to the ground and dug in. Supported in part by the 93rd Ohio of William B. Hazen's brigade, these troops suffered heavy losses until darkness brought a close to the firing. Among the casualties were three of Hazen's officers. Lieutenant Ambrose Bierce, topographical officer, suffered a severe head wound; Captain Friedrich Nierhoff of Company I, 6th Kentucky, was killed, and Captain John Eastman of Company H, 93rd Ohio, was fatally wounded. "It was a mistake to require us to advance closer," Hazen reflected, "being already so near."

As brigade officer of the day, Eastman was commanding Hazen's skirmishers when he was toppled from his horse by a Confederate sharpshooter, the fall breaking his sheathed M1850 foot officer's sword and scabbard. Standing nearby was Captain Jarvis Lake of the 93rd's Company B, who tried to help the stricken officer. Lake repaired his friend's equipment and carried the sword through the rest of the war. Many years later, he donated the memento to the Mulharen-O'Cain Post, Grand Army of the Republic, at Eaton, Ohio, where it remained until the hall disbanded.

could make a breach anywhere near the rebel centre, and thrust in a strong head of column, that with the one moiety of our army we could hold in check the corresponding wing of the enemy, and with the other sweep in flank and overwhelm the other half." Eight days earlier, writing to Washington, he had entertained similar thoughts. "[I] am now inclined to feign on both flanks and assault the center. It may cost us dear but in results would surpass an attempt to pass around .... If, by assaulting, I can break his line, I see no reason why it would not produce a decisive effect." [8]

During the morning of the 24th Sherman moved from Big Shanty to a knob he called Signal Hill, located behind the army's center on Thomas' front. Telegraphers quickly strung field wire and connected the new headquarters with those of Thomas, McPherson and Schofield. Later in the day Sherman issued Special Field Orders No. 28, outlining for his subordinates the plan of battle. Two days were allotted for reconnaissance and preparations. With offensive movements scheduled to commence at 8 a.m. on June 27, the orders read:

I. Major-General Thomas will assault the enemy at any point near his center, to be selected by himself, and will make any changes in his troops necessary by night, so as not to attract the attention of the enemy.

II. Major-General McPherson will feign by a movement of his cavalry and one division of infantry on his extreme left, approaching Marietta from the north, and using artillery freely, but will make his real attack at a point south and west of Kenesaw.

III. Major-General Schofield will feel well to his extreme right and threaten that flank of the enemy with artillery and display, but attack some one point of the enemy's line as near the Marietta and Powder Springs road as he can with prospect of success.

IV. All commanders will maintain reserve and secrecy even from their staff officers, but make all the proper preparations and reconnaissances. When troops are to be shifted to accomplish this attack the movements will be made at night. At the time of the general attack the skirmishers at the base of Kenesaw will take advantage of it to gain, if possible, the summit and hold it.

V. Each attacking column will endeavor to break a single point of the enemy's line, and make a secure lodgment beyond, and be prepared for following it up toward Marietta and the railroad in case of success. [9]

Schofield was exempted from the attack order the following day after Sherman inspected the right wing and determined the Confederate defenses there were too imposing. Schofield instead was directed

to begin "demonstrations" south of the Powder Springs Road and across Olley Creek. It was hoped this would draw enemy troops away from the center where the primary assaults were to be delivered. [10]

That task fell to Thomas, who spent most of June 25 in quiet frustration trying to find a suitable point of attack. Few, if any, places appeared promising. With misgivings stoically concealed, he finally selected a sector just south of the Marietta-Dallas Road where the opposing lines were fairly close, yet separated enough for unseen deployment of a large assault force. Because of Sherman's insistence on strict secrecy, it was morning of the 26th when Thomas notified his 4th and 14th corps commanders — Generals Howard and Palmer, respectively — that a division from each would deliver the main blow. Those chosen were commanded by General Newton (4th Corps), a veteran of Antietam, Chancellorsville and Gettysburg, and Brigadier General Jefferson C. Davis (14th Corps), an Indianan who 21 months earlier shot and killed an ex-commanding officer in a Louisville hotel lobby. [11]

McPherson, too, was apprehensive but kept his feelings hidden. Portions of his 16th and 17th corps, assisted by General Garrard's cavalry division, were to feign attacks on Big Kennesaw from the north and northeast while Logan's 15th Corps assaulted Pigeon Hill on both sides of the Burnt Hickory Road. In order to do so, Logan's troops were transferred the nights of June 25 and 26 from their breastworks north of the mountain to those being vacated by Davis' and Baird's 14th Corps' divisions, which shifted further south at the same time. [12] Three brigades from Logan's command would spearhead the Pigeon Hill operation, an assault intended to be secondary to the main push on Thomas' front.

While preparations proceeded, musketry on the skirmish lines and the bellow of dueling cannon never ceased, though artillery fire slackened substantially on June 26, an uncomfortably hot Sunday. Religious services beckoned to many soldiers in camp. Others penned letters home or updated their diaries. "This is a day that goes to prove that the saying 'The Sunny South' is a correct idea — at least, as far as the heat is concerned," wrote Sergeant Elias Cole of Company C, 26th Ohio, in his journal. He compared the stifling weather to "heavy drop dumplings and hot mush in a bake oven." Over several previous days the soaring temperature

Mass. MOLLUS, USAMHI

Brigadier General John Newton

spawned an explosion of insect populations, and this added to Cole's discomfort. "We found it necessary to keep the fly brush in motion to prevent the blue-bottles from blowing our dinner before we could eat it. For illustration, the flies blowed a pair of clean socks, clothing of any kind, and mess pork just out of the barrel." [13]

Corporal Ambrose Remley of the 72nd Indiana concurred. "The flies are worse down here than I ever seen them. Green flies especially. If our blankets get a little damp they will blow them. They blow our salty pickeled pork and if we draw any fresh meat we have to cook it right away and then eat it before it gets cold." [14]

Such things, wrote Lieutenant Colonel Samuel Merrill of the 70th Indiana to his wife, "may appear only disgusting to you, but I consider them as constituting the chief hardships of the soldier. One of the horrors of this kind of life is that the mens bod-

ies and clothes are alive [with vermin] and nothing can be done to relieve them as they have no change of clothing and seldom any opportunity to bathe. The officers if they exert themselves and change their clothes frequently can escape the affliction, but the poor private drags his tormented carcass in utter hopelessness to the end of the campaign. Another trouble is produced by wearing thick wool clothes and by eating fat salt pork. Everyone from Colonel to Private is broken out horribly, and cannot enjoy a moments rest for the intolerable itching." [15]

William F. King, the 124th Indiana's assistant surgeon, informed his wife that "the worst plague we have in this army is body lice. The boys in the ranks and in the Hospitals are literally covered with them and I suppose there is not an officer that escapes. They will get on us in spite of every precaution. At first they worried me awfully but I have got so I can stand them pretty well by changing clothes often and hunting them down. We manage to keep them from over running but it is impossible to keep clean entirely." [16]

In addition to flying and crawling bugs, Sergeant Alexander Downing of the 11th Iowa had endured the sun's broiling rays lying in a rifle pit on June 25, and looked forward to being relieved that evening. Minutes after falling back to the regiment's breast-works, one of his close friends, Private John W. Esher, peered through the aperture under the head-log toward Kennesaw Mountain. "All of a sudden," Downing recalled, "a ball crashed in, knocking him down, and as he fell back his heels kicked up. He was right by my side when he was struck [in the jaw and neck], and as he fell he cried out, 'oh, boys, I'm killed!' " Esher eventually recovered but was disfigured for life.

The following day Downing observed three brigades of the 15th Corps leave their defenses and march away, noting as well how quiet it seemed north of the mountain. He confided in his journal: "May God hasten the day when this cruel war will be brought to a close, so that our nation may enjoy peace once more. But we must remember that there may be many men yet who will fall for their country before it is free from this accursed secession. May God be with us and help us as we stand in need ...." [17]

Captain Joseph W. Young, commanding Company C of the 97th Indiana, was among those of Logan's corps to move into position west of Little Kennesaw. Young, a Mexican War veteran, farmer and father of three children, was homesick. "I would like to come over this evening," he told his parents, "and take a good supper with you and have a big chat and see your corn, wheat and oats and that would take me out of the sound of the Battle that is going on. I had a fine visit with you all last fall [during a September 1863 furlough] but it seems like I want to see you all the worst that I ever did in my life. I would like to get a letter from you while I am down here in this God forsaken country for I think it is the poorest country I ever seen." [18]

These were the last thoughts the captain was able to mail home, for Young little knew that he had less than 24 hours to live.

As the day wore on those soldiers possessing a suspicious nature guessed that something big was brewing. "Appearances are ominous of an advance of our lines," wrote the 20th Illinois' sergeant major, Frank Chester. "No noise is allowed. Every man is furnished with about 50 rounds of ammunition." Corporal Henry Wright of the 6th Iowa observed: "Men of intelligence composed the rank and file of the army and it was perfectly natural that they should desire to know where and how far they were to march, and whether to battle or to camp. The secrecy which usually shrouded military operations left the brave men in the ranks in helpless ignorance of pending movements of the army; but there had been such a marked activity at the front and in the rear bringing up ammunition, filling the artillery chests, inspecting cartridge boxes, supplying stretchers and cots at the field hospitals, filling the medical chests, brightening up the surgeon's knives and saws, and marshaling the ambulances for duty, that all could understand that a conflict was pending." [19]

Three quarters of a mile from Wright's camp, the Confederates of Brigadier General Francis M. Cockrell's Missouri brigade found the stillness almost unnatural after 10 consecutive days fraught with heavy cannonading and skirmish fire. In many respects, Cockrell's soldiers spent June 26 like their blueclad counterparts. "Had preaching in A.M.," First Lieutenant Avington W. Simpson of Company F, 5th Missouri, penciled in his diary. "It being Sunday every thing more quiet." [20]

Near the railroad at the east base of Big Kennesaw, Columbus Sykes, the 43rd Mississippi's lieutenant colonel, luxuriated in the fighting's unexpected lull and shared the moment in a letter to his wife: "The day is beautiful, bright, warm — a brass band is discoursing sweet music from the mountain, and the strains, mellowed and softened by distance, come floating gently down the valley, while an occasional cannon, deep and low, plays the bass, accompanied with venomous minie balls from the enemy's sharpshooters. Rather a strange incongruous combination of sounds for a lovely Sabbath evening, is it not? But this being the 46th day to which we have been listening uninterruptedly at the last two, they fail to attract our attention, while the first, now but seldom heard, cheers and enlivens the men and is received with shouts of joy." [21]

The summer idyll was fleeting, however, as Georgian Hamilton Branch realized only too well. "The old saying of there always being a storm after a calm may be proved true up here. Some think that we are agoing to fall back whilst others think that we will have the big fight [and it] will take place here." [22]

Wrote Texas artillery captain James P. Douglas: "The enemy are strongly intrenched immediately in front of us along the entire line. If Sherman plans to attack us, I can see no reason for further delay." [23]

Like the tired men of his company, Captain Alvah S. Skilton welcomed the arrival of twilight. He watched them gather in little knots behind the breastworks following a frugal meal. Tobacco-filled pipes were lit, sparking chatter about the day's adventures and speculation concerning the campaign's probable outcome. Many conjectured as to what would, or should, be Sherman's next move. Nearly everyone who spoke thought himself competent to advise the general, but all agreed it would be another flank movement.

Darkness settled over the camp, mantling the rocks, trees, rifle stacks and the men themselves. For a while silence reigned, broken only by the low murmur of soldiers' voices as the talk changed to loved ones at home, dead or absent comrades, ribald tales and good-natured joking. It was a time-passing ritual, and Skilton listened intently until summoned for his own evening supper further back in a grove of pines. There, as senior captain of the 57th Ohio, he joined Colonel A.V. Rice, Lieutenant Colonel Samuel R. Mott, Adjutant William M. Newell and regimental quartermaster Louis L. Parker. The officers sat in a circle, a camp chest furnishing their table, a single tallow candle illuminating their faces.

"The meal was nearly finished," Skilton reminisced, "when an orderly was heard inquiring for Col. Rice. On being directed to him he delivered an envelope, gave a salute and rode away into the darkness. Col. Rice broke the seal deliberately, read the order and without comment passed it to Col. Mott, who read it and gave it to me. So it was read in silence and passed around the table."

The envelope contained an order for the 57th's brigade, commanded by Brigadier General Giles A. Smith, to leave its works that night and proceed to a designated spot near the depression between Little Kennesaw Mountain and Pigeon Hill. Then, shortly after daylight on June 27, the brigade was to form part of a storming column — a "forlorn hope," the soldiers called it — and force a lodgment inside the Confederate defenses. Skilton continued:

In an hour the regiment was underway and marched a greater part of the night before we arrived at the place assigned us, which was in a dense field of underbrush and close up to the enemy's works. Here we laid down for a little rest. It seemed as though I had scarcely fallen asleep when I was awakened by someone shaking me and whispering in my ear that Col. Rice wanted me. I reported at once and found that Gen. Giles Smith had sent an order requiring the three ranking officers of each

CHAPTER 7

The martial tread of trained heroes

L.M. Strayer

L.M. Strayer

Mass. MOLLUS, USAMHI

• *Three and a half weeks after the June 27 Kennesaw assaults, Captain Alvah S. Skilton, above, of Company I, 57th Ohio, was captured with some 90 members of his regiment during the battle of Atlanta. He spent seven of the next nine months confined in six different Rebel prisons. The 57th's field officers were Colonel Americus V. Rice, left, and Lieutenant Colonel Samuel R. Mott, right.*

regiment of the brigade to report at his headquarters. Cols. Rice and Mott, and myself, proceeded to report at once and were, I believe, the first to arrive.

Gen. Smith had established his headquarters under a hickory tree with a small, circular grass plot about 40 feet in diameter to the south of it. The plot was surrounded by a dense growth of underbrush. In a short time there were assembled here the three ranking officers from each regiment in the brigade and the members of Gen. Smith's staff. When all had reported Gen.

Smith addressed us as follows: "Gentlemen, I have sent for you to advise you of what is expected of us today and to make such provision as is possible to prevent confusion or misunderstanding. This column has been selected as a 'forlorn hope' and we are expected to carry the enemy's works in our front. Should we succeed in doing it, we are to hold them at all hazards for at least 10 minutes when ample reinforcements will be sent to enable us to hold the works. Gentlemen, this will be serious business and some of us must go down. I do not say this to frighten you, for I know that is impossible, but to impress on your minds that if I fall you must look to Col. [James S.] Martin of the 111th Illinois for orders. If he falls you must look to Col. Rice of the 57th Ohio."

Turning to Col. Rice, who stood nearest to him, he said, "Of course, Col. Rice commands his regiment. Should he go down, Col. Mott succeeds and in the event of his falling, Capt. Skilton will assume command." Gen. Smith addressed the officers of each regiment in like manner, calling each officer by name and rank, thereby showing how perfectly he was acquainted with them and how thorough was his knowledge of his command. When he was finished he said, "Gentlemen, go back to your respective commands, impart this information to your men and when the bugle sounds, charge. And may God bless and protect you all!" [1]

When news of the impending assault reached the line officers and enlisted men, many were dumbfounded. In Walcutt's brigade of the 15th Corps, slated to attack on the left of Giles Smith's, Captain Charles Wills and several other 103rd Illinois company commanders "did not particularly enjoy the prospect." Lieutenant Colonel George W. Wright told them to breakfast their men by daylight and be ready to charge the mountain at 8 a.m. Wills immediately sought his orderly sergeant, instructed him to have Company G up on time, then laid down to rest. "I thought the matter over a little while and after pretty fully concluding 'good-bye, vain world,' went to sleep." [2]

On the 14th Corps' front, where two of Davis' brigades were assembling for their part in the main assault, Captain James Burkhalter of the 86th Illinois was informed of the charge at 7 a.m. by Lieutenant Colonel Allen L. Fahnestock. Burkhalter, in utter disbelief, wrote: "So much for the foolish dream of our soldiers who thought that our few days in reserve presaged a new status as a pet brigade. Pet my foot. *Rested for the slaughter would be more like it.* The stupidity of this order is enough to paralyze me. However, I obeyed the orders so far as related to getting ready. This amounted to having plenty of ammunition, a musket, and to divest the men of all surplus baggage and equipment. But the role of Judas is more than I can swallow, and must here acknowledge myself as altogether too skeptical to have the least confidence in the success of the enterprise. I think it far better not to give the plan of operation to my men, lest I gag on my words and reveal that I have the horrors, which, in turn, would give them the horrors, too. I consider the folly of this undertaking of itself sufficient notice for their

Mass. MOLLUS, USAMHI

Brigadier General Giles A. Smith

own peace of mind. So the minutes passed." [3]

Captain Henry S. Nourse of Company H, 55th Illinois, another of Giles Smith's regiments, also was astonished at 7 a.m. when notified of the imminent assault. He, too, had supposed the brigade's night march was simply part of yet another flanking maneuver toward the right. Instead, Pigeon Hill was its intended objective, not much more than a half mile distant. Nourse later described his regiment's final preparations:

The men were at once instructed to strip for a fight, leaving everything but essentials at the bivouac. One man from each company was detailed to remain as guard over its property.

Few but tried soldiers were in that little band waiting in the forest glade for the dread signal. Though thus surprised with the knowledge that in a few minutes they were to make a desperate dash against ramparts bristling with natural difficulties and defended by practical fighters, yet probably a casual observer would have noted in the occupation or outward manifestations of feeling among these men little to distinguish this from an ordinary group of soldiers resting on a march. A quick breakfast was eaten with appetite, and the pipe smoking and discursive talk went on as usual. But comrades could read in each other's

Ray Zielin

Captain Jacob M. Augustine, 55th Illinois

faces signs not always to be seen there; in those of the promi-nent officers sterner and more rigid facial lines, indicating the load of responsibility they felt resting upon them; in all coun-tenances a more quiet and fixed expression, almost amounting to a slight pallor. The laugh sometimes heard had no heart in it, the arguments no vivacity, the sportiveness rare or spasmodic, and often a faraway look in some eyes told of thoughts wander-ing to a distant Northern home, perhaps never again to be seen. A few handed to one of the guards, or to the chaplain, a valued watch or keepsake, with brief words of contingent instruction. A few wrote brief notes and placed them in their knapsacks.

The tendency of old soldiers to become fatalists has often been commented on. Examples of this tendency were frequently

noticed in the 55th. Tales of premonitions justified by quick-following death or wounds were often in the mouths of com-rades, while the examples, probably far more numerous, of gloomy omens that came to naught, were all forgotten. Men who had marched confidently and undismayed into battle after battle were suddenly on the approach of a fight seen to be out of heart, and save for their pride almost willing to own that their courage had all but left them.

Perhaps these cases of dismal foreboding among us were not more numerous on the morning of June 27th than before other bloody days in our experience, but several are remembered. A sergeant whose past record had proved him exceptionally brave was exceedingly depressed and confessed to his company com-mander an immovable conviction that if he went into the im-pending battle he should never see the sun rise again. He asked if he could be saved from the death that stared him in the face, without disgrace. The officer reported the case privately to the senior officer commanding the regiment, Capt. Jacob M. Au-gustine, who, knowing the worth of the sergeant, ordered him detailed to be left in command of the guard over the regimental property.[4]

There was no one to excuse Augustine from the fight. Considered an ideal company commander, a veteran long tried by hard service since early 1862, and never known to falter, he had been in a jovial mood prior to General Smith's pre-battle confer-ence. Afterward, his demeanor suddenly changed. Seated next to Captain Nourse, Augustine quietly told him he "felt the oppressive shadow of death hanging over him." He handed Nourse a pocket knife "to remember him by," pulled out a small memorandum book and wrote:

Monday, June 27, 1864.

We marched last night until eleven — got up at seven this morning — are to make an assault upon the breastworks at half-past seven. Our division takes the lead. Now may God protect the right. Am doubting our success.[5]

In order to increase the chances of success, Sher-man's plan called for demonstrations by the 23rd and 20th corps to attract Confederate front line and reserve troops toward the southern flank. Diversion-ary attacks likewise were ordered on the opposite flank, where McPherson faced two-thirds of Lor-ing's firmly-entrenched corps as well as Wheeler's cavalry. Much of the Union effort here fell to the 17th Corps' division of Brigadier General Mortimer D. Leggett, whose three brigades were poised to ad-vance south astride Bell's Ferry Road. From left to right, these were commanded by Colonel Robert K. Scott, Colonel Adam G. Malloy and Brigadier Gen-eral Manning F. Force, and were composed entirely

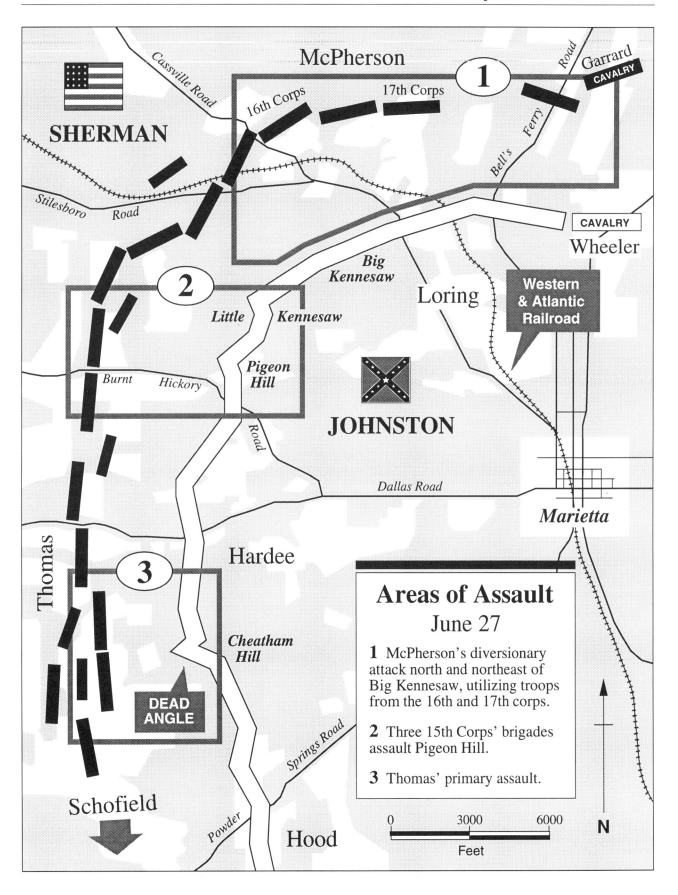

Areas of Assault
June 27

1 McPherson's diversionary attack north and northeast of Big Kennesaw, utilizing troops from the 16th and 17th corps.

2 Three 15th Corps' brigades assault Pigeon Hill.

3 Thomas' primary assault.

0   3000   6000
Feet

N

of Illinois, Ohio and Wisconsin soldiers. Precisely at 8 a.m., Leggett's troops moved forward.[6]

"Three lines of blue climbed over their works," wrote Private Jabez Cannon of the 27th Alabama, whose brigade on the far right end of Loring's sector was commanded by newly promoted Brigadier General Thomas M. Scott. "The woods being open timber, mostly tall pines, we could see them plainly from the time they left their works. On they came, maintaining their lines as perfectly as if on division drill, looking formidable enough and outnumbering us three to one; but having largely the advantage, and feeling confidence in our ability to hold our position, we waited patiently for our skirmishers to come in. The 12th Louisiana was on the skirmish line, and stood their ground until the front line of the enemy approached within 250 yards, when they retired.

"As soon as they were safely inside the breastworks we poured a deadly fire into the face of the advancing foe and at the same time the 12 cannon above us turned loose and grape, canister and minie balls mowed them down like grain before the sickle. Shells and solid shot tore limbs from the trees and split the tall pines like bolts of lightning. On, on they gallantly pressed forward, regardless of the wide gaps which were being cut in their ranks, until the front line was within a stone's throw of our breastworks; when mortal man could stand it no longer they halted, unable to advance and loath to retreat."[7]

From Force's rear battle line, the 20th Illinois' sergeant major, Frank Chester, watched the brigade's skirmishers deploy before the 31st Illinois and his own regiment stepped off. Converging fire from three masked Rebel batteries erupted, followed by volleys of musketry. As the 20th Illinois emerged from the woods it was fully exposed in a cleared field. Second Lieutenant Charles Taylor of Company I fell with a mortal wound. Eight others also were hit. Although the 12th Louisiana's skirmish line was pushed back, the Illinoisans' advance ground to a halt some 275 yards short of the main Confederate works. Chester explained:

The Rebs got two batteries in two positions and opened a cross fire with grape and shell. Some of the other regiments lost quite a number here but fortunately ours escaped unharmed during the whole fire which lasted some three hours. During the firing I was directed by the colonel to go back and have the

Brigadier General Thomas M. Scott, formerly colonel of the 12th Louisiana.

Generals In Gray

Richard W. Nee

Brigadier General Mortimer D. Leggett

stretcher bearers come up and help take off the wounded of the 31st. I found [Private] Ben Franklin, Co. E, coming up with his stretchers and stopped a moment to instruct him in case any of our musicians were seen by him lingering in the rear to have them come up and help bear off the wounded. I had just stepped from the position in which I was standing and moved on toward the regiment when a cannon shot from the enemies gun passed the very position which I had left, and had I stood still two seconds longer would have probably cut me in two — a consumation which would not have been at all satisfactory to the present occupant of this tabernacle of clay. [8]

Sergeant Ira Blanchard of Company H, 20th Illinois, recalled his own experience with a Confederate cannon ball:

[We] captured some prisoners and pushed close up to their main works, but halted under cover of some timber, where we lay flat down on the ground and let their artillery belch away at us for about two hours, but did not attempt to carry their works. The day was very warm and 'twas not so bad a thing to lay in the shade, but a hundred shells tearing around over our prostrate bodies was not altogether pleasant. I remember how a twelve pounder struck a large oak a little to our rear, then came bounding back to where we lay; as it rolled towards us I hit the thing with my foot and sent it back, but as luck would have it, it did not explode. The boys wanted to know if I had commenced a game of foot ball. It seemed that 'twas not in the program to storm their works at the point where we were, but to make a heavy demonstration to attract attention, while a strong effort was made at another point. So when our object was accomplished we withdrew, bringing our dead and wounded with us.[9]

At the center of Leggett's division, Major Asa Worden's battalion moved behind a screen of 17th Wisconsin skirmishers over broken, timbered terrain studded with large boulders. The battalion was an unusual, polyglot organization, comprised of three companies from the 14th Wisconsin and another culled from the 81st and 95th Illinois. As such, it was advancing into its first battle. Since Worden was absent sick, Captain Frederick H. Magdeburg of Company G, 14th Wisconsin, was commanding on June 27. He later wrote:

Soon we caught up with the skirmishers, who were unable to dislodge the Johnnies, who were posted on the crest of the hill, behind rifle pits, rocks and trees, making it rather lively for us. We halted, gave them a volley, loaded and then charged, which was too much for them and they got out of there speedily, some surrendering.

I ordered the skirmishers forward and again resumed our forward movement. We were now descending the hill and again overtook the skirmishers who were behind a rail fence, which enclosed an open field. Notwithstanding I had not received any orders to stop, I deemed it perfectly proper to order a halt, and ordering the men to lie down, I requested Adjutant [Benjamin

Milwaukee County Historical Society

Captain Frederick H. Magdeburg
Company G, 14th Wisconsin

F.] Goodwin to go to the right and ascertain our relative position to the balance of [the] Division, while I did the same to the left. The result of our joint reconnoitering showed that we were alone in our glory. Under the circumstances I assumed the responsibility of remaining and not advancing further, as midway between the fence and foot of the mountain in the open field there appeared to be an earth work and I could not risk going in there alone with about 300 men, as artillery seemed to be coming down the mountain road to assist the infantry in the field works. Some of our men while here were hurt, and had to be carried back. After being in that position about three-quarters of an hour we were called back toward the crest of the hill from whence we had dislodged the rebels. It must have been about eleven o'clock then, and here our trials began.

We were ordered to lie down, and we here had to take the artillery fire for about three or four hours without being able to return the compliment. Shells, solid shot and canister were flying around livelier than I had up to that time ever experienced, and many of the men were wounded. One had his gun shattered and others had very narrow escapes, among them Charles Beatty [Beattie] of Company F, whose cartridge box belt was cut in

L.M. Strayer

Colonel Greenberry F. Wiles, 78th Ohio, was known to his men as "Old Whiskers."

two by a bullet which also went through his coat extending about six inches along his backbone, while he was stooping over. We had seven men wounded. Two lost a leg and one a foot. The others, I believe, were slightly wounded. The heat during all this time was most oppressive. After about four hours we were returned to the position from whence we started in the morning.[10]

It was a similar story in front of R.K. Scott's brigade on Leggett's left. One regiment, the 78th Ohio, was pinned down by artillery fire for nearly seven hours, but miraculously escaped with only two men slightly wounded. Captain John W.A. Gillespie of Company G recounted the 78th's ensuing ordeal in a letter written the next day:

At half past three the batteries ceased firing and, having accomplished all that had been expected of us on that portion of the field, we were ordered back to the old position in front of our camp. We remained there only a few minutes, being ordered into line again. The fighting on our right at this time was simply terrific, the roar of artillery and musketry being almost deafen-

ing, while clouds of smoke kept us from seeing any part of the battle. However, we had enough to look after in our own immediate front, as we soon found out.

The brigade formed in line of battle, two regiments deep, and moved forward a quarter of a mile and prepared to receive the rebels should they charge from their rifle pits, as was reported they were going to do. I was put in command of Companies A and G of our regiment and ordered forward as skirmishers, to go as far as possible without being too much exposed. The woods we had to go through was so thick with a growth of red brush that we could scarcely work our way through it or see 10 steps ahead during our advance. We soon met the rebel skirmishers, however, and received their first fire when our boys let loose their dogs of war and drove them from the woods into their works in an open field.

On the left of our line the rebel rifle pits ran down into the woods and were thickly covered over with red brush. The left of my company got within five steps of the pits before they were aware of it. The rebs immediately opened on us from front and flanks, and being protected by their works had a big advantage and were enabled to pour a raking fire on my men without their being able to return it to much advantage, except to make the Johnnies keep their heads behind the works.

My company had advanced farther than the balance of the line of skirmishers, but owing to the dense undergrowth I did not become aware of it until the affair was over. The rebels had an enfilading fire on my boys for an hour and a half and during that time they tore the earth up all around us, cutting the limbs and leaves from the bushes so that they looked as naked as though a furious hailstorm had passed over them. I never heard balls come thicker or faster, and I hope I never get into such a place again without some chance to return the compliment in full.

Finding we could not advance or retreat, I passed the word along the line for the men to seek the best cover they could and then shoot every rebel who showed his head above the works, an order which was obeyed to the letter. As prisoners afterward stated, our boys killed and wounded several of their men in the works. One big Confederate jumped on top of the works and yelled out, "Surrender, you damned Yanks!" He raised his gun to fire, but before he could pull the trigger [Private] John W. Robinson, who was lying on the ground close to me and who had just loaded his Enfield rifle, raised up and fired, killing the fellow instantly. His gun went off in the air and I am sure I don't exaggerate when I say he jumped a full three feet up from the top of the works and fell on the brush outside, stone dead.

Col. Wiles, finding that we had gone farther than was intended we should go, ordered us to fall back to the balance of the line, Capt. [Gilbert D.] Munson [of Company B] calling in a loud voice for us to do so. Knowing it would be impossible to move as a body in any kind of safety, I had the order to fall back one at a time passed along the line, telling the men next to me that when they all got back to call me and then I would try it. The order was obeyed, but in every single instance my boys had a volley fired after them as they ran and dodged among the bushes. But they all got back.

When I heard the signal I jumped to my feet and I am certain

Blue Acorn Press

Brigadier General William A. Quarles

I never ran so fast in my life before as I did through the woods yesterday. When I got back the boys all seemed as pleased to see me as though I had been away from them a month. Gen. Leggett and Col. Wiles both said they never expected to see me alive again, after finding we had gone so much farther than was expected of us.[11]

West of Leggett, portions of six regiments from Brigadier General Walter Gresham's 4th Division, 17th Corps, charged the northern slope of Big Kennesaw but did not penetrate past the opposing skirmish line. This was held by Major Samuel L. Knox's 1st Alabama Infantry, a veteran regiment belonging to Brigadier General William A. Quarles' brigade. Quarles, accompanied by division commander Major General Edward C. Walthall and two staff officers, observed Gresham's Federals from an excellent vantage point atop the mountain. "To the First Alabama is due the whole credit of the most brilliant affair it has ever been my fortune to witness," Quarles wrote. "The steady, well-directed fire of the men drove the enemy back on the right. Moving, however, by the right flank to a point on my left where they had cover, they concentrated in three lines of battle. Major Knox re-enforced his left with his whole reserve, and without giving ground at any point repelled several obstinate and daring assaults. The Federal officers with great gallantry endeavored to bring their men up to a last and final charge, but succeeded only on the right, where the effort was as feeble as it was abortive."[12]

Knox reported "the enemy only succeeded in getting within twenty or twenty-five yards of the works; at other points they came within ten feet; at one or two points they leaped into the [rifle] pits, thinking they had carried them, but were forced to surrender." Captain Hezekiah Wakefield of Company A, 53rd Indiana, suffered this fate as well as 18 others from his regiment. Captain John H. Smith of the 16th Iowa, which furnished five companies of skirmishers in the assault, lost six men killed and 15 wounded. Believing the Confederates outnumbered him five to one, Smith wrote in his diary that evening, "this charge was one of the follies of the war." In addition to those captured, Gresham listed his division's casualties at 97 killed and wounded. By contrast, Knox lost one sergeant killed and five privates slightly wounded.[13]

Adjacent to Knox at his left, the 26th Alabama covered Colonel Edward A. O'Neal's brigade as skirmishers. It was assailed by the 66th Illinois, a 16th Corps' sharpshooter regiment armed with 16-shot Henry repeating rifles. Notwithstanding vastly superior firepower, the 66th only managed to approach within 30 to 100 yards of the Alabamians before it was "handsomely driven back."[14]

The 64th Illinois, however, enjoyed a modicum of success, at least temporarily. Brushing aside the 25th Arkansas skirmishing in front of Walthall's left flank, the 64th, known as Yates' Sharpshooters and partly armed with Henry repeaters, slowly clawed its way up Big Kennesaw's rugged northwest face. According to Major General Grenville M. Dodge, commander of the 16th Corps' left wing, the Sharpshooters "secured and held a position so close to the enemy's main line of works on top of the mountain

Lonn Ashbrook

• *Members of Company D, 66th Illinois, display the diversity of dress found in Sherman's western regiments, in marked contrast to many in the 20th Corps, derisively dubbed "Hooker's paper collar boys." At Kennesaw, the 66th carried 16-shot Henry rifles, as did a portion of the 64th Illinois. Private Truman S. Powell, who joined Company A early in 1864, extolled the Henry's virtues in a June letter home: "A man can load and fire 16 loads in the same length of time it would take to load and fire one shot with a muzzle loader. They have a metallic cartridge and do not need caps. We have to pay for our own guns and they cost $41 each. The rest of the regiment have Whitney or Windsor rifles and the Springfield rifle. These latter are good guns but half so good as the Henry rifle."*

The .44 caliber Henry rifle, showing attached leather sling

that [the Confederates] were obliged to keep closely inside of their works; its loss was heavy, and its position the most trying that soldiers could possibly be placed in. Three of its men were killed upon the enemy's works and several others within a few yards of the works." [15]

Nowhere north of Big Kennesaw did the Yankees make a lodgment in the Rebels' primary defense line, but that was not expected. Stalwart resistance and the mountain itself prevented the diversionary attacks from becoming anything more. Still, the fighting here kept the Confederate right wing occupied all morning, and its generals were unable to dispatch reinforcements elsewhere. In that regard the feint served its purpose.

Except for powder smoke drifting over Kennesaw's crest, virtually none of this activity was visible to the 5,500 infantrymen from Logan's 15th Corps who assaulted the western slopes of Little

Kennesaw and its spur, Pigeon Hill. The day's secondary attack, as it was deemed, fell to two brigades of Brigadier General Morgan L. Smith's 2nd Division and Walcutt's brigade from William Harrow's 4th Division. Walcutt was positioned opposite the depression between Little Kennesaw and Pigeon Hill. To his immediate right were the six regiments of Giles Smith, Morgan's younger brother. Giles Smith's right flank rested near the Burnt Hickory Road, which traversed Pigeon Hill's southern slope and connected with the Dallas Road, leading to Marietta. Brigadier General Joseph A.J. Lightburn's six regiments were slated to maneuver and storm south of the Burnt Hickory Road. His opponents occupied rifle pits and breastworks on the extreme right flank of W.H.T. Walker's division, Hardee's corps. The Confederates facing Giles Smith and Walcutt belonged to the left flank and center brigades of French's division, Loring's corps.

Illinois State Historical Library

Major General John A. Logan

Mass. MOLLUS, USAMHI

Brigadier General Morgan L. Smith

French, as usual, was awake early and about 7:30 found a sheltered position below Little Kennesaw's summit from where he could observe the Union camps. "There appeared great activity among the Federal staff officers and generals all along my front and up and down the lines. Artillery-firing was common at all times on the line, but now [just before 8 a.m.] it swelled in volume and extended down to the extreme left, and then from 50 guns burst out simultaneously in my front, while battery after battery, following on the right, disclosed a general attack on our entire line. Presently, as if by magic, there sprang from the earth a host of men, and in one long waving line of blue the infantry advanced ...."[16]

At first, French did not detect any enemy infantry on his immediate front owing to intervening woods at the mountain's base. But he could see Lightburn's Ohioans and Hoosiers advancing toward Walker. Several batteries on Little Kennesaw were directed to fire at this target. Lightburn was caught exposed in an open field when the shelling began. Double-quicking across, his brigade splashed over a tributary of Noyes' Creek onto low, boggy ground covered for 150 yards with thick underbrush and interwoven vines. Slashing and fumbling through the vegetation, the disordered Federals reached another open field. At its forward edge a string of rifle pits contained six picket companies of the 63rd Georgia, an untried regiment that just seven weeks earlier had been comfortably guarding the Atlantic coastline near Savannah. Lightburn's first battle line was within 60 feet of the Georgians before it loosed a volley, then rushed forward with upraised muskets.[17]

Mass. MOLLUS, USAMHI

Brigadier General Joseph A.J. Lightburn

"We held our pitts until they got in some places and clubbed the men with their guns," wrote Georgian William Norrell of Company B. "In our part of

Valentine Museum

Major General William W. Loring lost his left arm to amputation after being wounded in September 1847 at the battle of Chapultepec, Mexico.

the line [we] retreated after firing a few times. Our company went off it seemed to me like a flock of sheep though they had the company of other portions of the Regt. It is estimated that our Regt. lost in all 123 men killed, wounded, and missing."[18]

The overpowered Georgians' misfortune was compounded when their major, Joseph V.H. Allen, shouted for the regiment's four reserve companies to rush to the skirmish line's assistance. Apparently only one responded. These men collided with those in retreat, exacerbating the confusion and casualties. Pointing a finger in blame, Private Celathiel Helms of Company E, which remained in the breastworks, thought "this loss wold not have been verey mutch if it had not been for the Mager   he made them charge on the yankys and the yankeys had ten men to thir one   I recon the Mager wanted to git a Repertashion and I expect that he will git his wants but I think it will come Contrerey to his expectashion or at least the Privets will not think any the more of him for his Bravery and not so mutch of the Bravery as the fool." [19]

Although the 63rd's stand lasted just minutes, Lieutenant Colonel Robert A. Fulton of the 53rd Ohio believed "the rebels fought with a desperation worthy of a better cause." He also reported that his own men "never showed more gallantry, mounting the works, shooting the enemy, and beating them over their heads with the butts of their guns." The victory was momentary, however, as Confederate infantry and artillery on the heights increased their fire. Lightburn's troops moved forward again, reaching a slight knoll less than 150 yards from their opponents. Orders called for everyone to lie down and seek shelter. [20]

Major Thomas T. Taylor of the 47th Ohio crawled up the hill to escape incoming bullets and flying shrapnel that already severely wounded his colonel. "When I got up with the line," Taylor wrote his wife, "I laid down behind a small rock from which I could see the greater portion of the material part of the line. The rebs soon got the range of the rock & every time I opened my mouth or gave an order *Zip* came a bullet against the stone. At various points I sheltered myself behind trees and had the infinite time and again of hearing balls intended expressly for my body strike the tree behind which I stood or sat, and more than once the dirt & bark was knocked in my face." [21]

As did the rest of the 83rd Indiana in the brigade's center, Private Joseph Grecian of Company A discovered "the steeps of the mountain slopes were so rough and encumbered with huge rocks that we found it impossible to ascend far up under such a galling fire as they continued to pour into us." The 83rd's colonel, Benjamin J. Spooner, went down with a shattered left arm, which was amputated the next day. Four weeks earlier near Dallas the regiment lost Lieutenant Colonel Benjamin H. Myers who, Lightburn reported, "during a crazy fit of drunkenness, threw himself in violation of orders beyond the skirmish line and was killed." After

Mass. MOLLUS, USAMHI

• *Major Thomas T. Taylor, 47th Ohio, reported the regiment at Pigeon Hill faced "the sheeted flame filled with missiles, giving forth ten thousand shrieks and tones, intensified by the cries of agony and the torture of the wounded." Among those to fall was Private Samuel M. McCracken, below, of Company D, who died of his injuries on August 5.*

L.M. Strayer

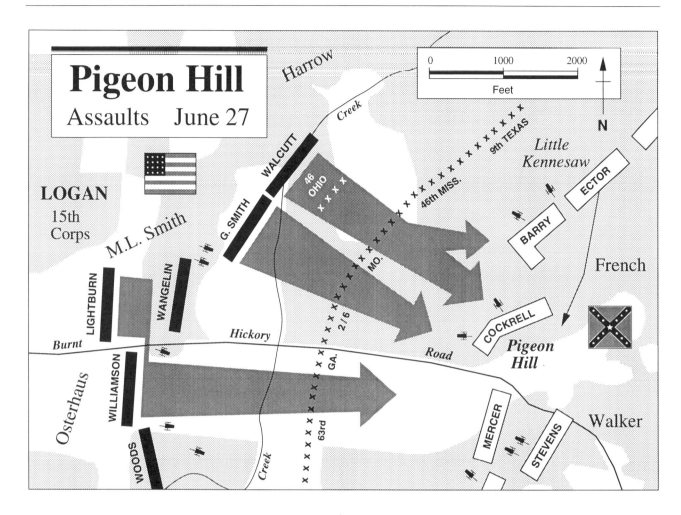

Pigeon Hill

Assaults   June 27

LOGAN
15th
Corps

M.L. Smith

LIGHTBURN

WANGELIN

Burnt

Osterhaus

WILLIAMSON

WOODS

Hickory

Creek

Harrow

Creek

WALCUTT

G. SMITH

46 OHIO
x x x

46th MISS.

9th TEXAS

MO.

2/6

GA.

63rd

Road

0   1000   2000
Feet

N

Little
Kennesaw

ECTOR

BARRY

French

COCKRELL

Pigeon
Hill

MERCER

STEVENS

Walker

Spooner's fall, command passed to Captain George H. Scott of Company H.[22]

"The scene of this days fight beggars all description," Grecian continued. "The ground all around the mountain is exceedingly rough — deep ravines, steep hills, sloughs, open fields and thickets are intermingled together in indescribable confusion. Over such and all of these we had to charge, so that it was difficult to tell our position, or see from what quarter danger threatened us most. Sometimes the missiles of death were showered upon us, and seemed to come down from over our heads, and shells would strike and plow up the ground, covering us with dirt and bursting in the earth would kill or wound some and hoist others from a chosen position. These things, mingled with the cries of the wounded and dying of both armies, made the scene terrible. The rebels fought desperately, but as they lay wounded and helpless in the excessive heat, they would call out, 'Oh, good Yankees, give me some water!' "[23]

With artillery raking the brigade's left flank and musketry enfilading its right, Lightburn after 10 minutes decided to pull back to the dense thickets west of the 63rd Georgia's former rifle pits. He remained there until dark, subjected to harassing shellfire, then withdrew to the brigade's old bivouac. His men had taken 40 prisoners at a cost of 171 killed and wounded. Sixty-seven of these casualties belonged to the 53rd Ohio.[24]

* * *

Eleven hundred yards to the north, Walcutt's bugles sounded his brigade's advance at 8:15 a.m. It was formed with a two-regiment front, the 46th Ohio, carrying Spencer rifles, deployed ahead in two lines as skirmishers. Before moving, recalled Captain Charles Wills whose 103rd Illinois was in the first line, the men piled their knapsacks and haversacks, shedding all unnecessary equipment except canteens, cartridge boxes and weapons. "While forming the line Corporal [Artemus] Myers of my company was killed by a bullet within six feet of me, and one of Company K's men wounded." [25]

In the second line, Captain John Alexander of Company D, 97th Indiana, thought of the previous night's meeting convened by Lieutenant Colonel Aden Cavins. "[He] sent for all the commissioned officers of the regiment, and told them an assault was to be made on the mountain the next day, and that our brigade had been specially named to form part of the assaulting column on account of our brilliant success on [June] 15th, and would be under command of Morgan L. Smith. He wanted to know how we felt about it. A few said, 'We'll go right up;' others said they would go as far as they could. Capt. James Jordan of Company K, a cool, practical officer, said, 'Well, you'll all smell fire before you get on top of that mountain!' " [26]

Walcutt's objective was the gorge separating Little Kennesaw from Pigeon Hill. Confederate artillerymen at once targeted his rapidly advancing troops, sending shrieking shells into the blueclad mass. One exploded directly in front of the 97th Indiana's Company C. Captain Joseph Young, the Mexican War veteran who had been so homesick to see his parents, wife and children during the past week, crumpled to the ground, his body sliced in half. "Your son until Death," read the closing words of his last letter home. Several files of the regiment stepped over the severed corpse and continued on. [27]

From the 6th Iowa's ranks, Corporal Henry Wright of Company D could see the 46th Ohio overrun the opposing skirmishers' rifle pits, located some 400 yards in front of the Rebels' main line. "The enemy's outposts and skirmishers were driven back along the entire front," Wright later wrote, "leaving their dead and wounded on the field and some prisoners. The ground advanced over proved to be worse than anticipated, part of the distance being over swampy ground densely covered by tangled brush and vines. After passing through the tangled brush, over the swampy ground and capturing the first line of rifle-pits, the lines were rectified and with fixed bayonets moved steadily forward against the enemy's main fortifications. The ascent of the mountain slope, leading up to the crest, was found to be steep and rugged, covered with brush and felled trees, ledges of rock, and an abatis ingeniously and firmly constructed, rendering the advance in the line of battle entirely impracticable. The fire

L.M. Strayer

Corporal Governor Duckworth, Company A, 40th Illinois, survived the June 27 assault that cost his regiment six killed, 31 wounded and two missing.

maintained by the enemy, with small arms and artillery, was terrific and deadly, officers and men falling thick and fast all along the lines in the assaulting column." [28]

Among those who fell near the mountain's base were two of Walcutt's regimental commanders. Lieutenant Colonel George Wright, 103rd Illinois, was wounded and helped to the rear. The 40th Illinois' lieutenant colonel, Rigdon S. Barnhill, was killed. His body later was retrieved by the Confederates. The 103rd Illinois and 6th Iowa were particularly hard hit, suffering half of the brigade's 246 casualties. [29]

"Our loss in killed and wounded was heavy," Corporal George S. Richardson of Company G, 6th Iowa, admitted to his parents two days later. "I was not hurt [though] a ball came near enough through to cut off my canteen and then put three holes in another man's coat but without any other injury." The assault was "an awful battle" to Richardson, who had been wounded at Shiloh in April 1862 and spent eight months in captivity. "I was thankful to get out so easy for it looked like almost certain death to charge where we did over the piles of fallen timber up a mountainside and right on to the very points of their bayonets. I have thought that I seen men look fiendish but I never did before. They stood by their work until we rushed within fifty yards of them. Then they poured death and destruction among us but we did not stop for that, but crouching as low as possible, we went up. They saw that we had come for everything they had .... We did not stay long for the Rebs were reinforced and our support was not coming in time."[30]

Charles Wills wrote that no one in the 103rd Illinois knew exactly where the Confederate breastworks were located when the regiment started. It

Illinois State Historical Library

Captain Charles W. Wills
Company G, 103rd Illinois

found them "as I did. I had with my company got within, I think, 60 yards of the Rebel works, and was moving parallel with them. The balls were whistling thick around us, but I could see no enemy ahead."

The 103rd inadvertantly had veered to the left and was receiving fire from the left portion of French's center brigade of Mississippians, temporarily commanded by Colonel William S. Barry. Wills, whose company lost five killed and four wounded, continued: "I did not even think of them being on our flank, until one of the boys said, 'Look there, Captain, may I shoot?' I looked to the right. and just across a narrow and deep ravine were the Rebel works, while a confused mass of greybacks were crowding up the ravine. These latter, I suppose, were from their skirmish line [probably the 46th Mississippi], which was very

Ray Zielin

Sergeant Robert B. Evans Jr., Company A, 103rd Illinois

heavy, and trying to escape us. The Rebels in the works were firing vigorously and have no excuse for not annihilating our three left companies K, G and B. The right of the regiment had seen them before and already started for them.

"I shouted 'forward' to my men and we ran down across the ravine, and about one-third the way up the hill on which their works were and then lay down. There was little protection from their fire, though, and if they had done their duty, not a man of us would have got out alive. Our men fired rapidly and kept them well down in their works. It would have been madness to have attempted carrying their works then, for our regiment had not a particle of support, and we were so scattered that we only presented the appearance of a very thin skirmish line. If we had been supported by only one line, I have no doubt but that we would have taken their line of works. Colonel Wright was wounded a few minutes after we got into the hollow, and [Adjutant] Frank Lermond came to me and told me I would have to take command of the regiment. I went down to the center and the order was heard to retire. I communicated it to the left and saw nearly all the men out, and then fell back.

"I could not find the regiment when I came out, but collected about 30 of our men on the left of the 6th Iowa, and after a while Colonel Wright and Captain [Franklin C.] Post [of Company E] brought the regiment to where we were, when we formed a brigade line and threw up works within 200 yards of the enemy's. There we remained until 9 p.m., when we returned to the position we occupied in the morning. About 12 of our dead were left in the ravine under the fire of the enemy's guns. It was a rough affair, but we were not whipped. I had my canteen strap cut off by a bullet and a spent glancing ball struck my ankle." [31]

Many of his men "nearly reached the enemy's works, but it was useless," reported Colonel Walcutt. "A line never struggled harder to succeed, but

Lieutenant Colonel George W. Wright, 103rd Illinois, received a leg wound on June 27 but recovered to resume command of the regiment.

Ray Zielin

• *Looking slightly southeast from behind a line of Federal entrenchments, Colonel Charles C. Walcutt's brigade was presented with this view of the depression between Little Kennesaw, left distance, and Pigeon Hill. before starting its assault. The photograph was taken by George N. Barnard later in 1864.*

Mass. MOLLUS, USAMHI

it was not in human power." Captain Alexander of the 97th Indiana would have agreed. "We lay under their fire for some time, when we had to retire. Every one of the color-guards, without an exception, was killed or wounded. The flag was riddled with shot and the staff cut in two with bullets." After watching loaded ambulances pass to the rear later in the day, a private from the same regiment observed: "The contest for the rebel works was but a few minutes work and the troops got somewhat mixed and that was the reason that they could not hold the ground they had gained. Too much haste always makes waste. If they had not been in too much of a hurry and advanced more slow and cautious the reserve would have had time to have gotten up to support them. War is an awful thing." [32]

* * *

In the center of Logan's three attacking columns, General Giles Smith regretted that virtually no time was allowed to reconnoiter his objective, Pigeon Hill. His brigade had marched more than four miles the night before and little opportunity was provided him and his staff after daybreak to study the hill, its approaches and defenses. It was apparent the intervening terrain was wooded, thickly in places, but beyond that "Nothing further of the ground was known, and very little of the enemy's position, except what could be seen from a high point in our lines over the tops of the trees." [33]

Nine hundred yards to the east, General Francis Cockrell's Missouri Confederates possessed no such handicap. Three of Cockrell's recently consolidated regiments occupied strong entrenchments midway between Pigeon Hill's base and crest, while a fourth, the 2nd/6th Missouri, was on the skirmish line. Additionally, three batteries comprising 12 guns bolstered the Missourians, who had earned an elite reputation in the western theater for their marksmanship.

Behind the main line near the brigade's center, Second Lieutenant George W. Warren of Company A, 3rd/5th Missouri, had spent three consecutive days on picket and this morning was sleeping late. Suddenly, he was awakened "by the most terrific outburst of artillery that the enemy has yet treated us to. We knew what the shelling foreboded — every man sprang to his arms. Capt. [Patrick] Canniff shouted for each to take his place in the trenches,

Alabama Department of Archives and History

Brigadier General Francis M. Cockrell

and in a moment all was ready. I shall always wonder how I got safely across the bald mountain top, through the flying mass of shells and fragments of rock. The artillery soon slackened its fire and we could hear the volleys delivered by our skirmishers as they met the first line of the enemy." [34]

As was the case with Lightburn's and Walcutt's brigades, Giles Smith's six regiments initially had to contend with natural obstacles. "The ground over which my line of battle advanced proved even worse than was anticipated," Smith related the following day. "A part of the way was low swampy ground, and so densely covered with underbrush as to compel the men to crawl almost on their hands and knees through the tangled vines. These difficulties were finely overcome, and the open ground in front of the enemy's works gained." [35]

• *Captain John E. Maddux, right, Company K, 116th Illinois, was Morgan L. Smith's division provost marshal. While Smith and his staff advanced with the attacking troops, "a terrible thud was heard, and all turned to see who had been hit," recalled a member of the 47th Ohio. "At the same instant, Maddux, pale as a corpse, cried out, 'Oh, Gen. Smith, I'm killed, I'm killed!' The general answered, 'Then why in hell don't you go to the rear, and quit howling.' A minié ball had struck the [captain's] canteen buckle and fallen down, but his left breast had been bruised over a space six inches in diameter. The buckle saved his life."*
Maddux later was promoted to lieutenant colonel.

Ray Zielin

The left flank of Cockrell's skirmishers, anchored just north of the Burnt Hickory Road, was first to give way. Lieutenant Colonel Thomas M. Carter, commanding the skirmish line, threw all his reserves to the threatened point and momentarily checked the Federals — until the blue battle lines burst into view. Carter's left and center collapsed as the Yankees rushed forward. The Missouri right-flank skirmishers, still holding the enemy at bay immediately to their front, could not be reached in time to receive Carter's order to retreat. Portions of the 116th Illinois and 57th Ohio fired into their backs. Those not killed or wounded were compelled to run through the Federals' disjointed ranks if they hoped to escape. Forty-two of them did not succeed and were shot down or taken prisoners.[36]

The Union skirmishers, wrote Private Benjamin

With the deaths of two previous commanders earlier in the campaign, Captain John S. Windsor of Company E led the 116th Illinois during its assault on June 27.

The Veteran

F. Creason of Company D, 3rd/5th Missouri, "were so close that they captured some 30 of our men [from the 2nd/6th Missouri] when they took our picket line. They mistook it for our main line. Thinking they had us routed, they rushed forward with a shout, but alas before they were aware of it they were within 100 yards of our main works when we raised and poured volley after volley into them." [37]

Corporal James Bradley of the 3rd/5th's Company K was awed by the "grand sight, as they came out of the woods into the open field with swords glistening in the sunlight and colors flying, bayonets sparkling, and the martial tread of trained heroes. Here they came pouring on in column, in line, in mass, filling all the plain below and still pouring out of the timber in the rear." According to Bradley, some Missourians, unable to contain their excitement, climbed atop the breastworks and began waving their hats at the Federals. "Several of Cockrell's men lost their lives while standing upon the works, cheering the foe." [38]

From his sheltered position on the hillside, Lieutenant Warren also watched Smith's forwardmost regiments make their appearance, "a solid line of blue emerging from the woods a hundred yards below us. We gave them a volley that checked them where they stood. As this line was melting away under our steady fire another pressed forward and reached the foot of the mountain. Behind this came yet another line, but our fire was so steady and accurate that they could not be induced to advance, though their officers could be plainly seen trying to urge them up the hill." [39]

The unequal battle, thought First Lieutenant Joseph Boyce of Company D, 1st/4th Missouri, was "simply a slaughter. It was really sickening to see those brave fellows struggling up that valley. Our infantry did not return their rammers as usual, after loading, but stuck them in the ground and snatched them up when wanted, to save time. No troops could stand such a concentrated fire long." [40]

Cockrell reported that part of the 3rd/5th Missouri fired 60 rounds per man. Its commander, Colonel James McCown, heard cries that ammunition was dwindling in several companies and asked for a detail to fetch more from ordnance wagons parked near the hill's eastern base. Brothers William J. and John A. Ervin, Daviess County, Missouri, farmers serving as privates in Company E, volunteered. William Ervin remembered: "Side by side we climbed the rugged heights ... crossed over the summit and reached with safety the ordnance train, asking for three thousand rounds of Enfield ammunition. We found red tape there. The officer wanted a requisition. We had no time to comply. An old musket stood near by. I picked up the old and familiar gun, which was loaded and capped, and said: 'Here is my requisition. Give us three thousand rounds now, and do it quickly.' It was done. We took one box each on our shoulders and one between us. We climbed the rugged heights from the east and began the descent to the west. Two or three hundred feet from the summit a shell ... coming from the front, burst between us (front or rear, I know not which) and scattered us thirty or forty feet apart, the box between causing a lively miniature battle. It all exploded as so many firecrackers in a barrel, but more terrific. When the shock was over, I asked John if he were hurt, and he answered that he was not. In the

midst of bursting shell we gathered each one thousand rounds. Once in line, the ammunition was distributed." [41]

The Missourians' accurate shooting stopped cold Smith's three frontline regiments, the 111th Illinois, 116th Illinois and 57th Ohio. Captain Alvah Skilton, the 57th's commander of Company I, recalled that "in an almost incredibly short time we were in the very jaws of death. Gallantly the brigade endeavored to perform the task allotted it, but flesh and blood could not endure the withering fire poured into it, and the charge failed." Twenty yards from the breastworks Colonel Rice fell critically wounded with injuries to his right leg, left foot and forehead. Lieutenant Colonel Mott became stranded on the hillside where, Skilton wrote, "it was impossible for him to get out until night. He lay exposed to the burning rays of the sun without food or water, and at evening exposed to one of the most terrific artillery fires I ever witnessed." [42]

In the 111th Illinois, Private Ira Van Deusen of Company H likened Cockrell's defenses to a fort. "It was a hard fight," he informed his wife a day later. "Capt [Jacob V.] Andrews Co. A was kild. There was one of our co. got one of his fingers shot off. our Regt was in 2 lines & our Co. was in the rear line so you see we dident have any fiteing to do tho the bullets come as thick as hail." Van Deusen's regiment, relatively inexperienced in battle, could not, or would not, push past the Confederate abatis, a jumble of wooden stakes and tree limbs sharpened to knife-like points. It quickly recoiled, suffering just 17 casualties. Likewise, the adjacent 116th Illinois absorbed only a few volleys before falling back with two dead and 25 wounded. [43]

Coming up directly behind the 111th, Captain Jacob Augustine's veteran 55th Illinois double-quicked to the hill's base. Captain Nourse of Company H observed the first wave "was no longer a column or line, but a swarm of desperate men clambering up between boulders and over tree trunks, and struggling through a tangled abatis of gnarled limbs. The place was almost inaccessible to one unencumbered and unopposed. Nothing we had surmounted at Vicksburg equalled it in natural difficulties."

The impulse of the Illinoisans' first rush quickly dissipated with fatigue and the sight of so many obstacles above them. The 55th began fragmenting in-

Donovan G. Lucus

• *Private Olof Nelson, right, Company E, 55th Illinois, posed at a Springfield photography studio in March 1864 with fellow recruit John A. Hall, Company C, shortly before leaving Camp Butler to join the regiment in the field. A native Swede who immigrated to Chicago in 1860, Nelson tried to enlist earlier in the war but was rejected twice due to his "extremely youthful appearance." Although most of Nelson's service letters were composed in Swedish, by war's end he was writing in good English — aided by a copy of army regulations and a McGuffey Reader he purloined from a Georgia house.*

than to within 10 steps of their breastworks when it was impossible to go further .... The sight which I saw cannot be described — men fell around me in masses as we ran up, a bullet bored through the comrade at my side and smashed my rifle to pieces, and everywhere I felt the wind of the bullets as they whizzed around me, but thanks be to God that I was unharmed." [45]

Nelson's company commander, Captain William C. Porter, fell with a bullet through his left thigh, the wound gushing blood. Private Adam Gleisner no sooner leaped to his aid when he was shot in the head and tumbled lifeless by the captain's side. Three others in the company already were dead or dying of wounds. Two men finally succeeded in reaching the stricken officer and carried him downhill, but he died from massive blood loss the same afternoon. Porter, leader of a forlorn hope at Vicksburg, had married in Naperville, Illinois, while home during veteran furlough in May. As his life ebbed away, he spent his last moments dictating a consoling message to his young bride. Wrote Captain Nourse, "The men who placed his body in mother earth, their sad duty done, had not gotten out of sight of the grave when a shell from the rebel batteries struck fairly into the little mound, and bursting, almost uncovered the dead soldier again, as though begrudging him his six feet of Southern soil." [46]

Partway up Pigeon Hill's western slope, a bullet slammed into Captain Nicholas S. Aagesen's right arm, shattering it near the shoulder. He was assisted to a hospital where the limb was amputated. It was

to companies, squads and smaller groups, some diverging left into the gorge separating Cockrell's men from Barry's Mississippians on Little Kennesaw. "There could be no concert of action and little leadership," noted Nourse. "Each man had to climb or shelter himself and fight as best he could." [44]

Private Olof Nelson of Company E, a 21-year-old Swedish immigrant who joined the 55th less than three months before, believed "a special grace of God" was all that kept him alive on June 27. "Death and destruction held absolute reign among us," he wrote to his brother. "The regiment that was supposed to take the lead didn't dare advance, so our regiment rushed up, and the rebels turned in their breastworks to flee, but when their officers saw that we were alone and without support, they got their wavering men back and [we] came no closer

Mass. MOLLUS,
USAMHI

Captain Nicholas S. Aagesen, Company D, 55th Illinois

a hard blow for the Danish-born commander of Company D. He already had lost practically total use of his left arm, the effect of a wound suffered at Shiloh.

Similarly, while leading Company K, First Lieutenant Joseph Hartsook was struck in the left shoulder. The injury also ended his field service with the regiment. Minutes later, the company's second lieutenant, William D. Lomax, and Sergeant James W. Kays were hit by the same bullet as one of them gave the other a drink from a canteen. The ball passed through Kays' left thigh and buried itself in Lomax's right hip. [47]

For a brief time the Illinoisans' impetuosity alarmed General Cockrell. "They ... succeeded in getting within twenty-five paces of the works, and by secreting themselves behind rocks and other shelter held this position for fifteen or twenty minutes, and were distinctly heard by my officers in the main line to give the command 'fix bayonets.' They advanced up the gorge along the line as far as my right, and succeeded in gaining the spur of the main mountain in front of my right and on [Barry's] left at a point higher up than my main line, and for some time had a plunging fire on my works." [48]

Requesting reinforcements, Cockrell dispatched a courier to the division commander atop Little Kennesaw. General French at once directed Brigadier General Matthew D. Ector, whose Texas and North Carolina brigade sat unengaged on the division's right flank, to send two regiments to the Missourians' assistance. Another courier soon arrived with the same plea. Wasting no time, French ordered the balance of Ector's brigade to vacate its breastworks and follow him over Little Kennesaw to Pigeon Hill. [49]

Meanwhile, the 55th Illinois' advance was faltering. A few individuals, like Privates James Clark and Bartley Holden of Company A, climbed to within a stone's throw of the Confederates' rifle barrels. "But they were nearly all shot down which deterred

Mass. MOLLUS, USAMHI

Captain William C. Porter, Company E, 55th Illinois

the others from following," observed Lieutenant Warren of the 3rd/5th Missouri. "Our men shot with unusual accuracy because they had low stone breastworks, which we had constructed with so much labor, on which to rest their guns." [50]

Private Holden was killed several yards ahead of Captain Augustine, commanding the regiment. At this point, realized Captain Nourse of Company H, the assault "seemed at an end. Seeing this, and at the same minute hearing and probably misunderstanding the bugle signal for retreat sounded in our rear, Capt. Augustine, sword in hand, climbing in advance a pace or two, and shouting 'Forward, men!' stood erect, for one moment the grandest figure in the terrible scene. The next instant he lay prostrate, pierced through the left breast by a fatal bullet. His

Mass. MOLLUS, USAMHI

Lieutenant Henry Augustine, Company A, 55th Illinois

Ray Zielin

Lieutenant Joseph Hartsook, Company K, 55th Illinois

fall visibly disheartened the regiment, though a few men got closer under the rebel parapet, and attempt at further forward movement ceased. Many wounded were dropping back to the rear. Longer exposure to the crossfire from covered marksmen meant only useless slaughter. Gen. Smith again gave the order by bugle call to fall back, and most of the men swept down into the shelter of the forest across the brook." [51]

Augustine was brought off the hill by Privates John Sheneman of Company D and Joseph P. Putnam of Company F. He remained conscious, giving orders to nearby soldiers to seek cover behind trees and try to suppress fire from Rebel sharpshooters until those still on the slope could escape. His younger brother, First Lieutenant Henry Augustine of Company A, was summoned to his side, but within an hour the captain died in his sibling's arms.

Simultaneously not far away, another pathetic scene was witnessed by Captain Nourse. "Joseph Putnam ... having helped bring the dying captain to the sheltered spot where he lay, ran to find a stretcher to bear him to the rear. Before he had gone many steps a bullet pierced his thigh, breaking the bone and severing an artery. A sweet singer, jolliest of messmates, loved for his invincible good nature, and respected by all for his courage and cheerful attendance to duty, his heroic death was in harmonious keeping with his life. The rosy-cheeked, curly-headed boy knew that his wound was mortal and told a comrade, George W. Curfman, who attempted to aid him, that he had but a brief time to live. Then he began singing: 'We're going home to die no more.' As his life's blood pulsed away his voice grew fainter and fainter, but murmured the refrain until forever stilled on earth."

The 55th's casualties for the day tallied at 16 killed and 31 wounded, the regiment's largest loss in battle since Shiloh. [52]

By the time General French with Ector's brigade in tow reached Cockrell's Missourians, the issue had been decided. Yet, some Federals remained trapped on the hillside, uncomfortably close to their opponents. The largest body of these belonged to the 57th Ohio, whose flags were in imminent jeopardy of being captured. Captain Skilton of Company I recalled: "When we stopped it happened that I was about 10 feet below the place where both color bearers lay. After remaining quiet in the brush for a time and seeing no chance to do anything more, I whispered to one of the boys to work the national banner down to me, which he did. I hugged the mountainside as close as possible, twisting the flag staff in my hand until the flag was rolled around it. Waiting a while until there was a lull in the firing, I made my way down the mountainside some five or six rods. By this time the boys were beginning to creep out. I gave the flag to Sergeant Samuel Winegardner of Company C, placed him in a protected place and commenced forming the regiment on the colors." [53]

Eventually, a majority of the 57th extricated itself and joined Skilton's makeshift line near the creek. General Smith sent forward tools, which the Ohioans and Illinoisans to their left used to construct breastworks. They stayed until nightfall, when orders arrived withdrawing the brigade to its original early-morning position. [54]

Five hundred and seventy-one members of the 15th Corps were killed or wounded in the Pigeon Hill assault. Correspondingly, Confederate casualties in French's and Walker's divisions totalled less than 300, nearly 120 of these being prisoners. "The charge cost us the lives of many, many brave men and inflicted but little injury upon the enemy," Skilton wrote. "It was barren of any good results ...." A fellow Federal officer concluded: "The trial had been gallantly made, and, as generally happens where human flesh is hurled against earth and stone defended with military skill by brave veterans, nothing had been gained at all commensurate with the frightful loss of valuable lives." [55]

At the same time little more than two miles to the south, the day's main assault was exacting an even greater toll.

CHAPTER 8

Powder and lead instead of the bayonet

Eight thousand troops from five Army of the Cumberland brigades listened for the signal guns and bugles to start them on their way. A 20-minute preparatory bombardment already was over, and still the soldiers waited. The delay was unavoidable; it took almost an hour longer than expected for all the regiments to assemble. For many Federals this proved to be the difference between life and death.

The cessation of shellfire, which had pounded the Rebel-occupied ridge three-quarters of a mile south of the Marietta-Dallas Road, alerted its defenders that an attack was certain to follow. The sector was held by two divisions of Hardee's corps, Cleburne's to the north and Major General Benjamin F. Cheatham's to the south. They joined near a promontory of the ridge which jutted some 1,000 feet toward the Union lines. Two of Cheatham's four seasoned Tennessee brigades filled the entrenched salient, which was about to erupt in "perfect pandemonium." Although the area was selected for the day's primary push because the assaulting columns would not have far to go, little reckoning was given to the opposition. Cleburne's and Cheatham's men were among the toughest fighters in the entire Confederacy.

From the elevated Southern fortifications, bolstered in front with thick, intertwined abatis, chevaux-de-frise and rows of sharpened stakes, the ground sloped irregularly westward to a narrow valley cut by a tributary of John Ward Creek. Confederate rifle pits lined the slope's base. Two large open fields had been carved out of the wooded valley, one of them directly below the salient in Cheatham's line and the other facing Cleburne's far-left brigade, Lucius Polk's old command. Beyond were wooded hillocks hiding the 4th and 14th corps' troops chosen to spearhead the attack.

Delegated for the effort from the 4th Corps was Newton's entire division of three brigades, commanded from left to right by Brigadier Generals Nathan Kimball, George Wagner and Charles G. Harker. Newton and corps commander O.O. Howard had examined with field glasses the terrain to be traversed, and decided to organize the brigades in close-packed columns of regimental divisions, each presenting a two-company front and a depth of 30 lines. "That formation," wrote Howard years afterward, "seemed best for the situation; first, to keep

Mass. MOLLUS, USAMHI

Brigadier General Nathan Kimball

the men concealed as well as possible beforehand and during the first third of the distance, the ground being favorable for this; second, to make as narrow a front as he could with many men, so as to make a sudden rush with numbers over their works." In other words, they were to become a human battering ram.[1]

The minutes passed in muted apprehension, wrote a *Cincinnati Daily Commercial* correspondent from a vantage point near Newton's headquarters. "There was no evidence in the movement or bearing of the men that they were so soon to essay "the deadly imminent breach,' though they must have been conscious that the task laid out for them was one which none but men hoping to meet death would covet. During the brief respite that ensued before the word *'charge'* was given, the men rested silently in their places, and no one could have guessed

from their undisturbed faces, that all the latent gallantry of their natures could be aroused, and lashed into a fury of heroism during the next ten minutes. Here was a man carefully replacing his shoe and tucking away the strings; the proposition that 'forlorn hopes' should be well and tightly shod plainly expressed in his movements. Letters were torn and crumpled and thrown furtively aside. Doubtless [photographic] miniatures came from their hiding places for a moment that morning, but such things are done in the army in profound secrecy. The soldier hates a scene, and none more than the purely sentimental variety." [2]

At 9 a.m., one hour behind schedule, the advance began. In front of Wagner, Lieutenant Colonel Willis Blanch's 57th Indiana deployed as skirmishers, each man five paces apart. Following close behind were the brigade's five other regiments, headed by the 40th Indiana. The Hoosiers no sooner had crossed the Union breastworks when the left of Cleburne's line exploded in a blaze of musketry. "Unmindful of the terrific havoc in their ranks," Wagner reflected, "the column moved forward." [3]

Before the Rebel pickets' rifle pits could be overrun, their occupants loosed a volley and ran up the slope to safety. The opposing lines here were separated by only 500 yards, so little time was consumed by Wagner's leading elements in reaching the Confederate obstructions, 40 yards from the trenches. The 40th Indiana, having caught up with the 57th Indiana skirmishers, began tugging and slashing at the abatis in order to clear a pathway. Captain Absalom Kirkpatrick, commanding the 40th's Company G, drew abreast of Wagner and asked him, "Where shall I strike the enemy's lines?" The general pointed and Kirkpatrick passed on. Suddenly, wrote Sergeant Walter Wilson of the 57th, the hillside was transformed into "the hottest place I ever was in." [4]

At that moment, two Napoleon 12-pounders loaded with canister fired into the Hoosiers' faces. The guns belonged to a section of Captain William B. Turner's Mississippi battery, and were commanded by Second Lieutenant W.W. Henry. The young officer's cannoneers immediately swabbed the barrels, reloaded and fired again into the tightly-packed blueclad mass. Among those instantly killed were Kirkpatrick, Captain Charles T. Elliott of Company A and First Lieutenant John C. Sharp commanding Company F. An eyewitness recalled: "The enemy reserved their artillery fire till the 40th advanced to within a short distance of their works, had raised the yell, and were moving forward on the double-quick, when they opened a withering fire of grape and canister .... The assaulting party [was] checked, and the men laid down."[5]

Behind them, the rest of the brigade pushed on, as did Kimball's seven regiments supporting Wagner's left. Kimball advanced en echelon with a three-regiment front, the other four trailing in two compact columns. In the center, Lieutenant Colonel James B. Kerr's 74th Illinois absorbed the brunt of Confederate rifle fire as it pressed for the junction of Polk's and Brigadier General Mark P. Lowrey's troops on Cleburne's line. The 74th's much-reduced ranks (it took 17 officers and 190 enlisted men into the fight) were shredded at point-blank range. Kerr went down with a mortal wound and was captured. Four company commanders likewise were killed or fatally wounded. Regimental command devolved upon Captain Thomas Bryan of Company H, who

Franklin Brandt

Colonel Silas Miller, 36th Illinois

blamed a Rebel battery for the "fearful execution," although some of his men "advanced so far that they crept up under the very muzzles of these guns." Near the works, Color Sergeant John Wilson was felled by a bullet but managed to keep his flag waving.[6]

Left of the 74th, the 36th Illinois "seemed now fast melting away." Its boyish-looking colonel, Silas Miller, already was hit through the right shoulder, a wound he succumbed to one month later. One man was killed and 38 others wounded, three of them mortally. Another casualty fighting in Miller's ranks, however, never showed up on the 36th's tally sheet. According to the regimental historian, Henry Hatch's case deserved special attention:

Al Camblin

Brigadier General Mark P. Lowrey

[James S.] Hatch of Company E, the youngest and the tallest of the one hundred who first joined the company [in August 1861], had a brother Henry, only fifteen years old, who was extremely anxious to go with the 36th. At Camp Hammond, the flag in some way became entangled, and he climbed the pole in sight of all, freeing the flag, and the boys made up a collection for him. After the 36th left, he ran away and enlisted in the 57th Illinois; was at Shiloh and most of the battles up to Resaca, when he became footsore, and dropping back, fell in with the 127th [Illinois], in which he was acquainted; fought with them, and when near Dallas, passing near the 36th, he joined his old friends once more, remained with them until the charge at Kenesaw, in which he was mortally wounded, dying the same day. Both the Colonel and his captain promised to have him transferred to the 36th, but his death, and also the Colonel's, so soon after his coming, prevented it.[7]

"The charge was made on quick time, or run, and with a yell that could not be equalled," wrote Corporal Alexander Cassaday of the 73rd Illinois. "The lead came so thick that no troops could live before

Cleburne and his Command

Captain Irving A. Buck
Assistant adjutant general, Cleburne's division

and 40th Indiana were stymied at the abatis, unable to punch through or find shelter rearward as the 28th Kentucky, 100th Illinois, 26th and 97th Ohio bunched inextricably together behind them. To Captain Robert D. Smith, a Tennessean serving on Cleburne's staff, "the slaughter was terrific as our troops literally mowed them down." Cleburne's adjutant, Captain Irving A. Buck, stated that Polk's Arkansans and Tennesseans "coolly and rapidly poured a murderous fire into the massed Federals, causing losses to them entirely out of proportion to those inflicted upon the Confederates." [9]

First Sergeant William Jones, writing to his brother four days later, felt the 26th Ohio was fortunate losing 23 killed and wounded. With his captain and a lieutenant absent sick, Jones led Company B in the charge. "Men were falling all around but we pressed forward. The Rebels had pointed stakes driven in the ground in front of their works and our men were shot down while trying to pull them out. The firing became too heavy. We were repulsed. I came out all right with the exception of a slight bruise on the right hand. The same ball killed one of the boys in our regt. He was some three feet to my right when the ball struck him in the center of the forehead." Also killed was the 26th's color sergeant. "The flag-staff was shot in three places," remembered First Sergeant Walden Kelly of Company E, "and the colors bore the evidence that 56 bullets had passed through them." [10]

Wagner's men twice surged uphill, but all efforts to bypass the inhibiting obstructions failed. In the column's hindmost regiment, the 97th Ohio, First Sergeant John W. Marshall saw his company had no chance to proceed further. "As advance was impossible, the line falters, breaks, and comes rushing back on the next line, which in turn breaks, causing the wildest confusion." Another non-commissioned officer, Asbury Kerwood of the 57th Indiana, wrote: "The order was given to fall back by companies from the rear, but in the confusion and excitement it was misunderstood, and a general retreat commenced. The slaughter among our troops at this moment was even greater than when they advanced, for the enemy now rose from behind their works, fearless of danger from the retreating force, and fired with greater precision than when the column advanced." [11]

The assault cost Kimball 194 dead, wounded and

it." Kimball's third regimental commander, Lieutenant Colonel George W. Chandler of the 88th Illinois, was killed just as he ordered his men to deploy into battle line behind the beleagured 74th. With hopes of success fast sinking, Kimball was ordered by division commander Newton to halt, then withdraw. Before Captain Bryan's 144 survivors did so, Corporal John Waldie of Company G crawled over to where his dying friend John Wilson still held the 74th's national flag aloft. Acting Adjutant Andrew J. Potter recalled that Waldie "seized the colors, and though but a very few yards from the rebels, and they clamoring for the 'damned Yankee to bring in them colors,' halted long enough to politely request them to 'go to hell,' and carried them safely back to the works, thereby saving the pride and good name of the regiment." [8]

It was a nightmare on Wagner's front. The 57th

War Scenes, Views and Pointers on Western & Atlantic RR

missing. Wagner's losses totalled 215. Not all of these casualties, however, resulted from bullets or cannon shot.[12]

While the battered Federals headed rearward, orange flames began flickering along the ground where the fighting had raged fiercest. Soon a sizeable brushfire, ignited by embers from hundreds of discharged weapons falling amidst dry leaves, twigs and pine needles, crackled in front of Polk's brigade. The Confederates watched in horror as the flames crept toward the bodies of dead and severely wounded Yankees still lying on the battlefield. Screams rent the air. Lieutenant Colonel William H. Martin of the 1st/15th Arkansas realized that if something was not done instantly, dozens of helpless men would be burned alive.

"At this stage," recounted William T. Barnes, an Arkansas private in Company G, "our colonel sang out, 'Boys, this is butchery,' and mounting our head

Museum of the Confederacy

• *From atop his regiment's breastworks, Arkansas Lieutenant Colonel William H. Martin, above, looks on during a temporary truce as Federal soldiers rescue wounded comrades from an approaching brushfire. Left, Private Henry A. Hill was among those of Martin's command watching. Less than four weeks later Hill was killed in battle east of Atlanta.*

logs, with a white handkerchief, he sang out to the Yanks as well as to our own men: 'Cease firing and help get out those men,' It is needless to add that the Feds never once refused to comply with this request. Our men, scaling the head logs as though for a counter charge, were soon mixed with Yankees, carrying out dead and wounded Feds with those who, a few minutes previous, were trying to 'down our shanties.' Together, the Rebs and Yanks soon had the fire beat out and the dead and wounded removed to the Federal side of the fence." [13]

* * *

Harker's 3rd Brigade, in the meantime, was having serious troubles of its own. Harker, a 28-year-old New Jersey native and U.S. Military Academy graduate, was promoted to brigadier general just 11 weeks earlier, earning his stars for distinguished service at Stones River and Chickamauga. General Howard, who first met cadet Harker while teaching mathematics at West Point in the mid-1850s, "was surprised and pleased to find that so young a man had won the complete confidence of the Commanding General of the Department [Sherman]. On my taking command of [the 4th] corps Harker was still a Colonel, and as I was a comparative stranger in the corps, I was anxious to get him to serve as my Chief of Staff. He assured me he would do everything in his power to aid me in my duties, but if I would excuse him he greatly preferred command in the field. His choice I soon learned to appreciate. Strict and exact in the performance of his own duty, he obtained the most willing and hearty cooperation from all his officers without apparent effort. The only complaint I ever heard was that if Harker got started against the enemy he could not be kept back. Yet I never found him other than cool and self-possessed. Whenever anything difficult was to be done, anything that required pluck and energy, we called on Gen. Harker." [14]

Before daybreak on June 27, Harker's tent was visited by the brigade's postmaster, Corporal Lyman Root of the 125th Ohio. "The General seemed a little depressed in spirits," Root recalled, "and I had to wait a little for him to finish up and seal his last letter home. He said to me as I was starting that he was ordered to take his brigade to the right rear, as I understood him, or in front of the 14th Corps, and charge the rebel breastworks. I said to the General

L.M. Strayer

Brigadier General Charles G. Harker

that I was sorry, for I knew there had been trouble on that part of the line just a day or so before, and that I expected when I returned to find himself and half the brigade killed. He remarked, 'I hope not.' " Later, the story circulated that Harker had had a premonition. Prior to leaving the tent he carefully arranged his private papers, entrusting them to a member of his staff, saying, "I shall not come out of the charge today alive." [15]

The brigade formed in the same manner as Wagner's, in column by division with a two-company front. The 125th Ohio was selected to cover as skirmishers. Its colonel, Emerson Opdycke, was division officer of the day and responsible for Newton's entire skirmish line, so command of the 125th passed to Lieutenant Colonel David H. Moore. His officers were informed of the regiment's role in the

L.M. Strayer

Colonel Emerson Opdycke, 125th Ohio

assault only two hours before it began.

In Company B, the men divested themselves of knapsacks and haversacks. Captain Elmer Moses told his first lieutenant, Ralsa Rice, to detail someone to watch over the pile. Rice later commented: "I saw that he was shirking a dreadful responsibility. One man had to be left to guard such baggage as we could dispense with in our run. I looked the boys over. There was not one wishful look; to do or die was in the face of each and all. I selected the oldest man present." [16]

Rice, whose company was on the extreme left of Harker's skirmish line, surveyed the ground while waiting for the bugles to blow. Not so much as a stump could be seen in the open field beyond the creek. The opposite hill or ridge rose abruptly and was timbered, masking the waiting enemy at the point where Cleburne's and Cheatham's divisions connected.

Sometime between 9:30 and 10 o'clock — the accounts vary — bugle blasts signalled the charge. The skirmishers clambered over the breastworks, spaced themselves four feet apart and, at quick time, trotted forward without firing. Their objective lay 400 yards away. [17]

Lieutenant Rice was amazed how quickly the Confederate pickets were encountered. "So sudden had been our dash that the Johnnies in this line surrendered almost to a man. The main line was plain to be seen, and from the point where I reached the first line was about 75 yards [further] up a steep incline. My first thought was that with these prisoners among us we would not be targets for those above us, but in this we were mistaken. Their bullets kept coming regardless of whom they hit. We compelled the captured men to go back over the ground to the rear." [18]

The prisoners ran headlong into Harker's seven other regiments, now advancing with uncapped weapons and bayonets fixed. Most of the brigade's officers were on foot, wrote Captain John Tuttle, acting major of the 3rd Kentucky. "It was ordered that all [field and staff] officers should go into the charge mounted but just before we started the order was modified to the extent to leave it optional with us to go in mounted or on foot. I chose to go on foot and turned my horse over to the supports who remained in the breastworks and took my place ... at the right of the [regiment's] rear line." [19]

Some officers, however, decided to accompany their men on horseback. Captain Nahum L. Williams of Company D, 65th Ohio, refused to dismount while acting as the regiment's major. During the assault he was unsaddled, a bullet striking him in the forehead. "He was laid upon a blanket, still alive but unconscious, and four officers and men carried him from the field under a terrific fire," wrote Wilbur Hinman, recently promoted to captain of Company F. "One or more bullets passed through the hat or clothes of each of the four, but no blood was drawn and they reached the rear in safety. How they escaped death or wounds is a marvel. Captain Williams died soon afterward ...." [20]

Harker and his adjutant, Captain Edward G. Whitesides, also chose to ride their horses, becoming conspicuous targets. The general already had

Union officers from the Bluegrass State

Lotz House Museum

Captain John L. Gilmore, Company D

Janis Pahnke

Captain George Roberts, Company K

• *The line officers pictured here belonged to the 3rd Kentucky Infantry and all survived the assault of Harker's brigade on June 27. The portraits were made at three different photography establishments in Nashville.*

Lotz House Museum

First Lieutenant Samuel D. Powell Company F

Lotz House Museum

Second Lieutenant Samuel Newton, Company B

four mounts killed under him in the previous nine months — two at Chickamauga, one at Missionary Ridge and another at Resaca.[21]

"The enemy," Captain Tuttle related, "opened a murderous fire on us with such effect that our commanders deployed their regiments as best they could and resorted to the use of powder and lead instead of the bayonet as was first intended." Halfway across, Tuttle noticed that his good friend Harrison Carter, first lieutenant of Company H, was bleeding. Carter, wounded at Stones River and again at Chickamauga where he was captured, rejoined the 3rd Kentucky early that morning. With graveyard humor some of his men had chided the officer as he entered camp, "Yonder comes Lieut. Carter ready to get wounded again."

The lieutenant fell but regained his feet just as Tuttle came up. "I asked him if he was hurt and he said he did not know. I looked and saw that the skin was peeled up on his forehead in a place about as big as a dollar (by a ball as I suppose which had passed through a small black-jack sapling and become flattened), and that blood was streaming down over his face. He asked me what he must do and I told him to get back inside of our works. A few paces to the right and front of where he fell I saw five or six rebel pickets in a pit. They had been run over by our charging columns before they could get away. As I passed them I called out to them, 'Get out of there John.' One of them jumped up and said excitedly, 'My name is not John. I don't know you. I don't know nobody. What must I do?' I told them to get back inside of our works but did not look back to see whether they did so or not. I suppose they did as they had no other place to go."[22]

As the bulk of the brigade surged across, Moore's 125th Ohio skirmishers valiantly tried to suppress the Confederates' vicious fire. Lieutenant Rice, an accomplished marksman and amateur gunsmith, joined in the shooting while lying prone behind a pile of fence rails. "Three of the boys loaded and passed me their muskets. While thus engaged one of them misfired. I drew it back and proceeded to recap it. I was compelled to shift my position to kneeling. Just then a bullet found a weak spot in the [top] rail and struck me fairly on top of the head. For a brief period there was a blank spot in my memory. I lay there long enough to be reported among the slain in a dispatch sent to a Cleveland

newspaper." Rice's scalp wound, though painful and the cause of recurring headaches over the next 47 years, did not force him from field duty. "I can attribute my escape to my new army hat; it was impregnable to anything but bullets, and these must not be hindered in their flight."[23]

Opdycke Tigers, 125th O.V.I.

• *First Lieutenant Ephraim E. Evans, above, Company D, 125th Ohio, was mortally wounded at Kennesaw, dying on July 8. Company B private Adrian Fitch, below, was killed.*

The head of Harker's column, reported Moore, "no sooner reached the abatis than it, too, was unable to stand the fire, and the men immediately threw themselves flat on the ground; all attempts to again rally them were unsuccessful, although several men struggled through the dense abatis and were cut down while climbing the outer slope of the enemy's works. There was no concerted action ...."[24]

The 65th Ohio, Wilbur Hinman believed, "never found a hotter place during all our four years of army service. Men fell by scores ... but the survivors pressed on." Singly or in small groups, "They reached the works and looked into the very muzzles of the hostile muskets, but it was not possible for mortal men to pierce that strong and well defended line. The color-sergeant of the Twenty-seventh Illinois, of our brigade, planted his flag upon the parapet. At the same instant he received a bullet in the

Courtney B. Wilson

• *Posing in Tennessee during the summer of 1863, half of this group from Company G, 27th Illinois, was dead a year later. From left: Private Frank A. Wood, Private Joshua F. Thornton (killed June 27 in Harker's charge), Corporal John Webber (killed November 25, 1863 at Missionary Ridge), Corporal Edward H. Castle, Sergeant Garrett Debaun, and Private Amisa G. Wood (killed June 18 at Mud Creek near Kennesaw Mountain).*

face and a bayonet thrust in the shoulder." Sergeant William J. Woltz of Company I, 29th Tennessee, leaped atop the breastworks and seized the 27th Illinois' banner, bringing it over to the Confederate side. Inscribed with the battle honors "Belmont, Union City and Stone River," the flag had been given to the regiment by its former colonel, Brigadier General Napoleon Bonaparte Buford, a half-brother of Army of the Potomac cavalry division commander John Buford. "Woltz ... wrested it from its bearer," reported an Atlanta newspaper, "and brought it triumphantly to camp, for which daring act Gen. Hardee presented it to the gallant sergeant." [25]

The 64th Ohio's national color, still stained with blood from its bearer killed early in May at Rocky Face Ridge, was shot down. A bullet shattered the staff, but the flag quickly was picked up and borne off safely. Near the works, one of the 3rd Kentucky's color bearers was instantly killed. [26]

Half of this regiment shoved past the ranks of those in front and managed to pass through the abatis. "All were mixed together," stated Captain Tuttle, "some of them immediately at the foot of the enemy's works. [Private] James Isbell of Co. H fell there. Harry Phillips was in about 15 paces of the works and stood up all the time firing under the enemy's head logs until he was shot down. Poor Harry is I fear mortally wounded. Capt. [William H.] Hudson of Co. H stood near him. Several of us begged them to lie down but they would not do so. Most of the men lay down most of the time, except when urged by their officers would get up and move up a little closer. I was sometimes up and sometimes down. The concussion from the enemy's cannon nearly unjointed my neck and the heat from them burnt my face." [27]

Near the right flank of Cheatham's line, two 12-pounder howitzers belonging to Captain John W. Mebane's Tennessee battery were responsible for much of the havoc. Commanded by First Lieutenant L.E. Wright, the howitzers, wrote a Southern staff officer, "had remained silent, masked with brush, notwithstanding shot & shell had been poured over and around them for several days, and when the assault was made the enemy were surprised, as they said, at receiving the fire from these guns, which did great execution ...." [28]

Seeing the brigade stalled, its commander put spurs to his horse, trailed by Captain Whitesides.

"General Harker rode up to the front and wanted to push the boys forward," thought Private Jesse Luce of the 125th Ohio. The two officers pounded up the slope, shrouded in battle smoke. Passing Luce's regiment Harker cried, "Come on, boys!" Company I rose to follow, urged on by Lieutenants Alson Dilley and Thomas Burnham. In seconds both went down, Dilley killed and Burnham perforated by five separate bullets. Nearby, Major John Brennan and two 3rd Kentucky company commanders were prostrated with wounds, as was the 65th Ohio's lieutenant colonel, Horatio N. Whitbeck, who was hit in the chest. [29]

As Harker approached the abatis in the midst of the 42nd Illinois, horse and rider suddenly sank to the ground. A bullet had torn through an arm and buried itself in the general's chest. "He must have known that nothing but a miracle could save his life, yet he never flinched," surmised an Illinois private. "Several of the men nearest him sprang up to carry him off the field; of these some were struck down at once, but others filled their places .... They

Janis Pahnke

• *After Lieutenant Colonel Horatio N. Whitbeck, left, was wounded, command of the 65th Ohio passed to the regiment's senior captain, Charles O. Tannehill, above, of Company B.*

USAMHI

carried the brave officer back to our works. He was still alive, a surgeon took him in charge, and on examination, his wound was pronounced mortal."[30]

Whitesides likewise was shot, a ball drilling into his right thigh. Dismounting, he guessed the leg was not broken, but while trying to get back on his horse the animal was killed, throwing the captain to the ground. Two soldiers bore him to the rear, from where he was jostled by ambulance to a 2nd Division field hospital and placed on a cot adjacent to the dying general.[31]

Following Harker's fall, the right of the brigade buckled. Command passed to its senior colonel, Luther P. Bradley of the 51st Illinois, but all his exertions failed to stem the rearward rush. Realizing that further prosecution of the assault was pointless, Bradley ordered buglers to sound retreat. According to Captain Tuttle, "when we gave way [the Confederates] rose up and poured a murderous fire into our backs. Our men rushed back like an immense herd of infuriated buffaloes running over and trampling each other under foot. I was run over and badly bruised but glad to get off so well." Adjutant Brewer Smith of the 65th Ohio shared a similar experience. "As I started back," he recollected, "when the order to retreat was given, some fellow as big as a steer ran over me and knocked me into a brush pile, heels over head, my cap going one way and my sword another. Of course I couldn't go back without them, and picking up scattered accouterments under the circumstances wasn't as pleasant as picking blackberries in one's own garden at home. But I got them and fell back in good order."[32]

At the Rebel rifle pits, Smith, several other officers and Sergeant Major Stanley G. Pope rallied

USAMHI

Sergeant Major Stanley G. Pope 65th Ohio

Janis Pahnke

First Lieutenant Brewer Smith, adjutant, 65th Ohio

some 40 members of the 65th around the colors. Lieutenant Colonel Moore of the 125th Ohio and Major Samuel L. Coulter, 64th Ohio, did the same as a preventative measure against counterattack. This line was held and "a vigorous fire" kept up for some time, until Bradley ordered a general retirement to the Federal breastworks. Once there, the new brigade commander accosted Captain Tuttle, who was now in charge of the 3rd Kentucky with Colonel Henry C. Dunlap taken violently ill and Major Brennan wounded. "A few minutes after getting back into our works Col. Bradley ... came to me and asked me where my flag was. I told him I did not know, that we went into the action with two superior officers to me and a color company, and that I had not specially looked after the colors of the regiment. And further, that in the retreat we were so mixed up I could not have told one flag from another if I had tried. He said he would go with me to hunt them and we climbed over our works and went towards the place from which we had been driven. When about half way to the rebel works we met some of the color company who were bringing them off together with a wounded color-bearer. A good many of our men from different regiments had gone back to the front to help off wounded comrades and the rebels fired on some of them and drove them back. Col. Bradley remained and looked after the wounded until all had been gotten away that was possible before he went back. I remained with him." [33]

Harker never learned that 245 members of the brigade were killed, wounded or captured. He died at 1 p.m. with two regimental chaplains at his side. Generals Stanley and Wood, 4th Corps' division commanders, reportedly were among officers who witnessed his passing, "and all were moved to tears by the sad event." His body was transported north and buried in Swedesboro, New Jersey. [34]

Four weeks before his death Harker had written to his sister, telling her of receiving a severe leg contusion in the battle of Resaca. "Though I suffered considerably, I did not leave the field. I am

Ray Zielin

Colonel Luther P. Bradley, 51st Illinois

now nearly well, and hope to conduct my brigade through the great struggle, which is almost hourly expected. The contending hosts now confront each other in a threatening attitude, and though no general engagement is now in progress, the blood of many a poor fellow is made to stain the dust by the enemy's sharpshooters. But a few steps from where this is being penned, I see several newly-made graves, the number constantly increasing by the fall of gallant officers and brave men, and before this reaches you thousands of others must fall. Who they will be, God in his infinite wisdom alone knoweth." [35]

CHAPTER 9

Hell had broke loose in Georgia, sure enough

After two days of waiting, marching and more waiting, Second Lieutenant Milo H. Lewis was uneasy. He knew that so much activity behind the lines meant an attack was sure to follow, and hoped his regiment, the 121st Ohio, would be left out of it. That prospect seemed unlikely, though, when its brigade formed in column following a daybreak breakfast. Two additional hours passed in anticipation of orders. The temperature soared under a sky nearly devoid of clouds or a stirring breeze. Soldiers clustered wherever a bush offered scant shade. The wait continued.

Finally, a courier arrived inquiring for Colonel Henry Banning. All eyes turned in their direction. Banning called for Lewis, telling the acting adjutant to carry a verbal message to the company commanders. Lewis recalled: "It was a simple matter to walk briskly through the scattered ranks and say to each proper officer, 'Have your men fall in without knapsacks' — a short announcement, but enough to settle the question as to who was going first. It was our lot. I had the opportunity to note the effect of these words; how the silence was only broken by company commanders repeating the order; how the men arose from their reclining positions with compressed lips and a faraway look of the eyes, each busy with his own thoughts of home and loved ones, and proceeded to lay aside such articles as must be left behind and might never be needed again. The feeling that pervaded the ranks may be shown in the remark of a comrade who met [me] 30 years after: 'Forget your face? Never. It rises before me whenever I think of Kennesaw, for it seemed to me you were carrying a death sentence to every man in the regiment.' " [1]

Lewis' corps commander, General John Palmer, also sensed disaster. The previous day he reconnoitered the 14th Corps' front, convincing himself that "this whole army could not carry the position of the Rebels." But the order stood, and Palmer's task of breaching the Confederate line south of Newton's sector was assigned to the 2nd Division of Jefferson C. Davis. [2]

The sometimes hot-tempered Davis conducted his own cursory reconnaissance, selecting as his point of attack the salient held by half of Cheatham's division. He deemed the salient's angle the most assailable, due to a perceived "absence of

Mass. MOLLUS, USAMHI

abatis, fallen timber, and other obstructions" generally found guarding the Rebel works. For his storming columns Davis selected the brigades of Colonel John G. Mitchell, to which Lewis' regiment belonged, and Colonel Daniel McCook Jr. The division's 1st Brigade under Brigadier General James D. Morgan was to remain in its forward breastworks as a tactical reserve, while General Geary's 20th Corps' division was ordered to provide support for Davis' right flank.[3]

Mitchell and McCook briefly were afforded time to familiarize themselves with the ground, inform their regimental commanders and designate troop dispositions. In McCook's brigade, Colonel Caleb J. Dilworth's 85th Illinois was chosen to lead as skirmishers, followed in rearward order by the 125th Illinois, 86th Illinois, 22nd Indiana and 52nd Ohio, McCook's own regiment. Their objective was the

• *Brevet Major General Jefferson C. Davis, left, photographed in his headquarters tent near the end of the war. Private Charles B. Dennis, who served 14 months as the general's secretary, "saw more in General Davis to admire, more that absolutely charmed me, than most of the officers of his staff. Dennis discovered, however, that Davis "was not a product of the Spencerian system, and his reports [were] quite long, and written on little tab sheets, all scratched up and underlined. He was careless about his writing, in the capitalizing, diction, syntax, orthography, etc., but he knew how it* should *be." Seated at right is Lieutenant Colonel Alexander C. McClurg who, at Kennesaw Mountain, was a captain and 14th Corps assistant adjutant general. He frequently was mentioned in dispatches and earned recognition as one of the ablest staff officers in the western armies. After the war McClurg became a prominent book dealer in Chicago.*

L.M. Strayer

Colonel John G. Mitchell, 113th Ohio, commanded the 2nd Brigade of Davis' division.

angle's apex. Each man was instructed to refrain from firing until the Confederate defenses were reached. [4]

During the final minutes of anxious waiting, the 86th Illinois' commander, Lieutenant Colonel Allen L. Fahnestock, loaned his Henry rifle and gave 120 rounds of ammunition to the regiment's principal musician, Fife Major Alason P. Webber. In battle, musicians usually were employed as stretcher bearers, but Webber insisted on participating in the attack. Fahnestock then crept ahead to the 125th Illinois, where Colonel Oscar F. Harmon and Company C's captain William W. Fellows, the brigade's acting inspector, sat talking behind a bush. "We three knelt down on our left knees," Fahnestock

wrote, "each facing the other in conversation. I unloosened my 'gorilla whistle' and tore up my letters. Col. Harmon asked me whether I thought we would carry the works. I replied that I thought not, as we had too far to run and the rebels were reinforcing their lines. I also told him that 'if we fail to carry the works I will surrender before my men should return over the open field.' He agreed with me, but said he thought we *would* carry the works." [5]

At the column's rear, Davis and McCook held a final consultation concealed in a hole behind a large tree stump. When the parley ended and McCook departed, a sergeant in the 52nd Ohio heard Davis call out, "Don't be rash, Colonel, don't be rash." The 29-year-old brigade commander, a student of military history, calmly walked forward. In an apparent attempt to inspire his men, McCook then began reciting verses from Thomas Macauley's 1842 poem depicting the legendary Roman warrior Horatius as he faced battle defending a bridge over the Tiber River:

> Then out spake brave Horatius,
> The Captain of the Gate:
> To every man upon this earth
> Death cometh soon or late,
> And how can man die better
> Than facing fearful odds,
> For the ashes of his fathers
> And the temples of his gods.[6]

Lieutenant Colonel Fahnestock, still conversing with Harmon and Fellows, did not witness this impressive scene. "I told them that I was sick and had been under the doctor's care all night, and had a dream that I was in a terrible battle but got out safe. Col. Harmon said that he, too, had a dream the previous night — that he was fighting 'copperheads up North' and then engaged in a big battle, but did not know how it terminated. Capt. Fellows said he also had dreamed — that his left foot was cut off with a cannon ball, and as he said this he brought his hand down across his left foot. Just as he did so the signal gun fired. The command was given: 'Right shoulder shift arms. Forward!' " [7]

Seven to eight hundred yards away, smoke from the pre-assault artillery barrage drifted over "Cheatham Hill," as the ridge here later became known. In the salient itself, Brigadier General Alfred J. Vaughan's command was positioned along the right flank,

Gil Barrett

Illinois State Historical Library

• *Prior to the 86th Illinois' charge up Cheatham Hill, the regiment's principal musician Alason P. Webber, above, borrowed Lieutenant Colonel Allen Fahnestock's Henry rifle in order to participate in the assault. Webber's use of the repeating weapon later that day earned him a Medal of Honor. Fahnestock, proudly displaying the privately purchased Henry at left, was photographed in 1863 while a captain in command of Company I.*

while that of Brigadier General George E. Maney (temporarily led by Colonel Francis M. Walker of the 19th Tennessee) held the left. The consolidated 1st/27th Tennessee of Walker's brigade occupied the angle, where McCook's and Mitchell's Yankees intended to strike.

"It was very hot," recalled Private James L.W. Blair of Company I, 1st/27th, "and we had our blankets stretched to shelter us in the trenches; but when the shells began to come our way blankets went down, and we kept out of sight until that part of the programme was finished. The shelling was to

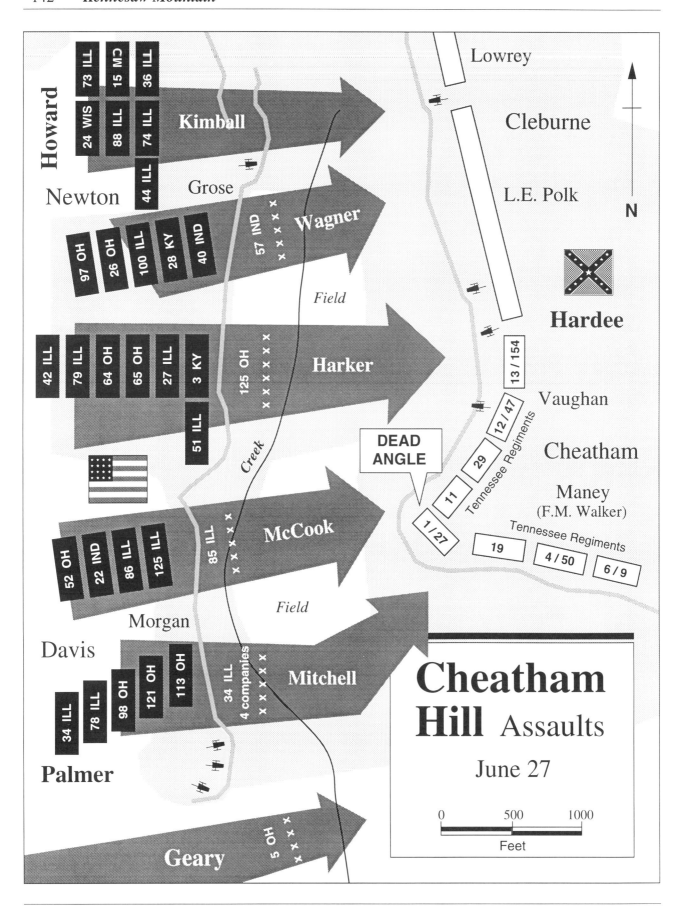

Lowrey

Cleburne

L.E. Polk

N

Howard

73 ILL | 15 CM | 36 ILL

24 WIS | 88 ILL | 74 ILL

Kimball

44 ILL

Newton

Grose

97 OH | 26 OH | 100 ILL | 28 KY | 40 IND

57 IND x x x x

Wagner

Field

Hardee

42 ILL | 79 ILL | 64 OH | 65 OH | 27 ILL | 3 KY

125 OH x x x x x

Harker

51 ILL

13 / 154

Vaughan

Cheatham

Creek

DEAD ANGLE

12 / 47

29

11

Tennessee Regiments

Maney
(F.M. Walker)

1 / 27

Tennessee Regiments

19 | 4 / 50 | 6 / 9

52 OH | 22 IND | 86 ILL | 125 ILL

85 ILL x x x x

McCook

Field

Morgan

Davis

34 ILL | 78 ILL | 98 OH | 121 OH | 113 OH

34 ILL
4 companies
x x x x x

Mitchell

Cheatham Hill Assaults

June 27

Palmer

5 OH x x x x

Geary

0   500   1000

Feet

• *Among the 34th Illinois veterans attacking Cheatham Hill were Private Joseph W. Matmiller, right, of Company H and Private William E. Willey, far right, of Company F. Companies A, B, F and I of the regiment covered Mitchell's brigade as skirmishers. The remaining six companies brought up the rear.*

Irwin Rider

USAMHI

cover the advance of the infantry, and as soon as it ceased we looked down the long, wooded slope and saw the enemy advancing, cheering as they came. Our cartridge boxes were quickly adjusted, every gun was in place, and when the order was given to fire a sheet of flame burst from under the head logs and the missiles of death crashed through the enemy's lines."[8]

Preceded by a skirmish screen of four companies from the 34th Illinois, Mitchell's brigade crossed Morgan's outside works to shouts of "Double-quick, charge bayonets!" The 113th Ohio, Mitchell's former command, led the assault trailed en echelon by the 121st Ohio, 98th Ohio, 78th Illinois and the rest of the 34th Illinois. Mitchell's attack plan called for a pivot when the 113th Ohio neared the Confederate entrenchments, each regiment successively moving into battle line as the brigade wheeled left to assault the angle's southern flank. The skirmishers rushed over the Rebel outposts and rifle pits, taking prisoners. "[Our] double skirmish line sprang away like a trained racer," wrote Sergeant Edwin W. Payne of Company A, 34th Illinois. "In less than sixty seconds every man of the [enemy] picket line was off his post, and all except perhaps a half dozen were in

our line as prisoners. The picket posts were separate pits, sufficient to accommodate four men, and the line did not run parallel with the main line of works, those in front of our right being farther from the main line than those on the left. The skirmish line pushed forward beyond the skirmish pits, out into open ground immediately in front of the main line of the enemy, without waiting for support. Nearly all of the casualties in the line occurred outside of the point to which proper orders for a skirmish line under such conditions would have taken it." The Illinoisans' impetuosity was so frenzied, reported Lieutenant Colonel Oscar Van Tassell, that "some of my men [pursued] the retreating foe so far as to die within twenty feet of the rebel works. Corporal George Phipps of Company A, carrying the colors, pressed forward with the intention of planting the Stars and Stripes on the enemy's works, but was wounded before he could accomplish his design."[9]

Lieutenant Colonel Darius B. Warner's 113th Ohio splashed across Ward Creek and swept uphill, diverging toward the angle. "Occasionally a man would stumble over some obstruction," observed First Lieutenant William H. Baxter, commanding Company K. "Several times I found it necessary to encourage and urge such on." Bullets zipped overhead, others smacked against tree trunks. Men began to fall. Privates Stephen Barr and Hiram Hancock were both shot through the head a few paces from Baxter. "In all dangerous places it had been my strong desire to live long enough to know that victory was ours. My thoughts in this instance were similar. They ran: 'This is a pretty hot place; I don't know whether I will get out or not; if I am killed I will not know anything about the result and it will make no difference, but if I am wounded I will know the result so there is no use thinking about the consequences, but take what comes.' "[10]

The regiment's left, where Warner was stationed, nearly reached the works when heavy abatis was encountered — a hindrance General Davis' reconnaissance had not discovered. At that moment the 19th Tennessee and left half of the 1st/27th Tennessee rose up and delivered a searing volley into the Ohioans' faces. The commanders of Companies E, G and F were instantly killed. Dozens more dropped to the ground, dead or wounded.

Lieutenant Baxter felt a sudden shock which he compared to "the terrific jar of a peal of thunder close at hand." He took another step but, like a ragdoll, slumped in a heap. "At once I knew I had been wounded. Immediately examining the wound, I found both bones of my [right] leg smashed into pieces a few inches above the ankle. Fearing that I might bleed to death, I rolled up my trouser leg above the knee, took a silk handkerchief from my pocket, tied it tightly about my leg just below the knee and, breaking off a stem of a bush, used it as a lever to twist the bandage so tight that all flow of blood was stopped."[11]

The 113th Ohio's progress likewise halted. Bedlam momentarily ensued as it recoiled from the

Gil Barrett Collection, USAMHI

Captain Toland Jones, Company A, 113th Ohio, was promoted to lieutenant colonel early in 1865.

L.M. Strayer

Lieutenant Colonel Darius B. Warner, 113th Ohio

deadly blasts of musketry. Warner sent word along the line for each company to seek cover and commence firing. "After I thought we were doing well and the men were well hidden under rocks and behind logs and trees, I discovered [Sergeant Francis M. McAdams of Company E] standing out in full view of the enemy, loading and firing as though we were at target practice. I was sure he would be killed, for the rebels seemed to be literally skinning the hill. I turned toward him, and began to motion to him with my right hand to lie down, and while in this position I was shot, and this was the last shake of my right hand."

McAdams somehow escaped without a scratch and two decades later wrote the regiment's history. Unfortunately for Warner, the wound necessitated amputation of his right arm.[12]

From the vantage points of other Ohioans in the brigade, it appeared the 113th had "broke and fled."

A member of the 121st Ohio estimated Warner's men were less than 60 feet from the enemy's parapets when they absorbed the initial fusillade. "Where the 113th went I never saw. I supposed they were all killed." That was not the case, but the 113th's losses were indeed grievous. Wrote Captain Toland Jones of Company A, "It is sufficient evidence of the nature of the contest to say that in a space of not over twenty minutes the regiment lost 153 men. Of the 19 commissioned officers who went into the charge 10 were killed or wounded." [13]

By now, two batteries situated on Cheatham's front near Maney's (Walker's) left flank were enfilading Mitchell's Federals as they debouched into line. Phelan's Alabama battery, commanded by First Lieutenant Nathaniel Venable, was spewing case shot and canister from the tubes of its 12-pounder Napoleons. These smoothbores, as well as the adjacent guns of Captain Thomas J. Perry's Florida battery, had remained masked prior to the attack by request of Hardee's artillery chief, Colonel Melancthon Smith. "The enemy for several days had occasionally opened with artillery," Smith explained, "for the purpose of finding out the position of our Batteries & most of our Division Comdrs. would insist upon replying with the Batteries on their line, thus discovering to the enemy what they required. Gen. Cheatham was about the only Div. Cmdr of our Corps who agreed with me to keep them concealed until the assault was made — on this occasion, I think the wisdom of this course was proven." [14]

William J. Worsham of the 19th Tennessee related: "Oh my! The cannons bellowed like so many mad bulls, sent shot and shell plowing the ground, scattering rocks, dirt and everything moveable, cutting down trees and felling limbs as if the air and tree tops were full of invisible sappers and miners. At times, from the roar and smoke of battle, we fought neither by sound nor sight. The air was so full of sulphurous smoke we could not see, and the roar of musketry so continuous we could not distinguish the report of our gun from that of the one by our side, and could only tell by the rebound of the gun whether it had gone off or not." [15]

Colonel Banning's 121st Ohio suffered much the same fate as the 113th to its left. The Rebels "opened upon my single line with grape and canister from both flanks and a full line of small-arms from

The Old Nineteenth Tennessee Regiment, C.S.A.

• *Colonel Francis M. Walker, 19th Tennessee, commanded Maney's brigade at Kennesaw Mountain while the latter was absent on medical leave. Walker was killed less than four weeks later near Atlanta.*

my front," he reported. "On the left, the captain of Company B was mortally wounded; the captain of Company G was shot dead; the captain of Company E was shot through the ankle, from which wound he has since died, while the major [John Yager] who was in charge of the left received three mortal wounds. Company I had lost 29 out of 56 men she took into action. Their commander was wounded in the knee, while most of the sergeants were either killed or wounded. In Company B, all of them were either killed or wounded." [16]

Columbus R. Warfield of Company H fixed his eyes on a spot where he intended to cross the Tennesseans' breastworks. But the withering fire and

Gary Delscamp

• **Opposite** — *Major General Benjamin F. Cheatham, center, is pictured on a rare, undated carte-de-visite with members of his division staff. His assistant adjutant general, Major Joseph Vaulx Jr., appears at top. Likely included among the other officers are Melancthon Smith (serving at Kennesaw as artillery chief of Hardee's corps); Major George B. Pickett, chief engineer; Major George V. Young, chief quartermaster; Major Joseph C. Lockhart, chief of commissary; Surgeon Joseph Bowers, acting medical director; and Lieutenant J. Webb Smith, aide-de-camp.*

Banning's order to halt stopped him. According to the 20-year-old private, "I knew too much about war to obey orders under such circumstances, and with haste retreated to the woods to find every tree occupied. I took my chances with [Sergeant] R.W. Whitney and [Private Ebenezer] Galpin behind a sapling about six inches through. I had not been there long before Whitney fell over, shot through the breast. I laid my gun down to get him in behind the tree as near as I could, when Galpin fell flat on his back in the spot where I intended to place Whitney. I noticed that his was only a wound in the arm, so I pointed to the rear and he went. I did not see him again until the war was over.

"I loaded until the bullets would not go down my gun. To remove a lodged bullet I placed my ramrod against the tree and used the weight of the gun as a rammer. After I had shot my gun I could not pull the ramrod from the tree. I took the ramrod from another gun, removed the paper from the cartridges, and kept on shooting until the command was given to retreat. This time I obeyed the command." [17]

To the 121st Ohio's right, the 98th Ohio and 78th Illinois forged within 100 and 125 yards of the works, respectively. It had not been easy. The 78th lost three officers to wounds caused by shellfire, one of whom died three days later. The 98th's ranks temporarily were broken when part of the 121st stampeded through them. Lieutenant Colonel John S. Pearce restored his line by ordering the regiment on its stomachs. "We had to lie under a front and cross fire from two batteries and front and cross fire from their rifle pits," wrote Private William Fulton of Company F. "But as we laid very flat we escaped

L.M. Strayer

Corporal John H. Boyd was one of 11 members from Company B, 121st Ohio, to be killed or mortally wounded on June 27.

with less loss than those who fell back." A member of Company C later was shown the regiment's national flag carried by Color Sergeant James W. Dickerson. "He says that it received more shots on that day than on any previous occasion; and I think if the citizens of Harrison [County, Ohio] could see the riddled condition it is in, they would try and

Dale S. Snair

• *The dead from Mitchell's brigade included Major James M. Shane, right, 98th Ohio; Sergeant William H. Pierce, left, of Company E, 78th Illinois; and Private Josiah N. Dillon, below, of Company I, 121st Ohio. Pierce and Dillon lie buried in Marietta National Cemetery, graves 9396 and 9325, respectively.*

L.M. Strayer

USAMHI

furnish us with a new one."[18]

While Pearce's men and their Illinois comrades hugged the ground, unable to advance further, the right-flank support expected from Geary's division barely materialized beyond the capture of a house and outbuildings opposite Cheatham's left center. Geary's skirmishers, the 5th Ohio Infantry, bagged 25 prisoners and managed to throw up breastworks several hundred yards closer to the Confederate line, but heavy Southern cannon fire held them in place. The Ohioans lost one killed and 28 wounded. Casualties in the rest of the division were negligible.[19]

In Mitchell's brigade, however, they were mounting at a steady pace. With the 113th Ohio repulsed, Banning's exposed left companies were taking a pounding. "It was a bloody day for the 121st Ohio — more bloody in numbers than Chickamauga," thought a private in Company G. His captain and three others from the company were dead. Thirteen were wounded and two more were missing. "The case was desperate — closely did we hug the ground and every tree and stump of any dimension was used for protection."[20]

After falling back "some twenty paces," still

ahead of the line occupied by the 98th Ohio and 78th Illinois, Banning rallied and ordered his men to entrench. Pearce and Colonel Carter Van Vleck, commanding the 78th Illinois, did the same. " 'Dig for your lives!' was the word passed along," wrote Lieutenant Milo Lewis, the 121st Ohio's adjutant. "With bayonets, tin cups, plates and hands they proceeded to dig themselves under cover while the front ranks were able, at such close range, to direct a continuous fire between the head logs of the enemy's works, creating such a spluttering of lead and splinters that the defenders lay low ....." [21]

 Private Warfield of Company H had sprinted a good deal further toward the rear, and once clear of immediate danger he discovered a trouser leg was badly torn. Underneath, blood trickled from his left calf — a flesh wound he surmised was caused by a bayonet during the crossing of Morgan's trenches. Warfield recollected:

Thinking of an old adage which I supposed would work in war the same as in peace, which says "a stitch in time saves nine," this I proceeded to put into practice at once. With needle and thread I began to repair the damage. Col. H.B. Banning, who had obeyed the same order which brought me to the rear, came from the left. When he saw me he said, "Boy, there is no time to sew. The rebs may charge us at any moment. Look up the boys that are left, and we will form here."

I made my stitches long and fast. In returning up the hill toward the breastworks I met one of the boys and told him what the Colonel had said, inquired for Capt. [Thomas C.] Lewis [of Company H], and was informed that he was on the top of the hill behind a certain black oak. I started in the direction indicated, and had not gone far before I saw Lewis drawn up behind the tree until he looked like a black chunk in the distance. I called him and he waved to me not to come any farther, but to go back. While stopping to think what was the next best thing to do I received a shower of bullets from the works, which caused me to seek shelter behind a tree which was near. Capt. Lewis had his boot-heels shot off.

I soon discovered that they had a cross fire on me, and I, like Capt. Lewis, became stationary. I had not been here long before there were two lines of dirt torn up by the bullets on each side of the tree. In Co. C there was an old man by the name of Henry Black, a recruit [Black was 41 when he enlisted in April 1864], who came along and lay down in full view of the rebs, with the remark, "This has been a pretty hot place today." I said: "If you are not prepared to die don't stop there." He said: "Well, I reckon I won't die until my time comes."

The words had not all passed his lips before a bullet tore up the ground not more than an inch from him. He arose, remarking that they did shoot close. I said: "Lie still." But he left.

Late in the evening [Private] Monroe Cockrell [of Company H] came from the front. I was squatting with my back against the tree. I raised and stood, and he squatted between my feet in

Mass. MOLLUS, USAMHI

Lieutenant Colonel John S. Pearce, 98th Ohio

the position I had been. Soon a shell struck the tree which we were behind about 10 feet from the ground, and away I went end over end. I remember seeing Monroe look up as if looking for game when the shell burst, and down came the tree-top while I still lay on the ground, and fell all over me.

Monroe led me down the hill and left me beside a rebel skirmish pit, which was a square hole in the ground, which I went into. What happened between this and some time in the night I am not able to say. I either slept or was unconscious. When I came to myself I could not think where I was or what had happened. After some time I remembered. I also was reminded that I had not eaten anything since morning. Besides, my canteen was dry, and what troubled me most was that I did not know which army had possession of the ground I occupied. I could hear some troops at work close by. I drew as near to them as I could to listen. I was not long in hearing a voice which I recognized to be that of one of the members of Co. H, 121st Ohio. I appeared amongst them as one from the dead. They supposed that I had been killed. [22]

Warfield soon learned that entrenching tools had been sent up the hill after dark and used to enlarge

Dennis Keesee

*Colonel Daniel McCook Jr., 52nd Ohio, commanded
the 3rd Brigade, 2nd Division, 14th Corps, in June 1864.*

the hand-scratched earthworks less than 100 yards
from the Confederates. It also was painfully apparent to the young private that his regiment was greatly reduced in size. Eighteen were dead and 126
wounded. Most of them remained lying unattended
between the lines.[23]

* * *

There were very few soldiers in his brigade who
did not respect and admire Daniel McCook. "Colonel Dan," his men universally called him, was a
scion of Ohio's "Fighting McCooks" — two fami-
lies that furnished 14 sons to the United States army
and navy, all but one becoming commissioned offi-

cers. Thus far the war had claimed two of his eight
brothers as well as their father, Daniel McCook Sr.,
who was mortally wounded in a skirmish during
Confederate Brigadier General John Hunt Morgan's
Ohio raid of July 1863.[24]

As an attorney in partnership with William T.
Sherman at Leavenworth, Kansas, in 1860, McCook
organized a volunteer militia company, tendering its
services to the Federal government in February
1861. The company, with McCook as its captain,
became part of the 1st Kansas Infantry which received a bloody baptism that August at Wilson's
Creek, Missouri, suffering 284 casualties. In July
1862 he was commissioned colonel of the 52nd
Ohio, and subsequently promoted to brigade command. One of McCook's subalterns, First Lieutenant Lansing J. Dawdy of the 86th Illinois, fondly remembered: "Dan was proud of his brigade, and
perhaps no brigade commander tried harder to have
the best drilled brigade in the service. He never
missed an opportunity to drill and instruct both officers and men. In fact, he went so far as to have only
one commissioned officer drill the regiments, and
sergeants command the companies. This for instruction. All were taught that no matter what happened
in battle, they must hang together — that their greatest strength was in unity of action."[25]

The morning of June 27 brought McCook to the
apogee of his military career. Perhaps sensing impending doom, he strolled through the brigade's
prone ranks, mouthing the words of Macauley's poem and admonishing everyone to lie low. "Bullets
whistled over us from the enemy's skirmishers,"
observed Private Theodore Neighbor of Company
D, 52nd Ohio. "Colonel Dan did not seem to think
there was any danger of himself being shot, and
when he told Jonathan Sills of Co. D to lie down —
Sills having raised up to look over into the woods
from whence the bullets came — 'You will get
your head shot off,' Sills replied: 'You might get
your head shot off.' Colonel Dan replied: 'Tis an
easy matter to fill my place and a very hard matter
to fill yours, now lie down.' Fifteen or twenty minutes later Sills was killed."[26]

Major James T. Holmes noticed an ominous
stillness pervade the regiment. "All knew that many
must fall and each heart communed with itself in
these few brief moments of rest. Some were gazing
upon a sun that would only shine in after days to

light their graves. Others were feeling themselves
perfect men for the last time. Here and there was a
talkative, restless, profane old soldier. I remember
one who had fought at Pea Ridge and many times
and places since. Said he, in my hearing, to a comrade: 'Aye! God, Jim, that hill's going to be worse'n
Pea Ridge. We'll ketch hell over'n them woods.'
This was uttered in a low tone with mysterious nods
toward the opposite ridge." [27]

By the time McCook reached the 125th Illinois,
a blast from nearby signal guns propelled everyone
to their feet. McCook waved his sword, shouting
"Attention battalions, charge bayonets!" The blue
column of nearly 1,300 men surged forward, Colonel Dilworth's 85th Illinois skirmishers out front
spaced at appropriate intervals. The tributary of
Ward Creek, its marshy bed threaded with trees and
matted vines, was passed quickly and Dilworth's
men wasted no time crossing 200 yards of open
wheatfield. Rebel rifle pits lined the field's eastern
edge, behind which stood a narrow belt of timber
leading to Cheatham Hill's abruptly sloped summit.
Almost directly at the center of the oncoming Federals was the projecting angle in the Confederate
defenses. [28]

The 85th, wrote First Sergeant Henry J. Aten of
Company G, "seized the enemy's rifle pits, capturing his skirmishers to a man. Even then the brigade
was under a heavy fire of both musketry and artillery, but the men moved through the field steadily
on the double quick. When the timber was reached
on the farther side, all ran eagerly up the hill, which
became steeper as we neared the crest. Now the enemy redoubled his efforts, and his cannon gave forth
a continuous roar. The air seemed full of bullets,
while a cross-fire of shot and shell tore diagonally
through our ranks." [29]

The 125th Illinois' flag went down, its bearer
shot, but reappeared waving in the hands of another
member of the color guard. Bodies were "dropping
as the leaves in the autumn." Bullets and canister
scythed through Company G, killing Captain Mar-
ion Lee, two sergeants and seven privates. "Oh!
how that fire of hell beat in our faces," wrote Sergeant Robert M. Rogers of Company B. Four of his
comrades were killed, and Second Lieutenant James
A. McLean was mortally wounded. He "was hit early in the fight, but pressed on in command of [Com-
pany B], until a ball, passing through his body,

Illinois State Historical Library

*Private Charles Spinks, Company B, 85th Illinois, sur-
vived his regiment's trial at Kennesaw Mountain but was
killed three weeks later near Peachtree Creek.*

felled him to the ground. Private James Knox had
his thumb shot off, but refusing to go to the rear,
pressed forward until a rebel ball also felled him to
the ground; rising on his hands and knees, for he
could not walk, he turned his face to the enemy, and
in that position crawled off the field, declaring he
would never turn his back to the foe." [30]

With only 30 feet separating each regiment in the
assaulting column, scant moments passed before the
first three compacted and started to mix. Lieutenant
Colonel Fahnestock of the 86th Illinois blamed this
on their opponents' unusually strong breastworks,
"in front of which were placed racks staked and

wired together. Our men were compelled to break through these obstructions, but after running so far, and receiving so galling a fire, many of them were spent." [31]

For the salient's occupants, the seething blue mass presented an incredible sight, and a point-blank target. "In this charge," recalled the 11th Tennessee's colonel, George W. Gordon, "the first line of the enemy came with guns uncapped, to take us with the bayonet; but when it reached our dense abatis, extending thirty paces in front of our line, well fortified and provided with head-logs, they halted and staggered with considerable confusion. Their other lines closed up on their first, and in this condition we swept them down with great slaughter, although our line had been so attenuated by being extended that we had not as much as one full rank in our works. The enemy were severely punished. They were exposed to a flank as well as front fire from our lines, which being provided with head-logs, the men were not only protected from actual danger, but being also free from the fear of it, delivered their fire with terrible accuracy." [32]

In the angle's apex, Samuel Robinson of the 1st/27th Tennessee later remarked that "our gun-barrels became so hot that we could scarcely hold them." Nearby, Private Samuel R. Watkins of Company H remembered that he "shot one hundred and twenty times that day. My gun became so hot that frequently the powder would flash before I could ram home the ball, and I had frequently to exchange my gun for that of a dead comrade." Watkins, who marked his 25th birthday the previous day, was awed by the bedlam boiling before his eyes. "Talk about other battles, victories, shouts, cheers, and triumphs, but in comparison with this day's fight, all others dwarf into insignificance. Afterward I heard a soldier express himself by saying that he thought 'Hell had broke loose in Georgia, sure enough.' " [33]

First Lieutenant Thomas H. Maney of Company B thought the Yankees "were fine-looking fellows and brave. There they stood, not firing for several moments, but we were pouring musketry into them, and a battery we had on our left was pouring grape and canister into them, and a battery still farther to our left was firing shot and shell among them. They looked as if they had come to stay. Erelong they made a rush on us, but, brave and gallant as they were, they had foemen to meet them who never

Ed Hibarger

Colonel George W. Gordon, 11th Tennessee

quailed. Our regiment was placed along in the works only in single file, about two paces apart, but we had the word passed to us to hold the works at all hazards, and it did look as if we would be pushed back by sheer force. But stand we must, and stand we did." [34]

More of McCook's men crowded the hill's brow, which soon received the chilling sobriquet "Dead Angle." Coming up behind the 125th Illinois, Fahnestock's 86th Illinois was stunned by the horrific violence. In the past month the regiment had lost only one man killed and nine wounded. It suffered 10 times that many casualties at the Dead Angle in less than 30 minutes. Company A was the hardest hit with 11 killed, 10 wounded and six missing, out of 39 officers and men present. Adjutant Lansing Dawdy recalled: "When the brigade made the

Co. Aytch

Private Samuel R. Watkins, Company H, 1st Tennessee

vanced toward the works. But in the meantime the line of rebels to our right poured an enfilading fire into our ranks in addition to that from our immediate front. Company A was virtually annihilated. There it was that I, at about 15 or 20 feet to the right of the angle, was wounded, being not more than 10 feet from the enemy's works. I was unable to get away."[35]

Dawdy collapsed several yards from Sergeant John H. Brubacker, who described Company A's ordeal:

When we reached the enemy's works at the "Dead Angle," the rebel battery on our right and the rebel musketry from the breastworks in our front had decimated our ranks to such an extent that my company, A, did not number quite three platoons. The rebel battery fire had the effect of pressing the right of the brigade toward the left of the "Dead Angle," before reaching which we were somewhat mixed. The regimental organization was pretty badly tangled up.

My company was clustered with the other men of the regiments until, in order to disentangle Company A, I gave the command, "Uncover to the right!" and seeing an opening in the abatis near the "Dead Angle," used by the rebels to pass out to and in from their picket line, I called on the men and led in a rush to gain possession of the passageway at the angle. I fell at this point, as did seven shot dead and 14 wounded who lay in a heap around me. Before we "uncovered" there was a surge of our men in an attempt to carry the rebel works. In the halt the men laid down; in fact, all had fallen to the ground, killed or wounded, or laid down for protection to escape the fate of their comrades. It was one of those times when veterans act quickly, governed by a judgment acquired by that experience which enables them to size up the situation and weigh the chances of success as clearly as anybody.

L.M. Strayer

Adjutant Lansing J. Dawdy
86th Illinois

It was at this moment that I gave the command "Uncover to the right." Lieut. Dawdy, our adjutant, led us; he fell to my right at the foot of the loose earth of the works. All who started with us were now down. As I lay there my stomach revolted and I do not remember ever having felt so sick in my life. As we started, someone said that it was hopeless and hesitated, but

charge I took my proper position behind the right wing of the regiment, and as we climbed the hill on which the rebel works were situated, I was just to the left and in front of the Dead Angle, being behind Company F. But the nearer I got to those works I could see that abatis was woven thickly in front of the works at that point, and to the right of the angle there was nothing but works with headlogs on top. So it seemed to me that our boys could cross the works at that point — so I pushed out to Company A with the intention of rushing them over.

"In the meantime the men had lain down, being as far advanced as those on their left who were to the works, or as near as they could get to them. Their officers did not try to carry them over, but when I called on them they rose to their feet and opened fire instead of going over, and yet they ad-

Illinois State Historical Library

about 20-odd of the boys of Company A went forward. As we made the first step in the forward movement I shall never forget the act of two of the boys who had been chums. They reached behind one of the men that separated them and clasped hands as though bidding each other goodbye. I thought it meant a pledge of succor in need or distress and that neither felt hope of surviving the attempt. Both fell, sealing their devotion with their lives.[36]

Corporal Caleb Chenoweth of El Paso, Illinois, was among those killed in Company A. Just 10 days earlier he had written to an uncle, telling him why he believed "the confederacy is so nearly played out and their army is becoming so badly demoralized." Asking his relative to send him a new hat, some postage stamps and two calico shirts, Chenoweth concluded: "All is going well. I am hearty and though under fire much of the time still cherish high hopes that I may live through it all and get back safe home again. I pray that it may be ...."[37]

As Brubacker lay retching at the side of his com-

• *Company A of the 86th Illinois suffered 61 percent casualties on June 27. Some of the survivors included the four privates above, all hailing from Woodford County, Illinois, and photographed earlier during a hardtack and coffee break. From left: Aaron C. Bullington, John E. Robeson, Eli E. Stewart and John T. Brown. Stewart, however, died in an Annapolis, Maryland, hospital on December 18, 1864.*

rades' bleeding bodies, his attention was attracted to McCook climbing the breastworks' outside embankment off to his left. "He stood erect facing the rebels," the sergeant disclosed. "I thought that they must have refrained from shooting him down to capture him unharmed. Our men were trying to reach the embankment which afforded some protection over the point-blank exposed position between us. Just then the right battalion of the brigade, for the regiments had become merged into one line, headed by one of the officers, made a surge to his rescue. His quick eye must have caught the movement, for he made a motion for them to come up to his position. He went forward in the lead and made a lodgment on the breastworks. A fusilading volley which they encountered swept most of them down, although some of them reached the outside of the works. Again the men, moved by the instincts of

veterans and the commands of the officers, faced for another effort to rally to our commander, now almost alone."[38]

Included in this second throng was Private Samuel M. Canterbury of Company C, 86th Illinois. Years afterward he related:

I found the brigade all mixed up in one line. In the space I was in I could not tell what was being done very far on the right or left of me. The rebel musketry fire was terrific; to stand still was death.

I realized the safest place was at the works. Col. Dan was in the lead. He said, "Forward with the colors!" When I first reached the works I fell or laid down, and hugged the works as close as I could for protection and to rest, as in running the distance we did, combined with the intense heat, I was about played out. Col. Dan climbed up on the works. For a moment my attention was taken with a rebel on the opposite side from me who was trying to fire under the headlog. When I looked up, Col. Dan was standing on the headlog above me. I heard him say, "Bring up those colors!" I don't know whose colors they were. He grabbed the colors in his left hand, holding them aloft and using his saber in his right hand, parrying the rebels on the other side of the breastworks who were trying to bayonet him. I

• *Posing in the Nashville studio of J.H. Van Stavoren, Sergeant Thomas F. Scott, below left, and Color Corporal George W. Berdine of Company B, 86th Illinois, fought on the regiment's left wing at the Dead Angle. Note cloth-backed crossed flags insignia tacked to Berdine's sleeves above his chevrons.*

Richard F. Carlile

Richard F. Carlile

reached up and took hold of the skirt of his uniform coat and said to him, "Colonel Dan, for God's sake get down, they will shoot you!" He turned partly around, stooping a little, and said to me, "G–d d—n you, attend to your own business." Then the gun was fired; they put the gun almost against him. I know the gun was not more than one foot from his hip when they shot him. I could not tell where he was shot. Had I not pulled on his coat I believe he would have fallen inside the rebel works. Some comrades took him back toward the rear. That was the last time I saw him.

Reunion of Col. Dan McCook's Third Brigade

Private Samuel M. Canterbury Company C, 86th Illinois

My eyes were on the works until I got a chance to crawl back to the top of a felled tree close to the works. The boys in our rear were pouring in a hot fire to keep the rebels down under cover, and to enable those of us at the works to hold our ground. When the colonel fell, we realized those in our rear could not come up and our only chance was to crawl back. While we lay there someone planted the colors in the trench and a rebel, attempting to capture them, was killed. The spot where Col. Dan stood on the works when he was shot was not far from where the south end of the works jogged off, and was north of the angle.[39]

The flag Canterbury alluded to probably belonged to the 52nd Ohio, which began the assault at the rear of McCook's column. Before arriving at the breastworks two color bearers were killed and two wounded. Captain John N. Beasley of Company I, 1st/27th Tennessee, attempted to wrestle the flag away, but its fifth bearer pulled a revolver and nearly blew off Beasley's head.[40]

"A perfect sheet of lead swept just over us," wrote Major Holmes in describing the 52nd's ascent. "Wounded and bloody men from what were then the front regiments began to pour back past us. 'Forward!' came the order at the same instant. The line of every regiment in front of us was broken. Men came rushing down the slope in crowds, breathing hard through fear and physical exhaustion. The tide of retreat swelled until I thought at one moment my part of the regiment, the left wing, would be swept away by the throng."[41]

The Ohioans persevered, taking with them to the angle a most unusual "soldier" who should have been left safe far in the rear. According to Sergeant Samuel M. Pyle of Company G: "[Private] Joe Swan and myself always had a negro servant, although we were not entitled to anything of the sort. We called him 'Tom.' He was about 16 years old and always on hand in the hottest of a battle. On this occasion, in the charge, Tom was right at my heels with a coffee pot full of coffee, waiting for a chance for me to drink it. As we advanced steady from the start the chance never came, and I heard Tom exclaim, 'Dar now, Sergeant, coffee all done spilled.' A bullet had struck the coffee pot, wrecking it. Throwing down the useless pot he picked up a dead or wounded soldier's gun and kept right along with us through the charge. All day he pumped lead out of that gun for all it was worth. He was a 'sticker,' and the boys had a proper consideration and respect for Tom."[42]

With McCook down gravely injured, brigade command passed to Colonel Harmon of the 125th Illinois, although he may have never realized it.

Reunion of Col. Dan McCook's Third Brigade

Major James Taylor Holmes, 52nd Ohio

Kennesaw Mountain National Battlefield Park Library

• *Photographed early in the war, brothers Edmond Brandon, left, and James M. Brandon served as privates in Company H, 1st Tennessee Infantry. The regiment was consolidated with the 27th Tennessee in January 1863 following the battles of Perryville and Stones River, in which both suffered heavy losses. Edmond survived the war but James was killed at the Dead Angle on June 27.*

Jumping to his feet he shouted "Forward!" and fell dead with a bullet through the heart. Nearby, Captain Fellows, the brigade inspector, was yelling "Come on, boys! We'll take ——," when his exhortation was cut short by a fatal bullet. Command next devolved upon the 85th Illinois' colonel, Caleb Dilworth.[43]

Meanwhile, the fight for the angle's breastworks rose to a crescendo. On the Confederate side, Colonel Hume R. Feild of the 1st/27th Tennessee mounted a skid log with a rifle, "loading and shooting the same as any private in the ranks," wrote Sam Watkins. Feild suddenly tumbled from the log and landed heavily in the ditch, his hair matted with blood. A minie ball had struck his forehead at the hairline, ranging backward over the scalp. He soon regained his senses but was forced to relinquish regimental

command to Lieutenant Colonel John L. House.[44]

Other officers joined in the close-quarters struggle, as described by Private Watkins:

Captain Joe P. Lee [Company H], Captain Mack Campbell [Company G], and Lieutenant T.H. Maney [Company B] ... threw rocks and beat them in their faces with sticks. The Yankees did the same. The rocks came in upon us like a perfect hail storm, and the Yankees seemed very obstinate, and in no hurry to get away from our front, and we had to keep up the firing and shooting them down in self-defense. They seemed to walk up and take death as coolly as if they were automatic or wooden men, and our boys did not shoot for the fun of the thing. It was, verily, a life and death grapple, and the least flicker on our part would have been sure death to all.

I never saw so many broken down and exhausted men in my life. I was as sick as a horse, and as wet with blood and sweat as I could be, and many of our men were vomiting with excessive fatigue, over-exhaustion, and sunstroke; our tongues were

Howard Norton

Lieutenant Colonel John W. Buford, 6th/9th Tennessee

parched and cracked for water, and our faces blackened with powder and smoke, and our dead and wounded were piled indiscriminately in the trenches. There was not a single man in the company who was not wounded, or had holes shot through his hat and clothing.

Captain Beasley was killed and nearly all his company killed and wounded. The Rock City Guards [Companies A, B and C] were almost piled in heaps and so was our company. Captain Joe P. Lee was badly wounded. Poor Walter Hood and Jim Brandon were lying there among us, while their spirits were in heaven; also, William A. Hughes, my old mess-mate and friend ... who loved me more than any other person on earth has ever done. I had just discharged the contents of my gun into the bosoms of two men, one right behind the other, killing them both, and was reloading, when a Yankee rushed upon me, having me at a disadvantage, and said, "You have killed my two brothers, and now I've got you." Everything I had ever done rushed through my mind. I heard the roar and felt the flash of fire, and saw my more than friend, William A. Hughes, grab the muzzle of the gun, receiving the whole contents in his hand and arm,

mortally wounding him. In saving my life, he lost his own. When the infirmary corps carried him off, all mutilated and bleeding, he told them to give me "Florence Fleming" (that was the name of his gun, which he had put on it in silver letters), and to give me his blanket and clothing. He gave his life for me, and everything that he had. It was the last time that I ever saw him ....[45]

One of Watkins' comrades, Samuel Robinson of Company C, recalled that Colonel Feild continued encouraging his men. "Above the din of battle the voice of the gallant Fields [*sic*] is heard, 'Give them the bayonet, if they come over,' while the work of death waxes warmer and more terrific. But here comes the fourth line to the aid of their wasted and confused comrades of the third line, whose foremost dead lay against our works, trampling over the bodies of the dead and the dying which beset their footsteps. Now the artillery comes to the rescue in earnest, and quick discharges of grape and canister cross the front, and do their appointed work like so many strokes of lightning. Our Colonel, though wounded, still urges his men to 'shoot for life,' and all, officers and men, stand nobly to their posts as if the fate of the army hung on their resistance. There was no time to think; action, under such circumstances, becomes intuitive, mechanical."[46]

Running desperately low on ammunition, the Tennesseans took what they could find from cartridge boxes of the dead and wounded. Brigade commander Francis Walker, needing reinforcements at the threatened angle, stripped Lieutenant Colonel John W. Buford's consolidated 6th/9th Tennessee from its position on the salient's far left. "At the time the assault was raging in its fury," noted Second Lieutenant William M. Latimer of Company H. "Colonel Feild's adjutant came running down the line to the left of the point where our regiment was stationed, with orders that we were to move to the right and fall in behind his regiment, which was out of ammunition. We were ordered to move by the flank, which was done amid a perfect shower of lead, and as we went we stooped very low."[47]

Captain James I. Hall of Company C remembered: "When I was trying to push my company as rapidly as possible to the right, I noticed one man, Jim Goforth, who had just finished loading his gun, suddenly halt and raise his gun to his shoulder thereby obstructing our movement to the right. I called to him to move forward. His reply was: 'Just wait Captain, till I kill this Yankee.' He immediate-

Howard Norton

Captain James I. Hall, Company C, 6th/9th Tennessee

ly fired across the breastworks and turning to me with 'I got him,' resumed his march.

"To show how hot the place was and how incessant the firing, one of my men brought his gun to me, choked and rendered useless by melted lead. The thin shaving of lead pared off from the minie ball by the grooves of our rifles when melted ran down into the tubes of the guns when held in an upright position. To prevent this I ordered the men to reverse their guns after firing so that the lead might run out at the muzzle. When they did this I saw small round pellets of melted lead poured out of their gun barrels on the ground. After the fight had gone on in this way for some time, a terrific cannonade of shell and grape was opened upon the three rear columns of the enemy from one of our batteries stationed on our left in such a position that their fire enfiladed the enemy lines. All this was more than

they could stand." [48]

More reinforcements bolstered the salient's rear with the arrival of the Florida Brigade, loaned from Bate's division. The Floridians, issued new Enfield rifles just a day before, hurried south along the ridge behind Cleburne's division. Adjutant W.M. Ives of the consolidated 1st/4th Florida recalled: "A battery of artillery began firing at us as we double quicked. Although their fire was accurate as to height none of our little band was struck — several shells passed just in my front. We passed [Turner's] battery ... and were then in rear of Maney's Tennessee brigade and not over eighty yards in its rear, when I heard Col. [Edward] Badger command 'By the left flank, march!' As I repeated the command as Adjutant I looked to the left; it seemed that every man was in his place, although we had double quicked over a half mile. The federals in our front had reached the breast works. Some were on the top, and had they broken the line not one of us could have escaped. As we reached the works the federals fell back and we were ordered 'Hold your fire!' " [49]

A second attempt to carry the works, led by Lieutenant Colonel Fahnestock on the left of McCook's brigade, had just failed. Fahnestock sent the 86th Illinois' sergeant major, Darwin E. Ward, to locate Dilworth, but Ward was wounded enroute. "I then went myself and found Col. Dilworth, and explained to him the situation on the left. I found the men nearly all killed and wounded on the right as they struck the angle of the rebel works. The 2nd Brigade on our right, Col. John Mitchell commanding, had retired toward the rear, leaving our right exposed to the enemy's cross fire. I asked Col. Dilworth what was to be done, and he asked me my opinion. I told him we could not retreat and I did not now feel willing to surrender, so we agreed to separate the men, make four lines and throw up fortifications while our sharpshooters held the enemy in check." [50]

The ground, wrote First Lieutenant Frank B. James of Company K, 52nd Ohio, "was thickly strewn with the dead and dying, and the living, crouched behind their dead comrades, still firing. Colonel Dilworth ... at once straightened out the tangled regiments; it being a well drilled brigade, order was quickly restored. The terrible artillery fire on the right flank, together with the musketry in

Mass. MOLLUS, USAMHI

Colonel Caleb J. Dilworth, 85th Illinois

front, had had the effect of disturbing and bunching up the right of the brigade and caused it to swing to the right rear; the center and left held fast, but later [relinquished] some ground to the rear. The whole line crept to the left and front again and began to make protection for themselves."[51]

McCook's Federals fell back 90 feet from the Rebel headlogs and, like Mitchell's men off to their right rear, "began to burrow like gophers." The effort was aided by taking advantage of a slight ledge in the hill's contour. "We lay flat on the ground," remembered Ohio private Samuel Grimshaw, "and threw up a line of works by digging with our bayonets and tin pans, scooping the dirt out with our hands."[52]

A sizeable number could not disengage, however, especially those lying closest to the breastworks. Captain Nathan M. Clark of Company E,

125th Illinois, was yanked to the Confederate side with two fractured ribs and a badly mangled left arm, which was amputated in Atlanta. He afterward shared a hospital room with the 86th Illinois' Jeremiah Parkhurst, orderly sergeant of Company D. Parkhurst described being taken prisoner: "I had fired three times and was in the act of firing the fourth time, when a ball pierced both arms. I fell at the foot of the breastworks, becoming unconscious from the shock and loss of blood, in which condition I remained for a brief time. Regaining consciousness, many thoughts passed rapidly through my mind. After a little I decided I would go over the breastworks and receive whatever care they would give me, as I thought it doubtful if I recovered. I walked up on the breastworks. The rebels saw my condition and assisted me down, relieving me of my accoutrements and also a good, new hat. Some of the stretcher-bearers that had been carrying the wounded back to the field hospital had been shot, so two rebel soldiers volunteered to help me back to the hospital where a rebel surgeon examined and dressed my wounds. He tried to cheer me by telling me it would be necessary to amputate both arms; then Uncle Sam would give me a good pension. There was only a flesh wound in the left arm, but the elbow joint of the right arm was fractured. I told him I intended to keep both arms. However, I suffered the amputation of the right arm later."[53]

Sergeant John W. Baltzly of Company D, 52nd Ohio, was marooned at the breastworks' base in front of the 11th Tennessee. Noticing he was unin-

John Gurnish

• *Metal clothing stencil belonging to 18-year-old Private Boyd Forbes, Company C, 52nd Ohio. Forbes was killed at the Dead Angle and is buried in Marietta National Cemetery, Section H, Grave 364.*

jured, several Confederates shouted, demanding he give up. Baltzly hesitated, but quickly realized there was no hope of escape. Hatless, he surrendered and spent the next six months in Andersonville prison.[54]

Closer to the angle, 17-year-old Ohioan Newton Bostwick was bleeding from a severe shoulder wound. The Company I private likewise was ordered to come over the works, which he attempted to do to save his life. Sergeant Major James A. Jennings of the 1st/27th Tennessee leaned across the headlog to assist him. Just then, a bullet fired at Jennings missed the sergeant major but hit Bostwick in the neck as the Tennessean pulled him over. Bostwick survived, recuperating in Macon, Georgia, until he was exchanged five months later. "The boys who captured me," he recollected, "were very proud of the conduct of the Yanks that day, and were never tired of telling of the gallant way our men walked up to the works in the face of their heavy fire of canister and musketry. They were Americans too, and that is what we went up against." [55]

Sergeant Nixon B. Stewart of Company E chanced gaining the 52nd's makeshift line, but not before enduring a harrowing experience. "Probably one-half of our regiment that were unharmed, lay within twelve feet of the earth works and not in a position to load and fire. One by one our men crawled back to the new line below, while many of us, with the dead and seriously wounded, lay near the works. Three of my comrades were struck just as our men lay down. Joseph Hanlon lay dead on my right. Isaac Winters, who was shot in the temple, but living, lay within my reach on the left. Frank Grace of Co. D lay dead just below me, and Joseph E. Watkins of the 22nd Indiana Regiment, rose to start for the line below, when he fell dead across my feet, as I lay near a chestnut stump within ten feet of the earth works. Who could describe the sensations of the forty minutes that passed. To run the gauntlet might be death; to lie there, a movement of the body would draw the fire of the enemy on the 'Dead Angle' to our right. Winters, shot in the temple, sat up and began to talk in delirium, which attracted the enemy. He plead for water. I pushed my canteen toward him and he reached out but failed to get it." [56]

Stewart's regimental commander, Lieutenant Colonel Charles W. Clancy, also waited for an opportunity to get out. When it came, he started to

USAMHI

• *Eighteen-year-old Corporal John W. Hance, Company C, 52nd Ohio, escaped injury on June 27, but 29 others of his company were killed or wounded at the Dead Angle, including most of the color guard.*

dash back but caught his feet in a discarded sword belt. Clancy sprawled to the ground, tumbling all the way to safety while dragging the belt and attached sword behind him. They belonged to Captain Salathiel M. Neighbor of Company D, who, having been seriously hurt near the works, stripped off the belt and staggered to the rear. He died of his wound on July 7 in Chattanooga.[57]

Clancy's fall exacerbated an injury inflicted during the assault's early moments. Before crossing the creek, his left leg was struck by a minie ball below

L.M. Strayer

• *Eight officers of the 52nd Ohio posed in their hutted camp at Lee & Gordon's Mills, Georgia, less than three months prior to June 27. From right: Major James T. Holmes, Lieutenant Colonel Charles W. Clancy (captured July 19 at Peachtree Creek), Captain Samuel Rothacker of Company G, Captain William Sturgis of Company B (wounded May 14 at Resaca), Second Lieutenant James H. Donaldson of Company E (killed July 19 at Peachtree Creek), First Lieutenant Frank B. James of Company K, Second Lieutenant Julius Armstrong of Company F, and Second Lieutenant David F. Miser of Company G. On July 2 Miser was mortally wounded by a sharpshooter's bullet while walking behind the 52nd's makeshift line near the Dead Angle. He died on August 2.*

the knee. At first he thought the limb was gone, but fortuitously, his boot tops had been folded down and the extra thickness of leather absorbed much of the bullet's force. Although suffering a bad contusion, Clancy hobbled up the slope using his sword as a cane.[58]

The 86th Illinois' adjutant, Lansing Dawdy, laid with a chest wound in front of the 1st/27th Tennessee's Company F. After more than five hours he finally signalled his willingness to surrender and was assisted to the Southern side by Company F's commander, Captain Benjamin F. Smith. The lieutenant was taken by wagon for hospitalization in Atlanta, where he was visited by General Cleburne. Dawdy eventually spent three months in Macon, Savannah and Charleston prisons, and was paroled on November 30, 1864.[59]

Captain Joseph Major, commanding the 86th's ill-fated Company A, spent almost 12 hours prostrate among a heap of bodies. He had been knocked senseless by a thrown rock just outside the angle, and afterward described his ordeal through the narrative of Private Julius B. Work, 52nd Ohio:

On the return of consciousness Capt. Major knew he must play himself for dead or he would be forced to crawl over the rebel works a prisoner — as several others were forced to do. Retreat was then impossible. About this time a venturous rebel crawled out over the works, probably for boodle, and crawling around among the dead and wounded, came to the captain, whom he relieved of his revolver, sword, haversack, canteen, pocket-book and hat. Noticing that Major was breathing, the rebel turned a little water into his mouth. But, although nearly dying of thirst, the Yank was afraid to swallow for fear his sham would be detected, and permitted the coveted fluid to run out of his mouth and go to waste in mother earth. The Johnny crawled away and left him, supposing there would soon be another dead Yank.

During all the balance of that hot 27th day of June, Capt. Major lay flat on his back with the merciless rays of the sun pouring down into his bare face, not even daring to scare the flies from his mouth or nose, or shift his body the least bit to gain a more comfortable position. He could hear the bang, bang of Yankee guns, and the crack of Col. Fahnestock's Henry rifle in the hands of Fife Major Webber — who had gained an advantageous position and was doing all he could to prevent the rebels from raising their heads above their breastworks, for which the government gave Webber a Medal of Honor. When the rebels would reply, the smoke from their guns would almost puff into the captain's face. With the bullets passing both ways, only a few inches above his body, there he lay, out-possuming any opossum that ever lived.

Finally, after a long, long wait, darkness came. Then was his time to attempt an escape from his perilous position. Gathering strength for a supreme effort, he got onto his feet and made a dash for the Yankee line. It was considerably down hill, and he came as near flying as he could. There were many dry twigs and dead leaves on the ground, so he made considerable noise which drew a volley of rebel bullets after him, but fortunately he was not hit.

Coming to our line he did not pause for ceremony or give the countersign, but running up the loose dirt placed his foot on top of the breastworks and leaped clear over men, guns and bayonets. It was my fortune to stand within six feet of where he lit; in fact, he jumped nearly over me, and when we saw who it was and what caused the noise and confusion, I can say of my own knowledge the feeling of surprise, joy and gratitude was simply beyond description. Of course, the first thing required of him was to "give an account of himself." This he did without even waiting for a drink of water. In relating how the rebel robbed him, he moved his hand from place to place, and was just saying "watch" when his hand struck his watch pocket and, to his great surprise, the watch was still there. When he drew it from his pocket and looked at it he could hardly believe his eyes.[60]

Colonel McCook was not so lucky. After being toppled from the breastworks he was borne from

Reunion of Col. Dan McCook's Third Brigade

Captain Joseph Major, Company A, 86th Illinois

the field by Fifer James Sheffler, 86th Illinois, Corporal James T. Seay, 85th Illinois, and two other enlisted men. Seay recalled: "While carrying him to the rear I had my gun in my hand with the bayonet on, and being at the back end of the stretcher it pointed to his head, and he said to me, 'Soldier, throw that gun down,' and I did so." The litter bearers deposited their commander at the hospital tent of brigade Surgeon Masena M. Hooten, who immediately examined McCook's injury and found an entrance wound in his right chest four inches below the clavicle.[61]

"The direction of the ball was very nearly straight toward his back," Hooten stated. "He must have been nearly facing the person that shot him. Col. McCook told me, 'I had just placed my left hand on the head log and turned to Capt. Fellows and called to him to tell Col. Harmon to bring the right wing up double quick. The next thing I knew the men were carrying me down to the ravine, and someone put some water on my face. This is to be my last battle, doctor.' I replied, 'Oh, let us hope not.' " [62]

McCook's words proved prophetic. Taken to a brother's home at Steubenville, Ohio, he died there on July 18, one day after receiving a brigadier general's commission. Years later, a member of the 52nd Ohio remembered that the colonel, while crossing the Ohio River with the regiment in August 1862, remarked, "Here's for a star or for death!" Ironically, he found both on a blood-soaked Georgia hillside. [63]

At army headquarters on Signal Hill, the telegraph lines continued humming. Frequent messages concerning the assault's progress flashed back and forth between Generals Sherman and Thomas, but news from the latter and the wing commanders was bitterly disappointing.

"McPherson and Schofield are at a dead-lock," Sherman informed Thomas at 1:30 in the afternoon. "Do you think you can carry any part of the enemy's line to-day? I will order the [general] assault if you think you can succeed at any point." Ten minutes later Thomas, having already told his chief of Newton's and Davis' repulse, answered negatively. Sherman persisted, still hoping that somewhere, somehow the Confederate line could be breached. Thomas responded bluntly about 3 o'clock: "We still hold all the ground we have gained and the division commanders report their ability to hold it. They also report the enemy's works exceedingly strong; in fact, so strong that they cannot be carried by assault except by immense sacrifice, even if they can be carried at all. We have already lost heavily to-day without gaining any material advantage; one or two more such assaults would use up this army."[1]

With this, Sherman relented. In a return message to the Army of the Cumberland commander, he expressed "regret beyond measure the loss of two such young and dashing officers as Harker and Dan. McCook. McPherson lost 2 or 3 of his young and dashing officers, which is apt to be the case in unsuccessful assaults. Had we broken the line to-day it would have been most decisive, but as it is our loss is small, compared with some of those East. It should not in the least discourage us. At times assaults are necessary and inevitable."[2]

Sherman's rationale and steeled mindset was displayed even more forcibly in correspondence to his wife Ellen. "I begin to regard the death and mangling of a couple thousand men as a small affair," he told her on the 30th, "a kind of morning dash — and it may be well that we become so hardened. Each day is killed or wounded some valuable officers and men, the bullets coming from a concealed foe." On July 9 he wrote: "I see by the papers that too much stress was laid on the repulse of June 27th. I was forced to make the effort and it should have succeeded; but the officers and men have been so used to my avoiding excessive danger and forcing back

CHAPTER 10

Would that this bloody affair was over

Illinois State Historical Library

First Sergeant Alexander Buchanan, Company K,
86th Illinois, was killed on June 27.

the enemy by strategy that they hate to assault; but
to assault is sometimes necessary for its effect on
the enemy."[3]

In this case the "effect on the enemy" was barely
noticeable in relation to the cost. Johnston lost less
than 600 men, nearly half of them prisoners. Cleburne's and Cheatham's divisions combined suffered only 206 casualties, and of these 94 were pickets captured on the skirmish line. By comparison,
Mitchell's and McCook's brigades lost 811 killed,
wounded or missing — 639 coming from five regiments alone. Total Federal losses exceeded 2,500,
and probably were close to 3,000. If such figures did
not discourage Sherman, many of those serving under him were hard pressed to understand why. One
only needed to look at the corpse-strewn battlefield,
or spend a few minutes at the field hospitals.[4]

"Gen. Sherman has been severely censured by
the surviving soldiers for this seemingly unnecessary
sacrifice of 2500 of the flower of his army and
country," observed Levi A. Ross, ordnance sergeant
of the 86th Illinois. The regiment's heavy casualties
meant a promotion to first sergeant of Company K
for Ross, who replaced his good friend Alexander
Buchanan, killed in the assault. "Went to the division
hospital where I saw suffering boys enough to un-
nerve the stoutest heart. Many are being carried out
dead and many more will be yet numbered with the
host of our fallen brothers. The weather is so intense-
ly hot that a large per cent of the wounded die."[5]

Second Lieutenant Jason Hurd of the 19th Ohio,
whose division supported Newton's, added to his
diary: "Large numbers of wounded began to come
in and such frightfull wounds it never befell my lot
to witness before. In following the advance, we
happened to come close to the ambulance train,
where the wounded were brought in. The day was
very warm and the wounds would swell and become
inflamed in a very short time. Some of the poor fellows were crazy, in particular, one lad not more than
eighteen years of age was raving upon the stretcher
as he was brought in with his bowels shot out. This
was a sad day's work for us and was the last time
we butted our heads against their works."[6]

Iowa corporal Henry Wright, among those participating in Walcutt's assault on Pigeon Hill, noted
that "The field hospitals were taxed to their limit ...
where arms and legs were amputated by the hundred. It was a supreme test of the confidence had in
the commanding general by the troops, and he saw
that the troops realized that it was his first mistake
in the campaign."[7]

At first, 125th Illinois sergeant Robert Rogers
was sorry he came to the hospital where, not long
before, Surgeon Hooten had cleansed and bandaged
Colonel McCook. But, Rogers later explained, he
was possessed by a compulsive need to do something to help his stricken comrades:

> The road [to the hospital] is flanked on either side by thick
> brush; going along I happened to look to my right, and see a
> sight that makes my blood stand still, so unexpected, and so aw-
> ful is it. There, in that clump of hazel, lays the body of our colo-
> nel, where he had been carried directly after he fell. A sickening
> feeling creeps over me as I stand in the presence of the dead,
> whom I had seen such a short time before in full health and vig-
> or. Yes, there he lay, his life ended, his heart's blood given for
> his country's good. Colonel Harmon was a christian man; what

Illinois State Historical Library

Colonel Oscar F. Harmon, 125th Illinois

more can I say? A strict disciplinarian, he had the solicitude of a father for his regiment, and he wanted his men to feel that in him they had a friend who would look after their welfare. With one sad, lingering look, I tore myself from the spot with my heart stirred with deep emotion.

The hospital tents, or rather "flys," were stretched in such a manner that their sides were raised some two feet from the ground, thus giving a thorough circulation of air. I enter; there lay our poor fellows, and as they see me they shout out a welcome. These fellows near the entrance are not so badly wounded as those farther on, so, returning their greeting with an assumed show of glee, I pass into the tent. And now I am in the midst of desperately wounded boys who are lying here, some of them without a vestige of clothing on them on account of the heat, slowly dying. Here is 2nd Lieut. James McClain [*sic*] with

his negro servant sitting by him, fanning him. I kneel down by the lieutenant. We had been old acquaintances before we left home, consequently no undue stiffness of official ceremony could come between us. Poor Jim, he was drawing his breath in gasps; I saw that death had set its seal upon his brow, and with a sorrow in my heart that I believe was the deepest I ever felt, I said: "Jimmy, is there anything I can do for you?"

Opening his eyes at the sound of my voice, and reaching out his hand, he exclaimed: "Oh, Bob! I am so glad to see you."

But my emotions overcame me, and in spite of all I could do, the tears would come. But I checked them as soon as possible and again repeated my question. Opening his eyes with his breath coming in convulsive gasps, he said: "Bob—write—to—my—mother,—tell her—that I died—doing my duty."

Oh! if I could have had at that moment a heart of stone, so that I could have talked to him, but it was too much; however, I managed to whisper to him a hope that he might get well, but no, he knew better, he knew that his life was fast drawing to a close, and moving his head slowly, he replied: "No, Bob, I am dying."

I could not stand it and gently stooping over him, I kissed him on the forehead and turned to the next man lying beside him, who proved to be orderly sergeant Benjamin F. Bonebrake [of Company B]. Ben presented a terrible appearance. He had been wounded in the head, and the blood had streamed down over his face and whiskers and over his once white shirt bosom, and dried there, giving him a ghastly appearance.

"Do you want anything, Ben?"

"Yes, I would like to have my face washed."

Oh! how quiet and gentle these poor boys were, no complaining, no harsh words, but there they lay, bearing their pain with true heroism. "All right," I reply, glad to be able to get outside for a moment, and away I went to the brigade hospital steward, with whom I was acquainted, for what I needed. I found him and on the strength of acquaintanceship procured from him a hospital bucket with some warm water and a sponge, and before I left him I had coaxed him to give me a clean shirt for Ben out of the sanitary supplies he had on hand. Rejoicing at my success I hastened back and proceeded to make Ben more comfortable; I washed his face, combed his hair and whiskers, and helped him on with the clean shirt. With a grateful acknowledgment he lay back in his place.

Next to him was Sergeant Wash. Cunningham [also of Company B], good natured, free hearted Wash; a man of large and powerful frame, he had received a rifle ball through the left arm; poor fellow, he had gotten down in such a shape that his wound was paining him, and in reply to my question as to what I could do for him, he said: "Nothing, only if you could help me to raise up a little." I looked at his massive form and felt afraid to touch him for fear of giving him pain; I told him so, and he replied: "All right, Rob, I can stand it." I wanted to get away. I was feeling sick and was afraid to stay longer, but there was one more boy whom I must find before I went, and this was Patrick Sullivan of Co. G. I searched and searched and at length I found him, lying on his back on his rubber blanket without a stitch of clothing on him; he was lying in a pool of his own blood with his eyes closed, and his face pale and bloodless; I thought at first he

I feel as though I have lost a brother

Not all Federal casualties at Kennesaw on June 27 fell fighting in the assaulting columns. After Newton's repulse, Colonel Isaac M. Kirby's 4th Corps' brigade was brought up to support the front line. Although it did not fire a gun, the 101st Ohio lost eight men wounded, including Captain Milton N. Ebersole who was shot in the left side and arm. He succumbed to his injuries on July 7 and in May 1865 was buried in Fostoria, Ohio.

In Colonel William Grose's brigade not far from where Ebersole was hit, Corporal Edward E. Fielding also lost his life. His bunkmate, Corporal George W. Eastwood wrote the next day to Fielding's mother:

It becomes my painful duty of informing you of the life of your son. He was killed yesterday during the charge on the enemy's works. On the evening of the 26th we received orders to be ready to move on the enemy's works at six o'clock on the 27th. When we went into the tent for the night Edward told me what to do with all of his effects and also directed me to write to you if he should fall. On the morning of the 27th we moved out and took a position on the extreme left of the [4th] Corps. Consequently we were not in the charge. Our Co. was on the picket line. When Edward was killed he had found a snake in his rifle pit, killed it, and took it on a stick and slipped out and spoke to the boys in the next pit saying, "Boys, I have found a rebel spy in my camp." He then threw it down and turned toward his post again when one of the enemy sharpshooters on a ridge about 150 yards distant fired at him, the ball taking effect in the center of the forehead. He breathed a few times but was perfectly insensible.

I have got all his effects save his photograph album. This was in his coat pocket and I suppose buried with him. I have a watch, a ring, one portfolio, four miniatures, one pocket book, one money belt. I have disposed of his clothing and will send you the money for them as soon as the reg. is payed off. It was his request that his ring be sent to you. He did not say what to do with his watch ....

I feel as though I have lost a brother in him for the last two years I have slept under the same blanket and a more agreeable companion I have never found. As a non commissioned officer I have never heard of a complaint against him which is a very uncommon thing in the army.

Fielding's remains lie today in Grave 9376, Marietta National Cemetery.

Brad L. Pruden

Captain Milton N. Ebersole
Company K, 101st Ohio

Beulah Adams

Corporal Edward E. Fielding
Company C, 59th Illinois

• *This rope-tension drum sporting the Illinois state seal painted in a shield was carried at Kennesaw Mountain by Musician William A. Payton of Company C, 125th Illinois. Payton, a resident of Vermilion County, later was promoted principal musician of the regiment.*

Kennesaw Mountain National Battlefield Park

was dead, but kneeling down by him I spoke his name. The heavy eyelids opened, and with a smile on his countenance he reached me his hand. I grasped it and put the question: "Can I do anything for you, Patsey?"

For a second there was no reply, and then his lips opened and he said: "Oh, Rob, if I could only sleep. I want to sleep but can't. The doctor won't pay any attention to me, and there is such a noise."

He was a little delirious, and the roar of the cannon and the musketry was still in his ears. Leting go his hand I started out to find the surgeon. I ran across him and told him what I wanted, that one of the boys had been overlooked and needed help; this with an impassioned force. He would come, he replied, as soon as he could, but his hands were full. "No, doctor," I pleaded, "come now, come now," and catching hold of his coat I would not let him go. Dr. Hooten, our brigade surgeon, was a man of tender heart and he saw I was terribly in earnest. "Where is the boy?" he said. I quickly turned and conducted him to Patsey's side. Bending over him he examined him; he had been shot through the lungs. Getting up he motioned for me to follow. "Go to the steward," he said, "and tell him to mix you some morphine and whisky," telling me the right amount of each. I hurriedly left him and was soon returning with the medicine. Reaching his side I knelt down and told him to open his mouth. Inserting the tube of the hospital tin between his teeth, I gently poured the medicine down his throat, but it had no sooner touched his stomach than he vomited it up. I repeated the dose and had the satisfaction at last of seeing him retain it. Drying up the blood and wet in which he was laying with some old rags, I

left him with the assurance that he would soon be sleeping.

Having been away now from my command for a long time, I felt I must hurry back, however much I felt disposed to stay and do what I could for our boys, so going outside of the fly I started back to the command. But my mind was torn and rent with sad feelings. Yonder under that hospital fly lay boys whom I tenderly loved, wounded and helpless, breathing, slowly breathing their lives away, while others suffering pain almost unbearable, lay with teeth clenched and knitted brows, suffering on in silence. As I slowly walked along how I strove for the mastery of my feelings, but I could not help it, and in spite of all I could do I cried like a child. Sitting down by a tree until I had partially overcome my sorrow, I arose and again started for the company, while ringing in my ears were the words: "Vengeance is mine I will repay, saith the Lord."[8]

"Everybody sad & gloomy," wrote the 125th's quartermaster, Alexander M. Ayers, late on June 27. He assisted in the burial of Lieutenant McLean and helped place Colonel Harmon's body on a railroad car at Big Shanty. That night and into the following day, Ayers penned a melancholy letter home:

Dear wife

No doubt you have learned from the papers something of the result of this day with our Command. This has been the saddest day in the history of our Regiment. This morning at about 9 o'clock our Brig. made a charge on the enemys works .... Our men got so close up to the works that neither party could shoot to advantage & both parties threw stones over the works at each other. Several of our men who escaped bullets are badly injured with blows from rocks .... A great many of our killed & wounded are yet lying in front of the enemys line where we cannot reach them, but hear the wounded calling for water .... It has been really a bloody day & with all our loss did not gain a *single* thing nor (probably) killed one man among the enemy .... The fight did not last over 30 minutes but was terrible while it did last. The fight occurred about 4 miles from my quarters but I happened [to be] there just in time to see them go in. But I can assure you I kept a proper distance off. The scene in the Hospital was really heart sickening. I was there about 3 hours & saw much of their suffering. It is *terrible* ....

Our Brigade lost in killed & wounded 422. It is a very rare thing that one Regt looses as many men as ours did. The men that are now left are all very gloomy & despondent — they will probably be relieved from the front lines tonight. They are entirely worn out, but a few days rest will make them all right again .... Today I helped bury some of our dead. The manner in which it was done was to dig a hole about 2 feet deep — lay the body in — throw a blanket over it & then cover up with dirt — this is the most respectable way of soldier burying. For the last 52 days we have hardly been out of the sound of firing one hour day & night. I had become so accustomed to it that I hardly took any notice of it but now I shudder to hear a gun fired, especially in the direction of our men. Would that this bloody affair was over. [9]

Human suffering in the wake of Sherman's failure at Kennesaw disgusted Claiborne J. Walton, surgeon of the 21st Kentucky in Whitaker's 4th Corps' brigade. Upending a hardtack crate for a writing desk, the 40-year-old Munfordville doctor vented anguished thoughts to his wife on June 29:

I am sick. Yes sick and tired of bloodshed. Weary and worn out with it. We have been on this campaign fifty-six days and it has been almost one continued scene of carnage from day to day. I am not out of much of the groans of the wounded from morning till night. My hands are constantly steaped in blood. I have had them in blood and water so much that the nails are soft and tender. I have amputated limbs until it almost makes my heart ache to see a poor fellow coming in the ambulance to the hospital ....

I could tell you of many, yes, of the most distressing cases of wounds. Such as arms shot off, legs shot off. Eyes shot out, brains shot out. Lungs shot through and in a word *everything* shot to pieces and totally maimed for all after life. The horror of this war can never be half told. Citizens at home can never know one fourth part of the misery brought about by this terrible rebellion. We have been near Kennesaw Mountain for about two weeks and still the Rebels are resisting us at every step. It is true that we have driven them back a few miles but they only fall back a few hundred yards at a time and fortify and fight us again. Sometimes they make a charge upon us [and] we drive them back with dreadful slaughter. Day before yesterday we

The Mail Goes Through

• *Private George Drake, Company K, 85th Illinois, wrote his parents a few days after McCook's assault how "the rebbels shot our men down out of their breastworks. I tell you the men were mowed down like grass but fortunately I was spared. We had a hard time."*

made a charge upon their lines. They were well fortified. We were compelled to fall back. You may well imagine that they slaughtered our men with a vengeance. We lost in a few minutes in killed and wounded *Two Thousand*. It was really distressing to see the ambulances coming in loaded with the wounded. We have three operating tables in our division and we were all busy for several hours. [10]

A struggle for life

Although Sergeant Major James Skelton of the 27th Ohio was suffering with a severe bout of colic on June 27, his pain was eased with the arrival that morning of a second lieutenant's commission in Company F. His regiment belonged to the 16th Corps and was spared a direct role in the diversionary attack on Big Kennesaw. Still, he wondered for years afterward why the day's assaults were made at all.

That night the Ohioans were ordered out to the front line as skirmishers, taking position on Big Kennesaw's lower northwestern slope. At 2 a.m. on June 28, while carrying an order to Company G on the regiment's right, Skelton was shot in the right leg, the minie ball shattering his tibia. Sixteen hours later the limb was amputated.

"I remained in the Field Hospital about 4 days," Skelton recalled, "and was then sent back to Allatoona Hospital where I remained

Sergeant Major James Skelton

Captain Elisha G. Hamilton

about one month. I was furloughed back home and there took a relapse and had a tough pull for life for near 3 months. I walked on crutches on the 26th day from the day I was wounded. [On July 26], a few minutes after I got out on my crutches, Captain Hamilton, Company I, 27th O.V.I., who was wounded the same night I was, and occupied the same

tent with me, died. Poor noble fellow. What a struggle for life he made. He wanted to live so bad. When he saw me get up and walk on my crutches he said, 'Skelton, if I could do that I would do anything on earth.' Then without uttering another word [he] closed his anxious black eyes in death. Peace to his ashes."

William Baxter, the 113th Ohio lieutenant whose lower right leg had been smashed during the "dreadful enterprise," spent the next two nights under canvas lying upon a fly-blown blanket, the stump of his amputated limb supported by a bundle of dead leaves. "My work was done," he later wrote in muted anger. "Others would go on, but I must go back. I had suffered a great misfortune without any compensation. We were shot down by the hundreds while the rebels behind their strong works escaped with scarcely any loss. The whole affair was useless and a mistake, and Sherman's reason given is not creditable to him or any good general. Could we have felt that our enemies had also lost a reasonable number, there would have been some compensation, but for them to have lost almost nothing and to be damaged in nothing, made us feel that we had been a useless sacrifice. If any just reason had been given

for the charge we would have felt better. Or even if Sherman had said it was a mistake and should not have been made, but the reason given was not such as to justify him in the loss of a single life in that charge." [11]

Ironically, even before darkness enveloped the shot-torn slopes of Kennesaw on June 27, Sherman was contemplating another flanking maneuver. In what was termed "the only advantage of the day," Cox's division of the 23rd Corps pushed a mile beyond Olley Creek down the Sandtown Road, and occupied a densely wooded, chigger-infested ridge six miles from the Chattahoochee River. Schofield, after making a personal reconnaissance, telegraphed Sherman that Cox's position "threatens the enemy's left rear and seems to me more important than I at first supposed." The army commander pondered his maps and the possibilities Schofield's news presented, weighing the risks of swinging his forces toward the right and striking Johnston's rear eight miles below Marietta. It meant cutting loose again from the railroad for at least 10 days, but that necessity, to Sherman, was a far less bitter pill to swallow than remaining stalemated in front of Kennesaw's fortifications. Provided the Confederates stayed put, the flanking movement could begin as soon as enough supplies were stockpiled. [12]

While this transpired, Thomas was instructed to hold the gains bloodily won by Newton's and Davis' divisions. On the latter's front, the makeshift line carved out with bayonets, eating utensils and bare hands ranged only 100 to 30 yards from the Rebel breastworks. During the night tools were brought up to deepen and consolidate the holes, and empty cracker boxes filled with dirt were used in some places to construct a parapet. A tunnel was started, its entrance hidden behind Dilworth's trenches. All the commotion of so much activity was not possible to conceal. Fearful of a sneak attack, some wary Confederates pitched burning cotton balls soaked with turpentine over their headlogs, lighting up the intervening ground. The measure resulted in a spectacular pyrotechnic display, but only succeeded in charring a number of corpses lying between the lines.

"The flanks of McCook's brigade were bent back to meet connecting lines on the right and left for permanent works, which were erected during the night of the 27th," wrote a 52nd Ohio officer. "Thereafter our regiments took twelve-hour tours upon the front line, firing almost constantly. The guns of the dead and wounded were gathered, double-shotted, pinned down to the top of the front line and held in readiness for a counter-charge, an emergency for which we were continually on the lookout." [13]

With the opposing lines so close near the Dead Angle, a soldier invited almost certain death by raising his head above the parapet to fire. For some of McCook's men, the problem was solved by what they called the "gun glass."

Sergeant Nixon Stewart of the 52nd Ohio described this as "a small piece of looking glass, two and a half inches square, framed with zinc, with a wire stem by which it was attached to the stock of our Springfield rifles, so arranged that we could lie down in the trench, the rifle resting on the breast-

works, pointing toward the rebel head log, that you could look through the sights and with your hammer pulled back, pick off a rebel without exposing the body. Hundreds of these were made and used to the astonishment of the men opposite to us." [14]

Another Ohioan credited Sergeant Edwin C. Silliman of Company C, 86th Illinois, with introducing usage of "gun glasses" to the brigade. "Silliman met a 4th Corps man trying to sell the glasses; the idea struck him that they could be used to sight the guns of the men in sharpshooting. He bought the whole outfit consisting of one hundred and fifty; these he gave to the boys of the brigade." Samuel Grimshaw, a 52nd Ohio private who earned the Medal of Honor six weeks later, believed the mirrors were very effective. "We soon learned that by shooting at the lower bevel of the headlogs, the ball was deflected, and as [Rebel prisoners] afterward said, made them seek safety as far back as they could get from the front of their works." [15]

The Confederates actually got their first look at this ingenious device before Grimshaw and his comrades. On June 24, reported Colonel Ellison Capers

Illinois State Historical Library

Sergeant Edwin C. Silliman, Company C, 86th Illinois

of the 24th South Carolina, "we captured a sharp-shooter who had a small looking-glass attached to the butt of his musket, so that he could sit behind his breast-work, perfectly protected, with his back to us, and by looking into his glass, sight along the barrel of his piece." [16]

During the 28th a Rebel barrage swept the front, forcing everyone to lie low. Union gunners responded with a bombardment of their own, smothering the ridge and swiftly silencing the Confederate cannon. Things remained relatively quiet until supper-time, when a sudden commotion startled those in Dilworth's forwardmost trench. A 52nd Ohioan recalled: "A command from the other side was heard, clear and distinct, 'Make ready, take aim, fire!' Over came stones and clubs, pick handles and frying pans, and woe be to the man who was unprotected. Many on our line were struck and disabled. Capt. [Henry O.] Mansfield [of Company E] was crippled for life. Serg. Major William Freeman was struck with a pick handle, went to the hospital and never returned for duty." [17]

Retaliation, of sorts, occurred after dark. "The enemy lying so near us, we were required to watch all night and keep up occasional firing so that sleep was out of the question," explained 1st/27th Tennessee private James Blair. "We were finally relieved by a regiment of our brigade and allowed to retire a few hundred yards to rest. About midnight we were aroused by a terrific firing, and learned that a Yank had ordered in a loud voice, 'Forward, double-quick, charge!' just to see what would happen. The boys jumped to their guns and poured in volley after volley, which amused the Yankees very much, who were a short distance away lying in their trenches." A fellow Tennessean remembered: "We had just gotten to sleep, and the sudden awakening caused such a panic among the boys that we could scarcely get inside our fort [the Dead Angle]. The order 'Fall in line!' was obeyed by some with one leg in their pants, by others with pants in hand, while others were altogether minus." [18]

Lieutenant Thomas Maney of Company B was one of those literally caught with his trousers down:

In the darkness a fellow would imagine he saw someone crawling, and then — bang! The report would be answered by several, causing the alarm. Generally such sensations did but little harm. I did not get hurt that night, but got scared out of my pants.

Having pulled off my shoes, socks and pants, I folded them up nicely for a pillow, and was sleeping at a two-forty gait when the din began by bang! bang! boom! boom! while the cry went up all around us: "Fall in, fall in; the enemy are on us!" Some thought that we were still on the front line, and were nearly crazed from loss of sleep. Every man awoke with a start, too dazed to know where to go, but our guns were stacked just before us, and there were the works.

I jumped up, put on my socks, shoes and hat, grabbed what I thought was my pants, jammed one foot through a breeches leg, but it would not go on, simply for the reason that it was my jacket; gave that up as a bad job, looked for the pants and could not find them, so I put on my jacket and fell into line in Texas costume style. Everybody was too much excited to notice my white [underwear], so after the scare I wrapped my blanket around me and lay down to rest again, promising myself that I would be up with the first peep of day and find my pants before any of the boys could find it out. [19]

The morning of June 29 offered no such amusement to the soldiers occupying the closest stretches of breastworks. Dozens of dead still littered the intervening ground, having become blackened and bloated after two days exposed to a broiling sun. "Some of them were lying against our works and [presented] a most revolting appearance," observed a Confederate artillery officer. "They were as black as negroes — enormously swollen, fly blown & emitting an intolerable stench." With a breeze generally blowing the noxious odor toward the Southerners, many became sick and unable to eat. [20]

"The smell from the bodies was so offensive, the wind being in our favor, that the rebels requested us to cease firing and have an armistice to bury the dead," noted Lieutenant Colonel Fahnestock in his journal. "We notified our general, J.C. Davis, who came over and sent an officer half way between our lines to meet theirs to make the terms." Sergeant Rogers of the 125th Illinois claimed these representatives were his own lieutenant colonel, James W. Langley, and Horace Rice, colonel of the 29th Tennessee, Vaughan's brigade. "Colonel Rice was very anxious that the arms and accoutrements of our soldiers who fell at the rebel breast works should be given over to them, but to this Col. Langley objected, and proposed that they should be regarded as neutral property, and not touched by either party until one or the other should occupy the ground. To this Colonel Rice reluctantly consented, knowing that if he did not it would be equivalent to saying that the rebels were not going to hold their position." [21]

Courtesy
David & Frances Hall

• *Major Philip Van Horn Weems, 11th Tennessee, joined scores of soldiers fraternizing in front of Vaughan's brigade during the June 29 burial truce. The regiment's colonel, George W. Gordon, was awed by the slaughter: "I [saw] eleven dead Federals around one large tree in front of the position occupied by the 11th and 29th regiments, behind which tree they had evidently taken refuge, but where they were subject to a destructive enfilading fire. The carnage was frightful." Six days earlier "Van" Weems had written his brothers in Hickman County, Tennessee, that "We feel confident of whipping the Yankees if they ever attack us and woe be to Sherman then ... I hope to see you once again, but the daily risks I am under leave me little chance of hope." On July 22 while acting as colonel, Weems was mortally wounded in the battle of Atlanta and died two days later.*

Once terms were arranged, Adjutant W.M. Ives of the 1st/4th Florida witnessed a thin line of armed Federals walk to within 25 feet of the Confederate works, about face and sit down. Conversely, a line of Rebels did the same. Then the burial parties went to work, accompanied by knots of officers and other sightseers. "Our men mingled freely with the Yankees," recorded William Trask, "chatting as friendly as if they were on the best of terms. The truce lasted until near night fall and the men took advantage of it to trade tobacco for knives, coffee and so forth." Wandering over from Hood's corps, Colonel Newton N. Davis of the 24th Alabama thought "It was very interesting to listen at the conversation between the Yanks & our men. Their men looked as ragged and dirty as our men. The Yanks would trade any thing they had for Tobacco. A brisk trade was kept up all the while. The Yankee dead looked very badly. They were as black in the face as a negro. If they would only keep on butting up against our lines we could soon dispose of them all in the same way."[22]

Captain William P. Bishop of Company D, 29th Tennessee, remembered that "there was some indulgence in grim humor, notwithstanding the terrible surroundings. Our jolly, whole-souled Gen. Cheatham was never better pleased than when passing himself off as one of the boys. Col. Rice was always grave, dignified and courteous. On this occasion Gen. Cheatham wore his slouched hat and smoked his short pipe. Col. Rice, gay in full regimentals, was treated with the deference due his position by the Federals. The men met the General as an equal, and he was soon the center of a large crowd, talking, laughing, and occasionally taking a drink from the inevitable canteen. One son of the Emerald Isle was about getting on very intimate terms with him, even going so far as to try to put his arms around the General's neck, when Col. Rice, walking up, touched the man on the arm, and inquired if he knew to whom he was speaking. 'One of your boys, I suppose,' was the reply. 'That,' said Col. Rice, at the same time raising his voice, 'is Maj. Gen. Cheatham.' A forty-pound shot thrown into their midst would not have produced a greater sensation than did this announcement. Instantly all eyes were fixed upon the old hero, for they knew and respected him. Thenceforth he was given ample room for moving around."[23]

Among those "promiscuously mingling" was Sergeant Major Lyman S. Widney of the 34th Illinois. He wrote home the following day:

I had quite an interesting chat with a Reb lieutenant. While talking with him, Gens. Cheatham and Hindman came out with their staffs and met some of our officers. A Rebel colonel made

History of the Doles-Cook Brigade

• *Colonel James C. Nisbet, 66th Georgia, wrote of the temporary halt in hostilities along W.H.T. Walker's division front: "The 1st Confederate Regiment occupied our salient. Col. Geo. A. Smith asked, 'What do you want?' [The Federals] answered, 'To bury our dead lying between the works.' He granted the truce, and while it lasted the men poured over the fortifications and mingled together fraternally. When General Johnston heard of it, he was hot sure enough! He hurried to our position and ordered the truce called off, and put Colonel Smith under arrest for transcending his authority."*

the introduction and after bowing very politely the whole party sat down on the ground about six feet distant from where I sat on a log, and talked pleasantly together for almost an hour.

Cheatham looked very unlike I supposed a Rebel major general commanding a corps [*sic*] would look. He wore nothing but a rough pair of grey pants tucked under the tops of an unpolished pair of boots, a blue flannel shirt and rough felt hat completed his attire. He had neither coat nor vest and was without

any or manner to indicate his rank. Gen. Hindman was just the reverse. He has a handsome, good natured countenance, and wears an abundance of gold lace and cord. [24]

Fellow Illinoisan Robert Rogers also saw Cheatham up close, describing the division commander's uniform as consisting of "an old slouch hat, a blue hickory shirt, butternut pants, and a pair of cavalry boots. The supports to his unmentionables were an old leather strap, and a piece of web, the general appearance being that of a 'johnny' gone to seed." [25]

At least one other officer purposely "dressed down" in an attempt to escape notice while surreptitiously reconnoitering. General James D. Morgan, commanding Davis' 1st Brigade, donned a corporal's coat and mixed undetected with the grave diggers nearest the Rebel works, all the while making mental notes of what could be seen. [26]

As the putrefying condition of the dead precluded carrying bodies from the field, they were buried where they lay, each grave marked with the man's name and regiment. It was a sad, mournful undertaking. Many in the burial details discovered and laid to rest some of their best friends. [27]

Twenty-one members of the 52nd Ohio had been killed outright on June 27, and most of them were interred during the truce. Private John Moore of Company F recalled: "The night before the charge R.J. Stewart said to me that he did not expect to get home alive. I tried to cheer him up, but could not. He said, 'I don't want to be wounded. I want to be shot through the heart.' When we buried the dead I found him within 12 feet of the Confederate works. He was lying with his face to the foe, shot through the heart." [28]

The first body located by Private John D. Kirkpatrick of Company D proved to be that of his chum Jonathan Sills, the inquisitive soldier admonished by Colonel McCook minutes prior to the assault. Kirkpatrick found him "sitting with his back to a tree, dead. In his hands were three photographs. One was of his mother and the others his two sisters. I dug a grave at the tree. I also found a Testament, which I wrapped with the pictures and sent them to his mother. We had orders not to remove any arms, so I slipped his gun into the grave." [29]

Similar burial truces, though of shorter duration, were arranged on Newton's and Morgan L. Smith's division fronts. Sergeant Walter Wilson led an eight-man detail from Company C, 57th Indiana.

They were particularly anxious to locate the body of their company commander, Captain Joseph Stidham, killed on June 23. His badly decomposed corpse finally was found, wrapped in a blanket and deposited in a separately dug grave. "A lot of others from different Regts," Wilson recorded in his diary, "were covered with dirt as they lay."[30]

The enemy, wrote First Lieutenant William H. Newlin of Company C, 73rd Illinois, "lent a helping hand in the work on the 29th, some of them no doubt wishing they could bury all the 'Yankees,' and have the thing done with. The rebels were in a good humor, and groups of soldiers — half and half, Yankee and Confederate — were between the lines, talking and trading and exchanging papers; coffee for tobacco, and tobacco for coffee, being about the extent of the trading done."[31]

Where Harker's assault had failed, Captain Wilbur Hinman estimated the truce lasted two hours. "The soldiers in blue and gray mingled pleasantly together, engaged in chaffing and bartering. A strapping fellow of our brigade challenged to a wrestling match 'the biggest reb they could find.' A stalwart Tennessean accepted the challenge, and scores gathered about to witness the contest, evincing as keen an interest as though the issue of the war depended upon its result. The stars and stripes were triumphant, for the 'Yank' threw the 'Johnny' three times successively. When the work of interment was finished the truce came to an end; the soldiers returned to their respective posts, seized their muskets and began to blaze away at each other. Such is war!"[32]

"It was, indeed, a strange sight," felt 85th Illinois sergeant Henry Aten. "During the truce all was peace and apparent amity, but as soon as the last sad service the living can render to the dead had been performed, both sides resumed their efforts to kill, and maim, and cripple." Aten noted the armistice provided each side with an opportunity to plan future defense and aggression. "On the night after the truce the enemy, by the use of ropes, threw over their works a continuous line of chevaux-de-frise in front of [Dilworth's] brigade, and at night illuminated the space between the lines with fire-balls of cotton soaked in turpentine or tar. On our side it was determined to establish an advance line some ten yards higher on the hillside, and by daybreak on the 30th this work was completed."[33]

Construction also continued on the subterranean

Craig Dunn

Captain Joseph Stidham, Company C, 57th Indiana

gallery started behind Dilworth's trenches. Rumors circulated that it would be blown underneath the Confederate breastworks on the 4th of July, but progress was hampered by inexperienced tunnelers using unsuitable tools. In addition, a member of the 125th Illinois explained, "the Johnnies found out the scheme. Prisoners later stated that they suspected something of the sort was going on, so placing a drum on the ground, and on its head some small pieces of gravel, the digging of our boys caused the head of the drum to vibrate, and make the gravel move." Lieutenant Colonel Langley, the mining project's supervisor, undoubtedly was mortified by what an Atlanta newspaper correspondent wrote on July 1: "The enemy is reported to be trying the

Vicksburg plan of undermining Cheatham's works, which are very near their own, and as every one knows he is the last man to sit down quietly and wait for them to finish a work of this description, we may expect to hear of some one being hurt should the report prove correct." [34]

In the end, the tunnel was not completed and a mine never sprung.

Scattered popping of skirmishers' rifles and booming cannon punctuated the last day of June at Kennesaw. "The weather is too warm for fighting during the day," Ohio artilleryman George Hurlbut informed his fiancée. "Many of our soldiers are becoming sick. My health continues fair, yet I feel the fatiguing effects of the long, continued campaign." Lieutenant Colonel Samuel Merrill of the 70th Indiana complained more forcefully about ill health in letters home, telling his wife about a scurvy-ridden company commander and of his own "indolent disposition. I am so wretchedly weak that it is with the greatest difficulty that I can drag along with the regiment, but as an officer is worse off in a field hospital than here, and as the surgeon will not give a certificate on which to base a plea for resigning at this stage of the campaign I shall keep on as long as I can stick to [my horse's] back. You need not think from this that I am in a comparatively bad situation, for there are a half dozen officers and a hundred men belonging to the regiment, with us and behind, with whom I would not swap places." [35]

A mid-afternoon thunderstorm — the first in nine days — temporarily squelched the heat but did not dampen Sherman's resolve to once again try flanking. Wagon trains guarded by cavalry stripped from Garrard's division northeast of Big Kennesaw already were en route toward the right. A Michigan sergeant detailed to procure rations at Big Shanty found the sheds there "alive with Yankees who were handling army supplies." Sherman's timetable for beginning the general movement within two days proceeded apace. On July 1 he wired Washington: "I have been hurrying down provisions and forage, and tomorrow night propose to move General McPherson from the left to the extreme right .... By this movement I think I can force Johnston to move his army down from Kenesaw, to defend his railroad crossing and the Chattahoochee. Johnston may come out of his intrenchments and attack General Thomas, which is what I want, for General Thomas is well in-

trenched, parallel with the enemy, south of Kenesaw. The movement is substantially down the Sandtown road, straight for Atlanta." [36]

The Confederate commander, expecting this course of action for some time and seeing telltale activity behind Union lines, realized the occupation of Kennesaw was nearing an end. New breastworks and redoubts had been built with impressed slave labor six miles south on high ground between Smyrna and the Chattahoochee, the last significant water barrier north and west of Atlanta. Leaving his rugged bastion after 26 days of almost uninterrupted fighting was now imperative, for as Johnston pointed out, Sherman's troops "already were nearer to Atlanta than the Confederate left." [37]

During late afternoon of July 1 a fierce Federal bombardment designed to keep the Rebels guessing blanketed the mountain with flying metal and smoke. "The enemy," recorded General French, "turned fifty-two pieces of artillery on three guns I have on the west brow of Little Kennesaw, and continued the fire long after dark. Seldom in war have there been instances where so many guns have been trained on a single spot. But it was only in the darkness of the night that the magnificence of the scene was displayed — grand beyond imagination, beautiful beyond description. Kennesaw, usually invisible from a distance at night, now resembles Vesuvius in the beginning of an eruption." Although causing little material damage, the nocturnal barrage masked the withdrawal of a 15th Corps' division destined to reinforce Schofield, and resumed before daybreak on the 2nd. French continued: "Not content with the waste of ammunition last evening, the enemy commenced again at 4:15 this morning — the heathens — and kept it up until 6 a.m. from every battery, and from some guns until 11 a.m." [38]

Less than three hours later a circular issued by Johnston alerted subordinate commanders the army would vacate its Kennesaw defenses that night. Thick clouds blotted the moonlight as the artillery pulled out first, followed by Loring's, Hardee's and Hood's corps, their rear guards and finally, the skirmishers. "It had been predicted that our batteries could not be safely withdrawn in case of retreat," wrote French's artillery chief, Major George Storrs. Johnston's order specified all cannon be removed after sundown. If not, as Storrs understood it, they were to be spiked and the carriages destroyed. "But routes were trimmed out straight down immediately in rear of each section, and every gun arrived at the base of the mountain by dark, without attracting a single shot from the enemy. We had been keeping our embrasures covered with brush to conceal our movements when preparing to deliver a shot, so that every thing was hidden." [39]

Coincidentally, at almost the same hour north of Kennesaw, McPherson's cannoneers were leaving their own positions for the move toward the right. "Got the artillery off the stony hill without making noise enough to hear two rods," boasted Captain Edward Spear, a division artillery commander in the 17th Corps. "I have never seen a feat accomplished with more perfect success." Spear's three batteries rolled three miles to the 14th Corps' rear, where "it being so dark and meeting with such a nest work of roads we were compelled to wait for daylight." [40]

McPherson's infantry trudged along as best it could in the intense darkness, as described by Illinoisan Fenwick Hedley:

From the side of the road the moving column might be felt, but it could not be seen. The army literally walked by faith, each man following in the steps of one he believed to be in advance of him. The ground, sodden with heavy rains, gave no sound of foot or hoof, and feet and wheels rapidly converted the roadway into a sea of mud.

Now the troops "string out" in the darkness until they reach over three times their ordinary ground, even in marching order. The ranks are not compact and well dressed; each man goes as he pleases. The head of column halts on account of some obstacle, and those in the rear, not knowing what has occurred, "close up" on their comrades in front, and collide in the darkness. Then is heard angry dialogue, the men being forgetful of all injunctions to silence. "Why the hell don't you keep up?" "What the hell are you running over me for?" "Hold up your damn gun, and keep it out of my eye!" "Damn your eye!" and so on, with countless variations. Then one finds himself anchored to the ground by the depth and consistency of the mud; and, while endeavoring to extricate himself, those hurrying on from behind stumble over him in the darkness, until a score or more of men are piled on top of one another, before the words "ease up" can be passed back.

Oh! the profanity of that night march! The objurgatory division of the mother-tongue stood revealed in all its elaborateness and comprehensiveness; and yet, reinforced as it was by copious selections from foreign languages, it proved utterly inadequate for such an emergency. Oaths of the most intricate construction and far-reaching meaning were thrown upon the midnight air, with a vehemence which left no doubt as to the sincerity of the swearer. He damned all things, visible and invisible, known, unknown and unknowable. The United States and the "Confederacy" were alike relegated, side by side, to the grim sulphurous shades of the forever cursed; then the swearer

Fort Pulaski National Monument, Savannah

Colonel Charles H. Olmstead, 1st Georgia Volunteers

wished that Sherman and Johnston were both in hadean regions "to fight it out themselves;" and further expressed the conviction that it would be comparative bliss to be there himself. Nor was the swearing spasmodic and occasional, but persistent and unanimous. [41]

"The fall back was conducted in good order & we lost no men," commented a Georgia infantryman after his regiment passed through Marietta's quiet streets and marched silently south to Johnston's new defense lines straddling the railroad near Smyrna. But during the retreat many Confederates shared the experiences of their Union counterparts. [42]

Charles Hart Olmstead, colonel of the 1st Georgia Infantry Volunteers in W.H.T. Walker's division, later wrote: "The order for this movement came to me about eleven o'clock at night when the whole command was in the profound slumber that blessed our eyes in these days. In a few minutes the Regiment was formed and we filed out onto the road to take our place in the Brigade column. The night was dark and the little country road narrow, so progress was exceedingly slow because of the thousand and one obstructions to a march of troops under such conditions. We would go on for a few hundred yards and then halt for what seemed an interminable time — then go on again to be halted again in a few minutes. I sat on my horse taking little "cat naps," indifferent to surroundings, when suddenly the sense of being in a familiar spot aroused me; we were marching up the rear of the hill on which the old Georgia Military Institute was located. It was the school in which I had been educated and in which I had spent four happy years. Many had been my dreams of the future while there but never had there been forecast of such an event as marching with an army corps at midnight through this beloved spot. Every inch of its soil, every brick of its buildings was dear to me and it saddened my soul to believe that its destruction was near. It had furnished too many officers to the Confederate Army to be spared and Sherman ordered it to be burned on the following day. You may be sure that memory was busy and that my mind was full of the associations so strangely awakened." [43]

Until midnight the Rebel rear guard and pickets kept up a boisterous fire to prevent the evacuation's detection. On Cheatham Hill, however, Lieutenant Thomas Maney and 12 men from the 1st/27th Tennessee were assigned the ticklish task of lying 30 feet in front of the Dead Angle's breastworks to watch for any movement in the opposing entrenchments. Maney recalled with candor:

In crawling out to our posts that night we ran a great risk, for if we shook a bush or made the least noise we would hear the unwelcome "siz" of a minie ball. We had orders not to fire under any circumstances, so we could not reply. It was our province to watch and listen, and if crowded to jump and run. The men were placed, one by one, in a zigzag line, I having to crawl out in the dark and post each one. It was the officer's duty to go along the line and ascertain if all were doing their duty — lying down and keeping awake. Not much trouble to keep awake that night!

On one of the tours of inspection I got a little off the line, and, it being crooked, I went clear outside and became so confused that I could not tell whether I was going to my own men or not. Creeping along in this frame of mind, I felt the muzzle of a musket right against my bosom, and then heard the click, click of the cocked hammer. Well, the past life of the writer came up before him. All the mean things I ever did were passed in review in a few seconds, for the ordeal was of short duration. I was afraid to catch the gun, for it would make the man at the other end of it pull the trigger. So I asked: "Who is that?" No

answer. Then I said: "If you are Federals, I'm your meat." Still no answer. "If you are Rebs, I am your officer." No answer yet. The sweat was pouring down my face about that time.

The soldier took me for a Federal soldier, as my clothes were dark and my hat black, but he lowered his gun. The gun was down and I was down, lying prone on the ground by the soldier. When I realized that it was a man in our regiment who was considered unstable about the head, my scare came on good, for he had no more sense than to shoot. The reaction came to my nervous system and I was as weak as water. If the enemy had come on us then, it would have been impossible for me to rise from the ground. The poor fellow was frightened too, when he saw how near he came to sending me to my long home. At a given signal, about twelve o'clock, we moved back to the works and then on in quick time to catch up with the rear guard. [44]

Hunched down in a reserve-line trench no more than 50 yards from Maney's nervous men, Colonels Dilworth and Fahnestock were devising a plan. "[We] intended to make a feint about 2 o'clock," Fahnestock related, "have our men ready with guns loaded, fire a few volleys, give a yell and lay low, and if we drew the rebs' fire to immediately charge the works. About 1 o'clock while he and I were talking and making ready, all seemed so quiet that I suggested the rebels had retreated. In a short time a voice from their works asked permission to come over to us, saying the rebels had left. We sent over a guard and found it to be true." [45]

Not far away in Whitaker's 4th Corps' brigade, 51st Ohio sergeant Israel Correll also noticed the abrupt cessation of firing at 1 a.m. "Thinking it was only a ruse to deceive us, and that the rebs were up to some devilment, every man was up in line prepared for any emergency. In about an hour and a half it was ascertained that they had evacuated their works. Orders [were] given to get our breakfast as soon as possible." [46]

Near the Powder Springs Road on the 20th Corps' front, Lieutenant Colonel Charles F. Morse, 2nd Massachusetts, was field officer of the day commanding his brigade's pickets opposite Hood's corps:

That night I received notice that the enemy were expected to leave very soon, and to watch them closely. I went out to the picket line, intending to stay there till morning; the night was pretty dark, and though only about three hundred yards of open field lay between our line and the rebels', yet nothing could be seen at that distance. Occasionally, shots were fired. At one in the morning I ordered three men and a corporal, whom I knew to be cool, brave men, to crawl up within a few yards of the nearest rebel picket post, if possible, and see if they were still there. In about an hour they returned, and reported that they had been near enough to hear the enemy talking, and had been fired upon twice; however, from general appearances, I made up my mind that they were going, and so reported. At a little before daylight, the whole picket line was ordered forward. We advanced and got into the enemy's works without opposition, taking quite a number of prisoners. These works were the most formidable I have yet seen — more of the nature of permanent fortifications than ordinary field works. The breastworks were of the strongest kind; then about ten yards in front was a *chevaux de frise* of a double row of pointed rails, and in front of this, an almost impenetrable abatis about one hundred yards wide. [47]

From Little Kennesaw to Kolb's Farm, Federal soldiers were amazed by their opponents' massive fortifications once daybreak of July 3 revealed them abandoned. Passing over the works at 6 a.m., Sergeant Henry Morhous of the 123rd New York found them "to be very strong, consisting of a well intrenched skirmish line, two light lines behind it, and still back of these a most elaborate main line, the parapet being ten feet wide on top, with ditch and abatis in front." Captain Henry Richards of Company F, 93rd Ohio, wrote his father later in the day: "It was the strongest position, and best fortified, I have yet seen. And if we did not outnumber them largely, which enables us to flank them, they could not have been taken." [48]

Lieutenant Charles Cox enthusiastically broke the news to his sisters back in Indianapolis. "The Johnnies becoming aware Mr Sherman had played one of his pretty flank movements on them — packed up traps at daylight and 'scyugled' from their works at Kenesaw Mt. and in and around Marietta. Scarce had they turned their backs upon and retreated from their splendid lines of works than us Yankees were at their heels." [49]

Kennesaw Mountain was our golgotha and our Waterloo

General Sherman knew for certain that his adversary was gone from Kennesaw when, at dawn of July 3, he peered at the mountain through a tripod-mounted spy-glass. He could see Union pickets crawling cautiously toward the summit, then begin to throw their hats as they ran along its crest. "In a minute," he recalled, "I roused my staff, and started them off with orders in every direction for a pursuit by every possible road, hoping to catch Johnston in the confusion of retreat, especially at the crossing of the Chattahoochee River." [1]

Someone hauled a large flag up a pole, which drew cheers from thousands of throats. Brigade and regimental bands struck up patriotic airs. "It was Sunday," remembered Nixon Stewart, whose Ohio regiment had spent the past six days lying almost within spitting distance of the Dead Angle. "Our band played 'Old Hundred,' while we sang 'Praise God from whom all blessings flow.' It was joy to our boys as we had scarcely looked up for six days from our dangerous position. Marietta was ours, and our forces were pushing Johnston toward Atlanta." [2]

General Stanley's skirmishers entered nearly deserted Marietta at 8 a.m., followed by Newton's division. Lyman Root, the 125th Ohio corporal serving as postmaster of Bradley's brigade, immediately sought the town's post office. "We found letters — sweet missives from the misses to their Johnny boys — and the morning papers telling all about the battle [of June 27]." Root also noticed a large signboard erected in Marietta's center square. "The picture of a Yankee soldier [was] sketched on it, and also a rebel soldier at a charge bayonet, with the point of the bayonet entering the seat of the Yank's trousers, with this inscription written under it: 'Gen. Sherman fleeing to the rear!' We laughed some over this, but the 'flea' was on the other fellow's leg." [3]

Samuel French left Kennesaw "with regret. From its slopes we repelled the assaults of the enemy, and from its top I loved to sit and witness the almost daily conflicts, and hear the Rebel yell." Georgian John Hagan was convinced "We had a Strong position & could have whiped all the Yanks Shearman could have brought against us." Situated where his regiment was now, Hagan was unsure "wheather they will attack us or not but I hope they will for I am wore out marching and building breast works." [4]

Captain Mumford Dixon, whose 3rd Confederate Infantry watched approaching Federal pursuers from the Rebel skirmish line on July 3, thought "the move was occasioned by the enemy flanking us, but a man knows nothing here unless he sees it. There is one thing that we all know, or think so anyway, that is that we will whip the yankees whenever and wherever we fight. Our confidence in ourselves and Gen. Johnston is unshaken notwithstanding we have retreated eighty miles." A Tennessean in Cheatham's division concurred. "The enthusiasm of the troops and their confidence in 'Old Joe' amounts to fanaticism almost. We are willing to go where he says without a murmur, even if it be to Atlanta." [5]

One week later Johnston ordered the Army of Tennessee to abandon its Chattahoochee fortifications and fall back once more. The Federals had not obliged many Southerners' hopes of assaulting frontally, as they had with disastrous consequences on June 27. Instead, Sherman used McPherson to envelop the Rebel left flank along the river while Schofield's 23rd Corps and a cavalry division marched upstream and crossed on July 8 and 9. With Union forces south of the river, Johnston's vaunted Chattahoochee defenses became untenable and he was compelled to retreat to unfinished works on Atlanta's very doorstep. Citizens and politicians feared a catastrophe was in the offing, even though most soldiers retained trust in their general. The Confederacy's president, however, did not. On July 17, Jefferson Davis relieved Johnston of command, replacing him with John Bell Hood.

In a reversal of his predecessor's strategy during the previous two months, Hood wasted no time striking back. Between July 20 and 28 he launched three separate blows against portions of Sherman's forces outside Atlanta, losing in the process 16,000 irreplaceable men. The weakened Confederates withdrew to the sprawling entrenchments circling the city, and endured a month-long siege. It was a mode of warfare Hood and Sherman both detested. The deadlock finally was broken in late August when the Union commander moved south to sever one of the Rebels' last remaining rail supply lines. After a two-day battle resulting in defeat at Jonesboro, Hood ordered Atlanta's evacuation. On September 2, jubilant Federals marched in, accepting surrender from the city's mayor.

*   *   *

For thousands of survivors North and South, Kennesaw Mountain provided searing, unforgettable memories in an unprecedented campaign. As a field of battle it was perhaps unique in the war. "The country," observed a Union general that summer, "is all woods, deep ravines, muddy creeks, and steep hills, the most defensible positions by nature I have ever seen. Rods and rods of abatis, trees and bushes cut down and intertwined in front, and chevaux-de-frise of strong pointed stakes, fastened firmly in the ground in the midst of the abatis, making a network through which a man could hardly crawl in an hour. Just imagine a line of armed men making their way through and thousands of rifles firing upon it!" An enlisted man simply stated: Kennesaw "was the most perfect natural fortification Sherman's army ever encountered, and the enemy made the most of the advantages it afforded." [6]

The human toll exacted during June 1864 was computed at 13,478. The wild tangles surrounding Kennesaw were likened to a meat grinder, where soldiers chanced being shot while sleeping in the rear as they did fighting on the picket line. Lives were inextricably altered. Men like Missourian Thomas Wells and Illinoisan John D. Frazier lost their right arms. Georgian J.B. Holland and Iowan Abraham W. Morris underwent amputation of their left legs. Floridian Samuel J. Herod, Tennessean John White, New Yorker Charles Lapoint and Ohioan Augustus T. Dorsey were killed. Alabamian Francis Shubert and Pennsylvanian William H. Thomas suffered the ignominy of capture and both died in captivity, Shubert at Rock Island, Illinois, and Thomas at Andersonville.

For an Ohioan whose regiment lost severely on June 27, "There is no place where we were tested that to me finds so much interest, as Kennesaw Mountain was our golgotha and our Waterloo." The sentiment was echoed by another member of the same brigade: "It was awful. I never want to see the like again." [7] □

SOURCES & NOTES

Chapter 1

1. William T. Alderson, editor, "The Civil War Diary of James Litton Cooper, September 30, 1861 to January 1865," *Tennessee Historical Quarterly,* vol. 15, no. 2 (June 1956), p. 162.

2. Ephraim C. Dawes, "The Confederate Strength in the Atlanta Campaign," *Battles and Leaders of the Civil War,* vol. 4 (New York: The Century Company, 1886), p. 281-282.

3. *The War of the Rebellion: A Compilation of the Official Records of the Union and Confederate Armies,* vol. 38, pt. 1 (Washington: Government Printing Office, 1891), p. 3. Hereafter referred to as *Official Records.*

4. Hosea W. Rood, *Story of the Service of Company E, and of the Twelfth Wisconsin Regiment of Veteran Volunteer Infantry, in the War of the Rebellion* (Milwaukee: Swain & Tate Co., 1893), p. 274.

5. *Official Records,* vol. 38, pt. 4, p. 327.

6. Ambrose G. Bierce, "The Crime at Pickett's Mill," *The Collected Works of Ambrose Bierce,* vol. 1 (New York: Gordian Press, 1966), p. 280.

7. Norman D. Brown, editor, *One of Cleburne's Command: The Civil War Reminiscences and Diary of Capt. Samuel T. Foster, Granbury's Texas Brigade, CSA* (Austin: University of Texas Press, 1980), p. 88.

8. Diary of Sergeant Major Andrew J. Gleason, 15th Ohio, quoted in Alexis Cope, *The Fifteenth Ohio Volunteers and its Campaigns, 1861-1865* (Columbus: Press of the Edward T. Miller Co., 1916), p. 456.

9. Albert Castel, *Decision in the West: The Atlanta Campaign of 1864* (Lawrence: University Press of Kansas, 1992), p. 246, 592.

10. Bell Irvin Wiley, editor, "The Confederate Letters of John W. Hagan," *The Georgia Historical Quarterly* (September 1954), p. 273.

11. Columbus Sykes to his wife, June 1, 1864, Kennesaw Mountain National Battlefield Park (KMNBP) library.

12. John M. Carr diary, KMNBP library. Before his enlistment in August 1862 as a sergeant in Company G, 100th Indiana, Carr resided in St. Paul, Minnesota.

Chapter 2

1. Martin Litvin, editor, "Captain Burkhalter's Georgia War," *Voices of the Prairie Land,* vol. 2 (Galesburg, Ill.: Mother Bickerdyke Historical Collection, 1972), p. 489.

2. *Official Records,* vol. 38, pt. 1, p. 710.

3. Burkhalter, p. 489-490.

4. Charles W. Wills, *Army Life of an Illinois Soldier* (Washington: Globe Printing Company, 1906), p. 254, 255.

5. Andrew Bush to Mary Bush, June 4, 1864, Indiana Division, Indiana State Library, Indianapolis.

6. Milo M. Quaife, editor, *From the Cannon's Mouth: The Civil War Letters of General Alpheus S. Williams* (Detroit: Wayne State University Press, 1959), p. 315.

7. Samuel G. French, *Two Wars: An Autobiography of Gen. Samuel G. French* (Nashville: *Confederate Veteran,* 1901), p. 201.

8. J.M. Davidson to Julia Davidson, June 4, 1864, Special Collections, Woodruff Library, Emory University, Atlanta.

9. *Official Records,* vol. 38, pt. 3, p. 616-617; Joseph E. Johnston, *Narrative of Military Operations* (New York: D. Appleton and Company, 1874), p. 335.

10. William L. Trask journal, "The Georgia Campaign of 1864," KMNBP library.

11. Elbert D. Willett diary, KMNBP library.

12. Samuel Robinson quoted in John B. Lindsley, *The Military Annals of Tennessee. Confederate* (Nashville: J.M. Lindsley & Co., 1886), p. 164.

13. William O. Norrell journal, KMNBP library.

14. J.M. Davidson to Julia Davidson, June 6, 1864, Special Collections, Woodruff Library, Emory University.

15. John M. Carr diary, KMNBP library.

16. John W. Tuttle journal, KMNBP library.

17. Jacob D. Cox diary, KMNBP library.

18. Wills, *Army Life,* p. 254.

19. Willis J. Nugent to his mother, June 8, 1864, KMNBP library.

20. Castel, *Decision in the West,* p. 264; William T. Sherman, *Memoirs of Gen. W.T. Sherman,* vol. II (New York: Charles L. Webster & Co., 1891), p. 50.

21. John Gaddis letter of June 9, 1864, quoted in Rood, *Story of the Service of Company E, Twelfth Wisconsin ...,* p. 280.

22. *Ibid.,* p. 280; David M. Smith, editor, "The Civil War Diary of Colonel John Henry Smith," *Iowa Journal of History* (April 1949), p. 144.

23. Jesse B. Luce diary, KMNBP library.

24. John O. Holzhueter, editor, "William Wallace's Civil War Letters: The Atlanta Campaign," *Wisconsin Magazine of History,* vol. 57 (Winter 1973-1974), p. 98, 99.

25. *Ibid.,* p. 98.

26. John W. Tuttle journal, KMNBP library.

27. David Coe, editor, *Mine Eyes Have Seen the Glory: Combat Diaries of Union Sergeant Hamlin Alexander Coe* (Rutherford, N.J.: Fairleigh Dickinson University Press, 1975), p. 150.

28. William Walton, editor, *A Civil War Courtship: The Letters of Edwin Weller from Antietam to Atlanta* (Garden City, N.Y.: Doubleday & Company, 1980), p. 86, 87.

29. William L. Trask journal, KMNBP library.

30. Columbus Sykes to his wife, June 8, 1864, KMNBP library.

31. William J. Watson diary, Southern Historical Collection, University of North Carolina at Chapel Hill; Elbert D. Willett diary, KMNBP library; Columbus Sykes to his wife, June 10, 1864, KMNBP library.

32. *Official Records,* vol. 38, pt. 4, p. 408; pt. 1, p. 67.

Chapter 3

1. Olynthus B. Clark, editor, *Downing's Civil War Diary* (Des Moines: The Historical Department of Iowa, 1916), p. 195.

2. Dale E. Linvill, editor, *Battles, Skirmishes, Events and Scenes: The Letters and Memorandum of Ambrose Remley* (Crawfordsville, Ind.: Montgomery County Historical Society, 1997), p. 117; *Official Records,* vol. 38, pt. 2, p. 804, 848-849. Due to recurring illness, Colonel Wilder was granted sick leave on June 14 and did not return to the army again. On June 9, the Lightning Brigade was commanded by Colonel Abram O. Miller, 72nd Indiana.

3. "A Badger Boy in Blue: The Letters of Chauncey H. Cooke," *Wisconsin Magazine of History,* vol. IV (1920-1921), p. 84.

4. James R. Bentley, editor, "The Civil War Memoirs of Captain Thomas Speed," *The Filson Club History Quarterly,* vol. 44 (July 1970), p. 249-250.

5. Wills, *Army Life,* p. 259.

6. Williams, *From the Cannon's Mouth,* p. 318.

7. Israel Correll diary, KMNBP library.

8. Burkhalter, p. 492-493.

9. William C. Davis, editor, *Diary of a Confederate Soldier: John S. Jackman of the Orphan Brigade* (Columbia: University of South Carolina Press, 1990), p. 138.

10. William J. Crook to his fiancée, June 20, 1864, KMNBP library.

11. French, *Two Wars,* p. 202.

12. Samuel B. Barron, *The Lone Star Defenders: A Chronicle of the Third Texas Cavalry Regiment in the Civil War* (New York: Neale Publishing Co., 1908), p. 195.

13. Charles F. Morse, *Letters Written During the Civil War 1861-1865* (privately printed, 1898), p. 170.

14. George Hurlbut to his fiancée, June 13 and 23, 1864, KMNBP library.

15. *Official Records,* Vol. 38, pt. 4, p. 454; W.T. Sherman, *Memoirs,* vol. II, p. 51.

16. Wills, *Army Life,* p. 258.

17. Milo H. Lewis, "Closing on Johnston's Army at Kenesaw," *The National Tribune,* July 30, 1925.

18. Theodore C. Tracie, *Annals of the Nineteenth Ohio Battery Volunteer Artillery* (Cleveland: J.B. Savage, 1878), p. 331-332.

19. W.T. Sherman, *Memoirs,* vol. II, p. 52; J.E. Johnston, *Narrative,* p. 337.

20. W.T. Sherman, *Memoirs,* vol. II, p. 52-53.

21. J.E. Johnston, *Narrative,* p. 337.

22. Jackman, *Diary of a Confederate Soldier,* p. 141.

23. *Official Records,* vol. 38, pt. 1, p. 243; "Killing of Gen. Polk," *The National Tribune,* March 31, 1904; David H. Chandler diary, L.M. Strayer Collection. An eyewitness to this incident, Chandler was a 5th Indiana Battery artificer later promoted to second lieutenant.

24. William M. Polk, *Leonidas Polk: Bishop and General,* vol. II (New York: Longmans, Green and Co., 1915), p. 373-374; Jack D. Welsh, *Medical Histories of Confederate Generals* (Kent, Ohio: The Kent State University Press, 1995), p. 174.

25. Jackman, *Diary of a Confederate Soldier,* p. 142, 143; A.D. Kirwan, editor, *Johnny Green of the Orphan Brigade: The Journal of a Confederate Soldier* (Lexington: The University of Kentucky Press, 1956), p. 135-136.

26. Arnold Gates, editor, *The Rough Side of War: The Civil War Journal of Chesley A. Mosman, 1st Lieutenant, Company D, 59th Illinois Volunteer Infantry Regiment* (Garden City, N.Y.: The Basin Publishing Co., 1987), p. 214; W.H.H. Terrell, *Report of the Adjutant General State of Indiana,* vol. V (Indianapolis: Samuel M. Douglass, 1866), p. 53.

27. Castel, *Decision in the West,* p. 280.

28. Asbury L. Kerwood, *Annals of the Fifty-Seventh Regiment Indiana Volunteers* (Dayton: W.J. Shuey, 1868), p. 256-257.

29. *One of Cleburne's Command,* p. 95.

30. Frank L. Byrne, editor, *The View from Headquarters: Civil War Letters of Harvey Reid* (Madison: The State Historical Society of Wisconsin, 1965), p. 161.

31. Coe, *Mine Eyes Have Seen the Glory,* p. 154, 155.

32. *Official Records,* vol. 38, pt. 2, p. 374.

33. John L. Ketcham quoted in Samuel Merrill, *The Seventieth Indiana Volunteer Infantry in the War of the Rebellion* (Indianapolis: The Bowen-Merrill Company, 1900), p. 130.

34. Lorna L. Sylvester, editor, " 'Gone for a Soldier': The Civil War Letters of Charles Harding Cox," *Indiana Magazine of History* (September 1972), p. 203, 204.

35. Stephen Pierson, "From Chattanooga to Atlanta in 1864, a Personal Reminiscence," *Proceedings New Jersey Historical Society,* vol. XVI (1931), p. 343-345.

36. *Official Records,* vol. 38, pt. 3, p. 279, 317; Ezra J. Warner, *Generals in Blue* (Baton Rouge: Louisiana State University Press, 1992), p. 534-535.

37. John D. Alexander, *History of the Ninety-Seventh Regiment of Indiana Volunteer Infantry* (Terre Haute: Moore & Langen, 1891), p. 13; Henry H. Wright, *A History of the Sixth Iowa Infantry* (Iowa City: State Historical Society of Iowa, 1923), p. 285.

38. Wills, *Army Life,* p. 262, 263.

39. Rex Miller, editor, *Prison Echoes of the Great Rebellion* (Depew, N.Y.: Patrex Press, 1992), p. 14-18. Hundley's account originally appeared under the same title in 1874.

40. Rex Miller, *Hundley's Ragged Volunteers: A day-by-day account of the 31st Alabama Infantry Regiment, CSA 1861-1865* (Depew, N.Y.: Patrex Press, 1991), p. 59-62.

41. J.E. Johnston, *Narrative,* p. 338; William L. Trask journal, KMNBP library.

42. Mauriel P. Joslyn, editor, *Charlotte's Boys: Civil War Letters of the Branch Family of Savannah* (Berryville, Va.: Rockbridge Publishing Company, 1996), p. 250.

43. Jacob D. Cox diary, KMNBP library.

44. Mumford H. Dixon diary, Special Collections, Woodruff Library, Emory University.

45. William O. Norrell journal, KMNBP library.

46. J.E. Johnston, *Narrative,* p. 338.

47. Williams, *From the Cannon's Mouth,* p. 321.

48. J.E. Johnston, *Narrative,* p. 338-339.

49. Alexander Q. Porter diary, Special Collections, Woodruff Library, Emory University; Zachariah J. Armistead to his brother, June 15, 1864, KMNBP library.

50. William W. McMillan letter of June 21, 1864, KMNBP library.

Chapter 4

1. *Official Records,* vol. 38, pt. 4, p. 572-573.

2. Lydia M. Post, editor, *Soldiers' Letters from Camp, Battle-field and Prison* (New York: Bunce & Huntington, 1865), p. 392-393.

3. Fenwick Y. Hedley, *Marching Through Georgia* (Chicago: R.R. Donnelley & Sons, 1887), p. 108-109, 110-111, 113-114, 116-117.

4. *Johnny Green of the Orphan Brigade,* p. 137-138.

5. David P. Jackson, editor, *The Colonel's Diary: Journals Kept Before and During the Civil War by the late Colonel Oscar L. Jackson* (Sharon, Pa.: privately printed, 1922), p. 131-132. Private McCarter recovered from his wound, transferring March 29, 1865 to Company I, 6th Regiment, Veteran Reserve Corps.

6. Jabez P. Cannon, *Inside of Rebeldom: The Daily Life of a Private in the Confederate Army* (Washington: The National Tribune, 1900), p. 222-223.

7. Richard A. Baumgartner, editor, *Blood & Sacrifice: The Civil War Journal of a Confederate Soldier* (Huntington, W.Va.: Blue Acorn Press, 1994), p. 148-150.

8. *Wisconsin Magazine of History,* vol. IV (1920-1921), p. 87-88.

9. Burkhalter, p. 495.

10. *Charlotte's Boys,* p. 251-253.

11. Franklin Whitney to his father, June 20, 1864, courtesy of Kendyl Wallis, Sandwich, Illinois.

12. *The Georgia Historical Quarterly* (September 1954), p. 276-278.

13. William L. Trask journal, KMNBP library.

14. *Official Records,* vol. 38, pt. 1, p. 243-244.

15. *The Rough Side of War,* p. 220-221.

16. Israel Correll diary, KMNBP library.

17. Wilfred W. Black, editor, "Orson Brainard: A Soldier in the Ranks," *Ohio History,* vol. 76 (Winter-Spring 1967), p. 69-70.

18. Adam Hogle, "The 97th Ohio: An Incident at Kenesaw Mountain," *The National Tribune,* May 3, 1888. Hogle was wounded November 30, 1864 at Franklin, Tennessee.

19. "Civil War Journal of John Wesley Marshall recorded on a daily basis and sent when practicable to his fiancée Rachel Ann Tanner," Manuscript Collections, Ohio Historical Society, Columbus.

20. William F. King to his wife, June 23, 1864, courtesy of Dennis Keesee, Westerville, Ohio.

Chapter 5

1. George S. Storrs, "Kennesaw Mountain," *The Southern Bivouac,* vol. I, no. 4 (December 1882), p. 136-137; *Official Records,* vol. 38, pt. 3, p. 873; Ezra J. Warner, *Generals in Gray* (Baton Rouge: Louisiana State University Press, 1959), p. 93.

2. French, *Two Wars,* p. 205.

3. Storrs, *op.cit.,* p. 137-138, 139. One of Storrs' battery commanders, Captain John J. Ward, was mortally wounded by shellfire outside Atlanta on July 27, 1864.

4. William R. Talley reminiscences, KMNBP library; John D. Broadman to his father, June 25, 1864, KMNBP library; Charles M. Smith to his father, June 21 and 26, 1864, KMNBP library; Ashley Halsey, editor, *A Yankee Private's Civil War* (Chicago: Henry Regnery Company, 1961), p. 36.

5. William K. Armstrong diary, KMNBP library; John D. Barnhart, editor, "A Hoosier Invades the Confederacy: Letters and Diaries of Leroy S. Mayfield," *Indiana Magazine of History,* vol. 39, no. 2 (June 1943), p. 189.

6. Robert P. Findley journal excerpt published in the Xenia (Ohio) *Torchlight,* July 6, 1864.

7. Hedley, *Marching Through Georgia,* p. 115.

8. Clyde C. Walton, editor, *Private Smith's Journal: Recollections of the Late War* (Chicago: R.R. Donnelley & Sons, 1963), p. 155.

9. Daniel P. Smith, *Company K, First Alabama Regiment, or Three Years in the Confederate Service* (Philadelphia: Burk & McFetridge, 1885), p. 99; William W. McMillan letter of June 21, 1864, KMNBP library.

10. John S. Kendall, editor, "Recollections of a Confederate Officer," *The Louisiana Historical Quarterly,* vol. 29, no. 4 (October 1946), p. 1166.

11. Joseph Bogle, *Some Recollections of the Civil War* (Dalton, Ga.: The Daily Argus, 1911), p. 13.

12. *Blood & Sacrifice,* p. 152.

13. "Lieut. Isaac Lightner," *Confederate Veteran,* vol. IV, no. 8 (August 1896), p. 252.

14. Welsh, *Medical Histories of Confederate Generals,* p. 175.

15. *Official Records,* vol. 38, pt. 1, p. 121.

16. *A Yankee Private's Civil War,* p. 37-38.

17. *Official Records,* vol. 38, pt. 1, p. 122.

18. Morse, *Letters Written During the Civil War,* p. 173.

19. William B. Hazen, *A Narrative of Military Service* (Huntington, W.Va.: Blue Acorn Press, 1993), p. 348a.

20. Larry M. Strayer & Richard A. Baumgartner, *Echoes of Battle: The Atlanta Campaign* (Huntington, W.Va.: Blue Acorn Press, 1991), p. 157.

21. Benjamin F. Scribner, *How Soldiers Were Made* (Huntington, W.Va.: Blue Acorn Press, 1995), p. 266, 267, 268-270, 292-293, 294-295.

22. Cope, *The Fifteenth Ohio Volunteers,* p. 505.

23. William P. Fulton to his brother, June 25, 1864, KMNBP library.

24. K. Jack Bauer, editor, *Soldiering: The Civil War Diary of Rice C. Bull, 123rd New York Volunteer Infantry* (Novato, Calif.: Presidio Press, 1986), p. 129-130, 132, 133-134.

25. Henry C. Morhous, *Reminiscences of the 123d Regiment, N.Y. S.V.* (Greenwich, N.Y.: People's Journal Book and Job Office, 1879), p. 101-102.

26. Lorenzo R. Coy diary, KMNBP library.

27. *Official Records,* vol. 38, pt. 2, p. 655, 49.

28. Frederick Smith diary quoted in Cyrus K. Remington, *A Record of Battery I, First N.Y. Light Artillery Vols.* (Buffalo: Press of the Courier Company, 1891), p. 115.

29. Tracie, *Annals of the Nineteenth Ohio Battery,* p. 336-337.

30. John E. West quoted in *The "Dutchess County Regiment" (150th Regiment of New York State Volunteer Infantry) in the Civil War: Its Story as Told by its Members* (Danbury, Conn.: The Danbury Medical Printing Co., Inc., 1907), p. 94.

31. Samuel Toombs, *Reminiscences of the War, Comprising a Detailed Account of the Experiences of the Thirteenth Regiment New Jersey Volunteers in Camp, on the March, and in Battle* (Orange, N.J.: Journal office, 1878), p. 142, 141.

32. Edmund R. Brown, *The Twenty-Seventh Indiana Volunteer Infantry in the War of the Rebellion 1861 to 1865* (Monticello, Ind., 1899), p. 508-509.

33. *Official Records*, vol. 38, pt. 3, p. 815; John P. McGuire quoted in Lindsley, *Military Annals of Tennessee. Confederate*, p. 480.

34. R. Lockwood Tower, editor, *A Carolinian Goes to War: The Civil War Narrative of Arthur Middleton Manigault, Brigadier General, C.S.A.* (Columbia: University of South Carolina Press, 1983), p. 192.

35. *Ibid.*, p. 193.

36. *Official Records*, vol. 38, pt. 3, p. 769, 815; pt. 2, p. 478, 673; Captain Byron D. Paddock (Battery F, 1st Michigan Light Artillery) after-action report, August 15, 1864, KMNBP library.

37. Frank Elliot, "A June Evening Before Atlanta: Cothran's Battery and Knipe's Brigade Repulse Stevenson's Division," *The National Tribune*, October 26, 1905.

38. Reid, *The View from Headquarters*, p. 164; Weller, *A Civil War Courtship*, p. 90.

39. Williams, *From the Cannon's Mouth*, p. 328, 329.

Chapter 6

1. Richard A. Baumgartner & Larry M. Strayer, editors, *Yankee Tigers: Through the Civil War with the 125th Ohio* (Huntington, W.Va.: Blue Acorn Press, 1992), p. 109-110.

2. Kerwood, *Annals of the Fifty-Seventh Indiana*, p. 261.

3. *Ibid.*, p. 261; Terrell, vol. II, p. 548, 551, 553.

4. William Jones letter of June 26, 1864, Dennis Keesee Collection.

5. Henry T. Woodruff to George H. Woodruff, June 25, 1864, quoted in Kathy Johnson, *Colonel Frederick Bartleson* (Joliet: Will County Historical Society, 1983), p. 7.

6. Strayer & Baumgartner, *Echoes of Battle: The Atlanta Campaign*, p. 118; Hazen, *A Narrative of Military Service*, p. 264.

7. Walter P. Wilson diary, Smith Memorial Library, Indiana Historical Society; Burkhalter, p. 496.

8. W.T. Sherman, *Memoirs*, vol. II, p. 60; *Official Records*, vol. 38, pt. 4, p. 492.

9. *Official Records*, vol. 38, pt. 4, p. 588.

10. *Ibid.*, p. 589.

11. Castel, *Decision in the West*, p. 305; Warner, *Generals in Blue*, p. 115-116, 345.

12. *Official Records*, vol. 38, pt. 4, p. 595.

13. Elias Cole, *Journal of Three Years' Service with the Twenty-Sixth Ohio Volunteer Infantry in the Great Rebellion 1861-1864* (Chillicothe, Ohio, circa 1897), p. 63, 64.

14. Remley, *Battles, Skirmishes, Events and Scenes*, p. 121.

15. A.T. Volwiler, editor, "Letters from a Civil War Officer," *Mississippi Valley Historical Review*, vol. XIV (1928), p. 520.

16. William F. King to his wife, June 15, 1864, courtesy of Dennis Keesee.

17. *Downing's Civil War Diary*, p. 201.

18. Oscar F. Curtis, compiler, *The Personal Letters of Captain Joseph Willis Young, 97th Regiment Indiana Volunteers* (Bloomington: Monroe County Historical Society, 1974), p. 50.

19. Frank Chester diary, KMNBP library; Wright, *A History of the Sixth Iowa Infantry*, p. 288.

20. A.W. Simpson diary, courtesy of Paul Gibson, Bristol, Tenn.

21. Columbus Sykes to his wife, June 26, 1864, KMNBP library.

22. *Charlotte's Boys*, p. 255.

23. Lucia R. Douglas, editor, *Douglas's Texas Battery, CSA* (Tyler, Texas: Smith County Historical Society, 1966), p. 105.

Chapter 7

1. Alvah S. Skilton reminiscences, L.M. Strayer Collection.

2. Wills, *Army Life*, p. 269.

3. Burkhalter, p. 497-498.

4. *The Story of the Fifty-Fifth Regiment Illinois Volunteer Infantry in the Civil War 1861-1865* (Huntington, W.Va.: Blue Acorn Press, 1993), p. 323-324.

5. *Ibid.*, p. 324.

6. Accounts vary as to the exact time the assaults began on June 27. They range from 7:30 to 10 a.m. In his after-action report, Leggett stated his division's diversionary advance started at 8 a.m.

7. Cannon, *Inside of Rebeldom*, p. 228-229.

8. Frank Chester diary, KMNBP library.

9. Ira Blanchard, *I Marched With Sherman: Civil War Memoirs of the 20th Illinois Volunteer Infantry* (San Francisco: J.D. Huff and Company, 1992), p. 134.

10. *Worden's Battalion: A Paper Read by Capt. F.H. Magdeburg at the First Annual Reunion of the 14th Wisconsin Veteran Vol. Infantry, held at Fond du Lac, Wis., Wednesday and Thursday, June 16-17, 1886*, p. 3-5.

11. John W.A. Gillespie letter of June 28, 1864, published in *The Ohio Soldier*, December 24, 1887.

12. *Official Records*, vol. 38, pt. 3, p. 930.

13. *Ibid.*, p. 579, 923, 934; *Iowa Journal of History* (April 1949), p. 147.

14. *Official Records*, vol. 38, pt. 3, p. 381, 940.

15. *Ibid.*, p. 382.

16. French, *Two Wars*, p. 206.

17. *Ibid.*, p. 206-208; *Official Records*, vol. 38, pt. 3, p. 222.

18. William O. Norrell journal, KMNBP library.

19. Celathiel Helms to his wife, June 28, 1864, KMNBP library.

20. *Official Records*, vol. 38, pt. 3, p. 253.

21. Thomas T. Taylor to his wife, June 29, 1864, Special Collections, Woodruff Library, Emory University.

22. *Official Records*, vol. 38, pt. 3, p. 221; Joseph Grecian, *History of the Eighty-Third Regiment Indiana Volunteer Infantry* (Cincinnati: John F. Uhlhorn Printer, 1865), p. 52-53.

23. *Ibid.*, p. 53.

24. *Official Records*, vol. 38, pt. 3, p. 222, 253.

25. *Ibid.*, p. 318; Wills, *Army Life*, p. 269.

26. Alexander, *History of the Ninety-Seventh Regiment of Indiana Volunteer Infantry*, p. 13.

27. Curtis, p. 50; Joseph W. Young pension records, National Archives, Washington, D.C.

28. Wright, *A History of the Sixth Iowa Infantry*, p. 291.

29. *Official Records*, vol. 38, pt. 3, p. 318, 324.

30. Gordon C. Jones, editor, *"For My Country": The Richardson Letters 1861-1865* (Wendell, N.C.: Broadfoot Publishing Company, 1984), p. 159.

31. Wills, *Army Life*, p. 270-271; *Official Records*, vol. 38, pt. 3, p. 901.

32. *Ibid.*, p. 318; Alexander, p. 14; Andrew Bush to his wife, June 28, 1864, Indiana Division, Indiana State Library.

33. *Official Records*, vol. 38, pt. 3, p. 194.

34. George W. Warren diary quoted in R.S. Bevier, *History of the First and Second Missouri Confederate Brigades, 1861-1865* (St. Louis: Bryan, Brand & Co., 1879), p. 236.

35. *Official Records*, vol. 38, pt. 3, p. 194.

36. *Ibid.*, p. 914.

37. Benjamin F. Creason to his cousin, undated June 1864 letter quoted in Phil Gottschalk, *In Deadly Earnest: The History of the First Missouri Brigade, CSA* (Columbia: Missouri River Press, 1991), p. 368.

38. James Bradley, *The Confederate Mail Carrier* (Mexico, Mo.: privately printed, 1894), p. 148.

39. Warren diary quoted in Bevier, p. 236.

40. Joseph Boyce memoir, Missouri Historical Society, St. Louis.

41. *Official Records,* vol. 38, pt. 3, p. 915; William J. Ervin, "Perilous Undertaking of Two Brothers," *Confederate Veteran,* vol. XV, no. 7 (July 1907), p. 308-309.

42. Alvah S. Skilton reminiscences; Strayer & Baumgartner, *Echoes of Battle: The Atlanta Campaign,* p. 160.

43. Ira Van Deusen to his wife, June 28, 1864, KMNBP library; *Official Records,* vol. 38, pt. 3, p. 203; J.N. Reece, *Report of the Adjutant General of the State of Illinois,* vol. VI (Springfield: Journal Company, 1900), p. 146.

44. *The Story of the Fifty-Fifth Regiment ...,* p. 325-326.

45. Olof Nelson to his brother, June 28, 1864, Gustavus Adolphus College archives, St. Peter, Minnesota. Transcripts of Nelson's wartime letters courtesy of Charles Band, North Vancouver, B.C., Canada.

46. *The Story of the Fifty-Fifth Regiment ...,* p. 327-328.

47. *Ibid.,* p. 328.

48. *Official Records,* vol. 38, pt. 3, p. 915.

49. French, *Two Wars,* p. 208.

50. Warren diary quoted in Bevier, p. 237.

51. *The Story of the Fifty-Fifth Regiment ...,* p. 326, 328.

52. *Ibid.,* p. 326-327, 330-331.

53. French, *Two Wars,* p. 208; Alvah S. Skilton reminiscences.

54. Ibid.; *Official Records,* vol. 38, pt. 3, p. 216.

55. Alvah S. Skilton reminiscences; *The Story of the Fifty-Fifth Regiment ...,* p. 330.

Chapter 8

1. O.O. Howard, *Autobiography of Oliver Otis Howard,* vol. 1 (New York: The Baker & Taylor Company, 1907), p. 582.

2. *Daily Commercial* account reprinted in George H. Woodruff, *Fifteen Years Ago: or the Patriotism of Will County* (Joliet, Ill.: Joliet Republican Book and Job Steam Printing House, 1876), p. 338-339.

3. Kerwood, *Annals of the Fifty-Seventh Regiment Indiana Volunteers,* p. 263; *Official Records,* vol. 38, pt. 1, p. 336.

4. *Ibid.,* p. 336; Walter P. Wilson diary, Smith Memorial Library, Indiana Historical Society.

5. Journal kept by unidentified officer on the staff of Colonel Melancthon Smith, Hardee's artillery chief, B.F. Cheatham Papers, Tennessee State Library and Archives, Nashville; Kerwood, *Annals ...,* p. 263; *Official Records,* vol. 38, pt. 1, p. 336.

6. *Official Records,* vol. 38, pt. 1, p. 304, 320; *Society of the Seventy-Fourth Illinois Volunteer Infantry: Sixth Reunion Proceedings and History of the Regiment* (Rockford: W.P. Lamb, 1903), p. 176.

7. L.G. Bennett & William M. Haigh, *History of the Thirty-Sixth Regiment Illinois Volunteers during the War of the Rebellion* (Aurora: Knickerbocker & Hodder, 1876), p. 609-610, 611.

8. Alexander M. Cassaday diary quoted in William H. Newlin, *A History of the Seventy-Third Regiment of Illinois Infantry Volunteers* (Springfield, 1890), p. 312; *Official Records,* vol. 38, pt. 1, p. 304; *Sixth Reunion Proceedings of the Seventy-Fourth Illinois Regiment,* p. 176.

9. Robert D. Smith diary, KMNBP library; Irving A. Buck, *Cleburne and his Command* (Wilmington, N.C.: Broadfoot Publishing Company, 1991), p. 225.

10. William Jones to his brother, July 1, 1864, Dennis Keesee Collection; Walden Kelly, "Kenesaw Mountain," *The National Tribune,* November 13, 1890.

11. "Civil War Journal of John Wesley Marshall ...," Ohio Historical Society; Kerwood, *Annals ...,* p. 263-264.

12. *Official Records,* vol. 38, pt. 1, p. 304, 336.

13. William T. Barnes, "An Incident of Kenesaw Mountain," *Confederate Veteran,* vol. XXX, no. 2 (February 1922), p. 49.

14. Warner, *Generals in Blue,* p. 207, 237; O.O. Howard to Colonel George P. Buell, July 15, 1864, published in *The National Tribune,*

January 17, 1895.

15. Lyman Root, "Kenesaw Mountain," *The National Tribune,* February 26, 1891; Hinman, *The Story of the Sherman Brigade,* p. 550.

16. Rice, *Yankee Tigers,* p. 112.

17. *Official Records,* vol. 38, pt. 1, p. 371.

18. Rice, *Yankee Tigers,* p. 114.

19. John W. Tuttle journal, KMNBP library.

20. Hinman, *The Story of the Sherman Brigade,* p. 551.

21. *Ibid.,* p. 549-550; Rice, *Yankee Tigers,* p. 116.

22. John W. Tuttle journal, KMNBP library.

23. Rice, *Yankee Tigers,* p. 115-116, 12-14.

24. *Official Records,* vol. 38, pt. 1, p. 371.

25. Hinman, *The Story of the Sherman Brigade,* p. 547-548; William L. Trask journal, KMNBP library; Warner, *Generals in Blue,* p. 53; The Atlanta *Southern Confederacy,* June 29, 1864.

26. Hinman, *The Story of the Sherman Brigade,* p. 548.

27. John W. Tuttle journal, KMNBP library. Private Harrison B. Phillips of Company H, 3rd Kentucky, died of his wound on September 6, 1864.

28. Melancthon Smith artillery staff journal, B.F. Cheatham Papers, Tennessee State Library and Archives.

29. Jesse B. Luce diary and John W. Tuttle journal, KMNBP library; Rice, *Yankee Tigers,* p. 116; Hinman, *The Story of the Sherman Brigade,* p. 550.

30. *Ibid.,* p. 549; *Official Records,* vol. 38, pt. 1, p. 361; *Private Smith's Journal,* p. 158.

31. Charles T. Clark, *Opdycke Tigers, 125th O.V.I.* (Columbus: Spahr & Glenn, 1895), p. 280-281.

32. *Official Records,* vol. 38, pt. 1, p. 355; John W. Tuttle journal, KMNBP library; Brewer Smith quoted in Hinman, *The Story of the Sherman Brigade,* p. 552.

33. *Ibid.,* p. 548; John W. Tuttle journal, KMNBP library.

34. Clark, *Opdycke Tigers, 125th O.V.I.,* p. 281; Warner, *Generals in Blue,* p. 208; *Official Records,* vol. 38, pt. 1, p. 296, 359. General Newton reported his division's losses on June 27 at 654. With losses in Wagner's and Kimball's brigades reported as 215 and 194, respectively, Harker's would have totalled 245. Colonel L.P. Bradley, however, reported 231 casualties for Harker's brigade — 28 killed, 179 wounded and 24 missing.

35. Excerpt from undated Charles G. Harker letter quoted in O.O. Howard, "Atlanta Campaign," *The National Tribune,* January 17, 1895.

Chapter 9

1. Milo H. Lewis, "Closing on Johnston's Army at Kenesaw," *The National Tribune,* August 6, 1925.

2. John M. Palmer, *Personal Recollections of John M. Palmer: The Story of an Earnest Life* (Cincinnati: The Robert Clarke Company, 1901), p. 205.

3. *Official Records,* vol. 38, pt. 1, p. 632; pt. 2, p. 133.

4. *Ibid.,* pt. 1, p. 632; Allen L. Fahnestock journal, KMNBP library.

5. Ibid., Strayer & Baumgartner, *Echoes of Battle: The Atlanta Campaign,* p. 179.

6. *Ibid.,* p. 176; Julius B. Work, *Reunion of Col. Dan McCook's Third Brigade, Second Division, Fourteenth A.C., Army of the Cumberland* (Chicago, 1900), p. 84.

7. Allen L. Fahnestock journal, KMNBP library.

8. James L.W. Blair, "The Fight at Dead Angle," *Confederate Veteran,* vol. XII, no. 11 (November 1904), p. 532.

9. Edwin W. Payne, *History of the Thirty-Fourth Regiment of Illinois Volunteer Infantry* (Clinton, Iowa: Allen Printing Co., 1902), p. 126, 128; *Official Records,* vol. 38, pt. 1, p. 686.

10. William H. Baxter quoted in F.M. McAdams, *Every-day Soldier Life, or A History of the One Hundred and Thirteenth Ohio Volunteer*

Infantry (Columbus: Charles M. Cott & Co., 1884), p. 343.

11. *Official Records,* vol. 38, pt. 1, p. 698; William H. Baxter quoted in McAdams, p. 343.

12. Darius B. Warner quoted in McAdams, p. 351-352.

13. William P. Fulton to his brother, July 1, 1864, KMNBP library; Columbus R. Warfield, "Charging Kenesaw," *The National Tribune,* September 6, 1894; *Official Records,* vol. 38, pt. 1, 698.

14. Melancthon Smith artillery staff journal, B.F. Cheatham Papers, Tennessee State Library and Archives.

15. William J. Worsham, *The Old Nineteenth Tennessee* (Knoxville: Press of Paragon Printing Co., 1902), p. 121.

16. *Official Records,* vol. 38, pt. 1, p. 703.

17. Warfield, "Charging Kenesaw," *The National Tribune,* September 6, 1894.

18. *Official Records,* vol. 38, pt. 1, p. 688, 692; William P. Fulton to his brother, July 1, 1864, KMNBP library; anonymous 98th Ohio letter of June 30, 1864, published in *The Cadiz Republican,* Cadiz, Ohio, July 20, 1864.

19. *Official Records,* vol. 38, pt. 2, p. 134, 173.

20. Correspondence of June 28, 1864, by an unknown member of Company G, 121st Ohio, published in *The Mount Vernon Republican,* Mount Vernon, Ohio, July 19, 1864.

21. *Official Records,* vol. 38, pt. 1, p. 693, 704; Lewis, "Closing on Johnston's Army at Kenesaw," *The National Tribune,* August 6, 1925.

22. Warfield, "Charging Kenesaw," *The National Tribune,* September 6, 1894.

23. *Official Records,* vol. 38, pt. 1, p. 704.

24. *The National Cyclopaedia of American Biography,* vol. IV (New York: James T. White & Company, 1897), p. 130-131.

25. William F. Fox, *Regimental Losses in The American Civil War 1861-1865* (Dayton: Press of Morningside Bookshop, 1985), p. 427; *Proceedings of the Twenty-Third Reunion of the Eighty-Sixth Regiment Illinois Volunteer Infantry* (Peoria, 1909), p. 20, 21.

26. Theodore D. Neighbor quoted in Work, *Reunion of Col. Dan McCook's Third Brigade ...,* p. 32.

27. James T. Holmes to his parents, September 14, 1864, published in James T. Holmes, *52nd O.V.I. Then and Now* (Columbus: Berlin Printing Co., 1898), p. 182.

28. Robert M. Rogers, *The 125th Regiment Illinois Volunteer Infantry* (Champaign: Gazette Steam Print, 1882), p. 91; Henry J. Aten, *History of the Eighty-Fifth Regiment, Illinois Volunteer Infantry* (Hiawatha, Kansas, 1901), p. 181-182.

29. *Ibid.,* p. 185.

30. Rogers, p. 92-93.

31. Allen L. Fahnestock journal, KMNBP library.

32. George W. Gordon quoted in Lindsley, *The Military Annals of Tennessee. Confederate,* p. 299.

33. *Ibid.,* p. 165; Sam R. Watkins, *Co. Aytch, Maury Grays, First Tennessee Infantry, Or a Side Show of the Big Show* (Jackson, Tenn.: McCowat-Mercer Press, 1952), p. 157, 158.

34. Thomas H. Maney, "Battle of Dead Angle on Kennesaw Line," *Confederate Veteran,* vol. XI, no. 4 (April 1903), p. 159.

35. Lansing J. Dawdy quoted in Work, *Reunion of Col. Dan McCook's Third Brigade ...,* p. 35.

36. *Ibid.,* p. 120-121.

37. Caleb A. Chenoweth letter of June 17, 1864, KMNBP library.

38. John H. Brubacker quoted in Work, *Reunion of Col. Dan McCook's Third Brigade ...,* p. 121.

39. Samuel M. Canterbury quoted in Work, p. 40-41.

40. Nixon B. Stewart, *Dan. McCook's Regiment, 52nd O.V.I.* (Alliance, Ohio: Review Print, 1900), p. 118; Frank B. James, "McCook's Brigade at the Assault upon Kenesaw Mountain, Georgia, June 27, 1864,"

Sketches of War History 1861-1865, vol. IV (Cincinnati: The Robert Clarke Company, 1896), p. 260; William L. Trask journal, KMNBP library.

41. Holmes, *52nd O.V.I. Then and Now,* p. 182-183.

42. Samuel M. Pyle quoted in Work, *Reunion of Col. Dan McCook's Third Brigade ...,* p. 62.

43. James, "McCook's Brigade ...," *Sketches of War History 1861-1865,* vol. IV, p. 260.

44. Watkins, *Co. Aytch,* p. 158; William H. Latimer, "Dead Angle, on the Kennesaw Line," *Confederate Veteran,* vol. XXV, no. 4 (April 1917), p. 167; *Official Records,* vol. 38, pt. 3, p. 654.

45. Watkins, *Co. Aytch,* p. 158-159.

46. Samuel Robinson, "Battle of Kennesaw Mountain," *The Annals of the Army of Tennessee and Early Western History,* vol. I, no. 3 (June 1878), p. 112-113.

47. Latimer, *op. cit.,* p. 167.

48. James I. Hall, "A History of Company C, 9th Tennessee Regt. from its Organization 1861 until the Surrender 1865," Southern Historical Collection, University of North Carolina at Chapel Hill.

49. W.M. Ives reminiscences, KMNBP library.

50. Allen L. Fahnestock journal, KMNBP library.

51. James, "McCook's Brigade ...," *Sketches of War History 1861-1865,* vol. IV, p. 260-261.

52. Samuel Grimshaw, "Doings at Kenesaw Mountain," *The National Tribune,* November 14, 1912.

53. Jeremiah P. Parkhurst quoted in *Proceedings of the Twenty-Fourth Reunion of the Eighty-Sixth Regiment Illinois Volunteer Infantry* (Peoria, 1910), p. 26.

54. Stewart, *Dan. McCook's Regiment, 52nd O.V.I.,* p. 120.

55. *Ibid.,* p. 120-121; Newton Bostwick quoted in Work, *Reunion of Col. Dan McCook's Third Brigade ...,* p. 51.

56. Stewart, *Dan. McCook's Regiment, 52nd O.V.I.,* p. 120.

57. *Ibid.,* p. 120.

58. Work, *Reunion of Col. Dan McCook's Third Brigade ...,* p. 32. Three and a half weeks later Clancy was captured in the battle of Peachtree Creek outside Atlanta.

59. *Proceedings of the Twenty-Fourth Reunion of the Eighty-Sixth Regiment Illinois Volunteer Infantry,* p. 21-25.

60. Work, *Reunion of Col. Dan McCook's Third Brigade ...,* p. 46.

61. *Ibid.,* p. 40, 41.

62. *Ibid.,* p. 42.

63. Warner, *Generals in Blue,* p. 295; Samuel Grimshaw, "The Charge at Kenesaw," *The National Tribune,* January 15, 1885.

Chapter 10

1. *Official Records,* vol. 38, pt. 4, p. 608-610.

2. *Ibid.,* p. 611.

3. M.A. DeWolfe, editor, *Home Letters of General Sherman* (New York: Charles Scribner's Sons, 1909), p. 299, 300-301.

4. J.E. Johnston, *Narrative,* p. 343; *Official Records,* vol. 38, pt. 1, p. 637; pt. 3, p. 703; pt. 4, p. 607. Fox, in his *Regimental Losses,* lists 153 casualties for the 113th Ohio, 147 for the 121st Ohio, and 104 for the 125th Illinois. Stewart's history of the 52nd Ohio gives a figure of 139 for that regiment, while 96 losses were reported in John R. Kinnear's 1866 *History of the Eighty-Sixth Regiment Illinois Volunteer Infantry.*

5. Levi A. Ross journal and reminiscences, Illinois State Historical Library, Springfield.

6. Jason Hurd diary, courtesy of Jason H. Moore, Southington, Ohio.

7. Wright, *A History of the Sixth Iowa Infantry,* p. 296, 297.

8. Rogers, *The 125th Regiment Illinois Volunteer Infantry,* p. 94-97. Lieutenant McLean died within an hour of Rogers' ministrations. Sullivan succumbed to his wound on July 26 at Chattanooga. Cunningham lost his arm and was discharged December 10. Bonebrake recovered and

subsequently was promoted to sergeant major and first lieutenant of Company B.

9. Alexander M. Ayers to his wife, June 27 and 28, 1864, Special Collections, Woodruff Library, Emory University.

10. Claiborne J. Walton to his wife, June 29, 1864, KMNBP library.

11. William H. Baxter quoted in McAdams, *Every-day Soldier Life ...*, p. 344, 345.

12. *Official Records,* vol. 38, pt. 4, p. 611, 617, 618, 631, 635; Jacob D. Cox diary, KMNBP library.

13. James, "McCook's Brigade ...," *Sketches of War History 1861-1865,* vol. IV, p. 262.

14. Stewart, *Dan. McCook's Regiment, 52nd O.V.I.,* p. 127.

15. Work, *Reunion of Col. Dan McCook's Third Brigade ...,* p. 121, 43.

16. *Official Records,* vol. 38, pt. 3, p. 716.

17. Stewart, *Dan. McCook's Regiment, 52nd O.V.I.,* p. 126.

18. Blair, "The Fight at Dead Angle," *Confederate Veteran,* vol. XII, no. 11 (November 1904), p. 533; Latimer, "Dead Angle, on the Kennesaw Line," *Confederate Veteran,* vol. XXV, no. 4 (April 1917), p. 168.

19. Maney, "Battle of Dead Angle on Kennesaw Line," *Confederate Veteran,* vol. X, no. 4 (April 1903), p. 160.

20. Melancthon Smith artillery staff journal, B.F. Cheatham Papers, Tennessee State Library and Archives.

21. Allen L. Fahnestock journal, KMNBP library; Rogers, p. 99.

22. W.M. Ives reminiscences and William L. Trask journal, KMNBP library; Newton N. Davis to his wife, July 1, 1864, Alabama Department of Archives and History.

23. W.P. Bishop quoted in Lindsley, *The Military Annals of Tennessee. Confederate,* p. 436-437.

24. Lyman S. Widney to his parents, June 30, 1864, KMNBP library.

25. Rogers, p. 99.

26. Levi A. Ross journal, Illinois State Historical Library.

27. Stewart, *Dan. McCook's Regiment, 52nd O.V.I.,* p. 126.

28. "Roll of Honor of Ohio Soldiers," *Official Roster of the Soldiers of the State of Ohio in the War of the Rebellion, 1861-1866,* vol. IV (Akron: The Werner Ptg. and Mfg. Co., 1887), p. 808-813; John Moore, "A Rebel Spy," *The National Tribune,* November 14, 1895.

29. John D. Kirkpatrick, "At Kenesaw Mountain," *The National Tribune,* May 28, 1914.

30. Walter P. Wilson diary, Smith Memorial Library, Indiana Historical Society.

31. Newlin, *A History of the Seventy-Third Regiment of Illinois Infantry Volunteers,* p. 313.

32. Hinman, *The Story of the Sherman Brigade,* p. 552.

33. Aten, *History of the Eighty-Fifth Regiment, Illinois Volunteer Infantry,* p. 189-190.

34. *Ibid.,* p. 190; Rogers, p. 98-99; The *Memphis Appeal* (then published in Atlanta), July 2, 1864.

35. George Hurlbut letter of June 30, 1864, KMNBP library; "Letters from a Civil War Officer," *Mississippi Valley Historical Review,* vol. XIV (1928), p. 520-521.

36. Coe, *Mine Eyes Have Seen the Glory,* p. 167; *Official Records,* vol. 38, pt. 5, p. 3.

37. J.E. Johnston, *Narrative,* p. 345.

38. French, *Two Wars,* p. 210, 212.

39. *Official Records,* vol. 38, pt. 5, p. 860; Storrs, "Kennesaw Mountain," *The Southern Bivouac,* vol. I, no. 4 (December 1882), p. 139.

40. Edward Spear diary, KMNBP library.

41. Hedley, *Marching Through Georgia,* p. 132-133.

42. "The Confederate Letters of John W. Hagan," *The Georgia Historical Quarterly* (September 1954), p. 281.

43. "The Memoirs of Charles H. Olmstead," *The Georgia Historical Quarterly,* vol. XLIV, no. 4 (December 1960), p. 430-431.

44. Maney, *op. cit.,* p. 160.

45. Allen L. Fahnestock journal, KMNBP library.

46. Israel A. Correll diary, KMNBP library.

47. Morse, *Letters Written during the Civil War,* p. 173-174.

48. Morhous, *Reminiscences of the 123d Regiment, N.Y.S.V.,* p. 107; Henry Richards, *Letters of Captain Henry Richards of the Ninety-Third Ohio Infantry* (Cincinnati: Press of Wrightson & Co., 1883), p. 40.

49. " 'Gone for a Soldier': The Civil War Letters of Charles Harding Cox," *Indiana Magazine of History* (September 1972), p. 207.

Epilogue

1. W.T. Sherman, *Memoirs,* vol. II, p. 62.

2. Stewart, *Dan. McCook's Regiment, 52nd O.V.I.,* p. 129.

3. *Official Records,* vol. 38, pt. 1, p. 890; Root, "Kenesaw Mountain," *The National Tribune,* February 26, 1891.

4. French, *Two Wars,* p. 212; "The Confederate Letters of John W. Hagan," *The Georgia Historical Quarterly* (September 1954), p. 282.

5. Mumford H. Dixon diary, Special Collections, Woodruff Library, Emory University; The Atlanta *Southern Confederacy,* June 29, 1864.

6. Williams, *From the Cannon's Mouth,* p. 334; Hedley, *Marching Through Georgia,* p. 103.

7. T.D. Neighbor quoted in Work, *Reunion of Col. Dan McCook's Third Brigade ...,* p. 35; Julia A. Drake, editor, *The Mail Goes Through or The Civil War Letters of George Drake* (San Angelo, Texas: Anchor Publishing Co., 1964), p. 90.

BIBLIOGRAPHY

Manuscripts

Armistead, Zachariah J. (42nd Georgia), letters, Kennesaw Mountain National Battlefield Park (KMNBP) library.

Armstrong, William K. (52nd Ohio), diary, KMNBP library.

Ayers, Alexander M. (125th Illinois), letters, Special Collections, Woodruff Library, Emory University, Atlanta.

Boyce, Joseph (1st/4th Missouri Infantry), memoir, Missouri Historical Society, St. Louis.

Broadman, John D. (Battery F, 1st Illinois Light Artillery), letters, KMNBP library.

Bush, Andrew (97th Indiana), letters, Indiana Division, Indiana State Library, Indianapolis.

Carr, John M. (100th Indiana), diary, KMNBP library.

Chenoweth, Caleb A. (86th Illinois), letter, KMNBP library.

Chandler, David H. (5th Indiana Battery), diary, L.M. Strayer Collection.

Chester, Frank (20th Illinois), diary, KMNBP library.

Correll, Israel A. (51st Ohio), diary, KMNBP library.

Cox, Jacob D. (3rd Division, 23rd Corps), diary, KMNBP library.

Coy, Lorenzo R. (123rd New York), diary, KMNBP library.

Crook, William J. (13th Tennessee), letters, KMNBP library.

Davidson, John M. (39th North Carolina), letters, Special Collections, Woodruff Library, Emory University.

Davis, Newton N. (24th Alabama), letters, Alabama Department of Archives and History, Montgomery.

Dennis, Charles B. (101st Ohio), reminiscences, Rutherford B. Hayes Presidential Center, Fremont, Ohio.

Dixon, Mumford H. (3rd Confederate Infantry), diary, Special Collections, Woodruff Library, Emory University.

Fulton, William P. (98th Ohio), letters, KMNBP library.

Garland, Daniel M. (7th Pennsylvania Cavalry), letters, Civil War Miscellaneous Collection, United States Army Military History Institute (USAMHI), Carlisle, Pennsylvania.

Hall, James I. (9th Tennessee Infantry), manuscript of regimental history, Southern Historical Collection, University of North Carolina at Chapel Hill.

Helms, Celathiel (63rd Georgia), letters, KMNBP library.

Hurd, Jason (19th Ohio), diary, courtesy of Jason H. Moore, Southington, Ohio.

Hurlbut, George (14th Ohio Battery), letters, KMNBP library.

Ives, W.M. (1st/4th Florida), reminiscences, KMNBP library.

Jones, William (26th Ohio), letters, Dennis Keesee Collection, Westerville, Ohio.

Keay, William F. (17th Indiana), letter, KMNBP library.

King, William F. (124th Indiana), letters, courtesy of Dennis Keesee.

Luce, Jesse B. (125th Ohio), diary, KMNBP library.

Madison, John W. (28th Alabama), letters, courtesy of Paul Gibson, Bristol, Tennessee.

Marshall, John W. (97th Ohio), journal, Manuscript Collections, Ohio Historical Society, Columbus.

McDill, W.J. (9th Tennessee Infantry), letters, KMNBP library.

McMillan, William W. (17th Alabama), letters, KMNBP library.

Nelson, Olof (55th Illinois), letters, Gustavus Adolphus College Archives, St. Peter, Minnesota.

Norrell, William O. (63rd Georgia), journal, KMNBP library.

Nugent, Willis J. (78th Pennsylvania), letters, KMNBP library.

Paddock, Byron D. (Battery F, 1st Michigan Light Artillery), after-action report, KMNBP library.

Porter, Alexander Q. (22nd Mississippi), diary, Special Collections, Woodruff Library, Emory University.

Ross, Levi A. (86th Illinois), journal and reminiscences, Illinois State Historical Library.

Simpson, Avington W. (3rd/5th Missouri Infantry), courtesy of Paul Gibson.

Skelton, James (27th Ohio), diary, KMNBP library.

Skilton, Alvah S. (57th Ohio), reminiscences, L.M. Strayer Collection.

Smith, Charles M. (16th Wisconsin), letters, KMNBP library.

Smith, Melancthon (Hardee staff officer), artillery journal, B.F. Cheatham Papers, Tennessee State Library and Archives, Nashville.

Smith, Robert D. (2nd Tennessee Infantry), diary, KMNBP library.

Spear, Edward (15th Ohio Battery), diary, KMNBP library.

Spencer, Daniel J. (25th Iowa), diary, KMNBP library.

Sykes, Columbus (43rd Mississippi), letters, KMNBP library.

Talley, William R. (Havis' Georgia Battery), reminiscences, KMNBP library.

Taylor, Thomas T. (47th Ohio), letters, Special Collections, Woodruff Library, Emory University.

Trask, William L. (Hardee staff courier), journal, KMNBP library.

Tuttle, John W. (3rd Kentucky Infantry), journal, KMNBP library.

Van Deusen, Ira (111th Illinois), letters, KMNBP library.

Walton, Claiborne J. (21st Kentucky), letters, KMNBP library.

Watson, William J. (53rd Tennessee), diary, Southern Historical Collection, University of North Carolina at Chapel Hill.

Weems, Philip Van Horn (11th Tennessee), letter, courtesy of David & Frances Hall, Clarksville, Tennessee.

Whitney, Franklin A. (36th Illinois), letter, courtesy of Kendyl Wallis, Sandwich, Illinois.

Widney, Lyman S. (34th Illinois), letters, KMNBP library.

Willett, Elbert D. (40th Alabama), diary, KMNBP library.

Wilson, Walter P. (57th Indiana), diary, Smith Memorial Library, Indiana Historical Society, Indianapolis.

Published diaries, journals & correspondence

Brainard, Orson (51st Ohio), "Orson Brainard: A Soldier in the Ranks," edited by Wilfred W. Black, *Ohio History,* Winter-Spring 1967.

Branch, Hamilton M. (54th Georgia), *Charlotte's Boys: Civil War Letters of the Branch Family of Savannah,* edited by Mauriel P. Joslyn, Berryville, Va.: Rockbridge Publishing Company, 1996.

Bull, Rice C. (123rd New York), *Soldiering: The Civil War Diary of Rice C. Bull, 123rd New York Volunteer Infantry,* edited by K. Jack Bauer, Novato, Calif.: Presidio Press, 1986.

Burkhalter, James L. (86th Illinois), "Captain Burkhalter's Georgia War," edited by Martin Litvin, *Voices of the Prairie Land,* vol. 2, Galesburg, Ill.: Mother Bickerdyke Historical Collection, 1972.

Chambers, William P. (46th Mississippi), *Blood & Sacrifice: The Civil War Journal of a Confederate Soldier,* edited by Richard A. Baumgartner, Huntington, W.Va.: Blue Acorn Press, 1994.

Coe, Hamlin A. (19th Michigan), *Mine Eyes Have Seen the Glory: Combat Diaries of Union Sergeant Hamlin Alexander Coe,* edited by David Coe, Rutherford, N.J.: Fairleigh Dickinson University Press, 1975.

Cole, Elias (26th Ohio), *Journal of Three Years' Service with the Twenty-Sixth Ohio Volunteer Infantry in the Great Rebellion 1861-1864,* Chillicothe, Ohio, 1897.

Cooke, Chauncey H. (25th Wisconsin), "A Badger Boy in Blue: The Letters of Chauncey H. Cooke," *Wisconsin Magazine of History,* 1920-1921.

Cooper, James L. (20th Tennessee), "The Civil War Diary of James Litton Cooper, September 30, 1861 to January 1865," edited by William T. Alderson, *Tennessee Historical Quarterly,* June 1956.

Cox, Charles H. (70th Indiana), " 'Gone for a Soldier': The Civil War Letters of Charles Harding Cox," edited by Lorna L. Sylvester, *Indiana Magazine of History,* September 1972.

Downing, Alexander (11th Iowa), *Downing's Civil War Diary,* edited by Olynthus B. Clark, Des Moines: The Historical Department of Iowa, 1916.

Drake, George (85th Illinois), *The Mail Goes Through or The Civil War Letters of George Drake,* edited by Julia A. Drake, San Angelo,

Texas: Anchor Publishing Co., 1964.

Hagan, John W. (29th Georgia), "The Confederate Letters of John W. Hagan," edited by Bell Irvin Wiley, *The Georgia Historical Quarterly,* September 1954.

Jackman, John S. (9th Kentucky), *Diary of a Confederate Soldier: John S. Jackman of the Orphan Brigade,* edited by William C. Davis, Columbia: University of South Carolina Press, 1990.

Jackson, Oscar L. (63rd Ohio), *The Colonel's Diary: Journals Kept Before and During the Civil War by the late Colonel Oscar L. Jackson,* edited by David P. Jackson, Sharon, Pa.: privately printed, 1922.

Mayfield, Leroy S. (22nd Indiana), "A Hoosier Invades the Confederacy: Letters and Diaries of Leroy S. Mayfield," edited by John D. Barnhart, *Indiana Magazine of History,* June 1943.

Merrill, Samuel (70th Indiana), "Letters from a Civil War Officer," edited by A.T. Volwiler, *Mississippi Valley Historical Review,* 1928.

Morse, Charles F. (2nd Massachusetts Infantry), *Letters Written During the Civil War 1861-1865,* privately printed, 1898.

Mosman, Chesley A. (59th Illinois), *The Rough Side of War: The Civil War Journal of Chesley A. Mosman, 1st Lieutenant, Company D, 59th Illinois Volunteer Infantry Regiment,* edited by Arnold Gates, Garden City, N.Y.: The Basin Publishing Co., 1987.

Reid, Harvey (22nd Wisconsin), *The View from Headquarters: Civil War Letters of Harvey Reid,* edited by Frank L. Byrne, Madison: The State Historical Society of Wisconsin, 1965.

Remley, Ambrose (72nd Indiana), *Battles, Skirmishes, Events and Scenes: The Letters and Memorandum of Ambrose Remley,* edited by Dale E. Linvill, Crawfordsville, Ind.: Montgomery County Historical Society, 1997.

Richards, Henry (93rd Ohio), *Letters of Captain Henry Richards of the Ninety-Third Ohio Infantry,* Cincinnati: Press of Wrightson & Co., 1883.

Richardson, George S. (6th Iowa), *"For My Country": The Richardson Letters 1861-1865,* edited by Gordon C. Jones, Wendell, N.C.: Broadfoot Publishing Company, 1984.

Sherman, William T., *Home Letters of General Sherman,* edited by M.A. DeWolfe, New York: Charles Scribner's Sons, 1909.

Smith, J.H. (16th Iowa), "The Civil War Diary of Colonel John Henry Smith," edited by David M. Smith, *Iowa Journal of History,* April 1949.

Soldiers' Letters from Camp, Battle-field and Prison, edited by Lydia M. Post, New York: Bunce & Huntington, 1865.

Wallace, William (3rd Wisconsin Infantry), "William Wallace's Civil War Letters: The Atlanta Campaign," edited by John O. Holzhueter, *Wisconsin Magazine of History,* Winter 1973-1974.

Weller, Edwin (107th New York), *A Civil War Courtship: The Letters of Edwin Weller from Antietam to Atlanta,* edited by William Walton, Garden City, N.Y.: Doubleday & Company, 1980.

Williams, Alpheus S. (1st Division, 20th Corps), *From the Cannon's Mouth: The Civil War Letters of General Alpheus S. Williams,* edited by Milo M. Quaife, Detroit: Wayne State University Press, 1959.

Wills, Charles W. (103rd Illinois), *Army Life of an Illinois Soldier,* Washington, D.C.: Globe Printing Company, 1906.

Young, Joseph W. (97th Indiana), *The Personal Letters of Captain Joseph Willis Young, 97th Regiment Indiana Volunteers,* compiled by Oscar F. Curtis, Bloomington: Monroe County Historical Society, 1974.

Memoirs, reminiscences & recollections

Blanchard, Ira (20th Illinois), *I Marched With Sherman: Civil War Memoirs of the 20th Illinois Volunteer Infantry,* San Francisco: J.D. Huff and Company, 1992.

Bogle, Joseph (40th Georgia), *Some Recollections of the Civil War,* Dalton, Ga.: The Daily Argus, 1911.

Bradley, James, (3rd/5th Missouri), *The Confederate Mail Carrier,*

Mexico, Mo.: privately printed, 1894.

Buck, Irving A., *Cleburne and his Command*, Wilmington, N.C.: Broadfoot Publishing Company, 1991.

Cannon, Jabez P. (27th Alabama), *Inside of Rebeldom: The Daily Life of a Private in the Confederate Army*, Washington, D.C.: The National Tribune, 1900.

Foster, Samuel T. (24th Texas Dismounted Cavalry), *One of Cleburne's Command: The Civil War Reminiscences and Diary of Capt. Samuel T. Foster, Granbury's Texas Brigade, CSA*, edited by Norman D. Brown, Austin: University of Texas Press, 1980.

French, Samuel G., *Two Wars: An Autobiography of Gen. Samuel G. French*, Nashville: Confederate Veteran, 1901.

Green, John W. (9th Kentucky), *Johnny Green of the Orphan Brigade: The Journal of a Confederate Soldier*, edited by A.D. Kirwan, Lexington: The University of Kentucky Press, 1956.

Hazen, William B., *A Narrative of Military Service*, Huntington, W.Va.: Blue Acorn Press, 1993.

Hedley, Fenwick Y. (32nd Illinois), *Marching Through Georgia*, Chicago: R.R. Donnelley & Sons, 1887.

Holmes, James T. (52nd Ohio), *52nd O.V.I. Then and Now*, Columbus: Berlin Printing Co., 1898.

Howard, Oliver O., *Autobiography of Oliver Otis Howard*, New York: The Baker & Taylor Company, 1907.

Hundley, Daniel R. (31st Alabama), *Prison Echoes of the Great Rebellion*, edited by Rex Miller, Depew, N.Y.: Patrex Press, 1992.

James, Frank B., (52nd Ohio),"McCook's Brigade at the Assault upon Kenesaw Mountain, Georgia, June 27, 1864," *Sketches of War History 1861-1865*, vol. IV, Cincinnati: The Robert Clarke Company, 1896.

Johnston, Joseph E., *Narrative of Military Operations*, New York: D. Appleton and Company, 1874.

Kendall, John I. (4th Louisiana Infantry), "Recollections of a Confederate Officer," edited by John S. Kendall, *The Louisiana Historical Quarterly*, October 1946.

Magdeburg, Frederick H. (14th Wisconsin), *Worden's Battalion: A Paper Read by Capt. F.H. Magdeburg at the First Annual Reunion of the 14th Wisconsin Veteran Vol. Infantry, held at Fond du Lac, Wis., Wednesday and Thursday, June 16-17, 1886.*

Manigault, Arthur M., *A Carolinian Goes to War: The Civil War Narrative of Arthur Middleton Manigault, Brigadier General, C.S.A.*, edited by R. Lockwood Tower, Columbia: University of South Carolina Press, 1983.

Morhous, Henry C. (123rd New York), *Reminiscences of the 123d Regiment, N.Y.S.V.*, Greenwich, N.Y.: People's Journal Book and Job Office, 1879.

Olmstead, Charles H. (1st Georgia Volunteers), "The Memoirs of Charles H. Olmstead," *The Georgia Historical Quarterly*, December 1960.

Palmer, John M., *Personal Recollections of John M. Palmer: The Story of an Earnest Life*, Cincinnati: The Robert Clarke Company, 1901.

Pierson, Stephen (33rd New Jersey), "From Chattanooga to Atlanta in 1864, a Personal Reminiscence," *Proceedings New Jersey Historical Society*, 1931.

Rice, Ralsa C. (125th Ohio), *Yankee Tigers: Through the Civil War with the 125th Ohio*, edited by Richard A. Baumgartner & Larry M. Strayer, Huntington, W.Va.: Blue Acorn Press, 1992.

Scribner, Benjamin F., *How Soldiers Were Made*, Huntington, W.Va.: Blue Acorn Press, 1995.

Sherman, William T., *Memoirs of Gen. W.T. Sherman*, New York: Charles L. Webster & Co., 1891.

Smith, Benjamin T. (51st Illinois), *Private Smith's Journal: Recollections of the Late War*, edited by Clyde C. Walton, Chicago: R.R. Donnelley & Sons, 1963.

Speed, Thomas (12th Kentucky), "The Civil War Memoirs of Captain Thomas Speed," edited by James R. Bentley, *The Filson Club History Quarterly*, July 1970.

Strong, Robert H. (105th Illinois), *A Yankee Private's Civil War*, edited by Ashley Halsey, Chicago: Henry Regnery Company, 1961.

Toombs, Samuel (13th New Jersey), *Reminiscences of the War, Comprising a Detailed Account of the Experiences of the Thirteenth Regiment New Jersey Volunteers in Camp, on the March, and in Battle*, Orange, N.J.: Journal Office, 1878.

Watkins, Sam R. (1st Tennessee Infantry), *Co. Aytch, Maury Grays, First Tennessee Infantry, Or a Side Show of the Big Show*, Jackson Tenn.: McCowat-Mercer Press, 1952.

Work, Julius B. (52nd Ohio), *Reunion of Col. Dan McCook's Third Brigade, Second Division, Fourteenth A.C., Army of the Cumberland*, Chicago, 1900.

Newspapers & periodicals

Memphis Appeal (published in Atlanta), July 2, 1864.

Norwalk Reflector, Norwalk, Ohio, July 19, 1864.

Southern Confederacy, Atlanta, June 19 and 29, 1864.

The Cadiz Republican, Cadiz, Ohio, July 20, 1864.

The Mount Vernon Republican, Mount Vernon, Ohio, July 19, 1864.

The Ohio Soldier, Chillicothe, Ohio, December 24, 1887.

Torchlight, Xenia, Ohio, July 6, 1864.

Barnes, William T. (1st/15th Arkansas), "An Incident of Kenesaw Mountain," *Confederate Veteran*, February 1922.

Blair, James L.W. (1st/27th Tennessee), "The Fight at Dead Angle," *Confederate Veteran*, November 1904.

Elliot, Frank (Battery M, 1st New York Light Artillery), "A June Evening Before Atlanta: Cothran's Battery and Knipe's Brigade Repulse Stevenson's Division," *The National Tribune*, October 26, 1905.

Ervin, William J. (3rd/5th Missouri), "Perilous Undertaking of Two Brothers," *Confederate Veteran*, July 1907.

Grimshaw, Samuel (52nd Ohio), "The Charge at Kenesaw," The National Tribune, January 15, 1885.

Grimshaw, Samuel, "Doings at Kenesaw Mountain," *The National Tribune*, November 14, 1912.

Hamilton, Posey, "Battle of New Hope Church, Ga.," *Confederate Veteran*, September 1922.

Hogle, Adam (97th Ohio), "The 97th Ohio: An Incident of Kenesaw Mountain," *The National Tribune*, May 3, 1888.

Howard, Oliver O., "Atlanta Campaign," *The National Tribune*, January 17, 1895.

Kelly, Walden (26th Ohio), "Kenesaw Mountain," *The National Tribune*, November 13, 1890.

"Killing of Gen. Polk," *The National Tribune*, March 31, 1904.

Kirkpatrick, John D. (52nd Ohio), "At Kenesaw Mountain," *The National Tribune*, May 28, 1914.

Latimer, William H. (6th/9th Tennessee), "Dead Angle, on the Kenesaw Line," *Confederate Veteran*, April 1917.

Lewis, Milo H. (121st Ohio), "Closing on Johnston's Army at Kenesaw," *The National Tribune*, July 30, 1925 and August 6, 1925.

"Lieut. Isaac Lightner," *Confederate Veteran*, August 1896.

Maney, Thomas H. (1st/27th Tennessee), "Battle of Dead Angle on Kenesaw Line," *Confederate Veteran*, April 1903.

Moore, John (52nd Ohio), "A Rebel Spy," *The National Tribune*, November 14, 1895.

Robinson, Samuel (1st/27th Tennessee), "Battle of Kennesaw Mountain," *The Annals of the Army of Tennessee and Early Western History*, June 1878.

Root, Lyman (125th Ohio), "Kenesaw Mountain," *The National Tribune*, February 26, 1891.

Storrs, George S., "Kennesaw Mountain," *The Southern Bivouac*, December 1882.

Warfield, Columbus R. (121st Ohio), "Charging Kenesaw," *The National Tribune*, September 6, 1894.

Unit histories

Alexander, John D., *History of the Ninety-Seventh Regiment of Indiana Volunteer Infantry,* Terre Haute. Moore & Langen, 1891.

Aten, Henry J., *History of the Eighty-Fifth Regiment Illinois Volunteer Infantry,* Hiawatha, Kan., 1901.

Barron, Samuel B., *The Lone Star Defenders: A Chronicle of the Third Texas Cavalry Regiment in the Civil War,* New York: Neale Publishing Co., 1908.

Bennett, L.G. & Haigh, William M., *History of the Thirty-Sixth Regiment Illinois Volunteers during the War of the Rebellion,* Aurora: Knickerbocker & Hodder, 1876.

Bevier, R.S., *History of the First and Second Missouri Confederate Brigades, 1861-1865,* St. Louis: Bryan, Brand & Co., 1879.

Brown, Edmund R., *The Twenty-Seventh Indiana Volunteer Infantry in the War of the Rebellion 1861 to 1865,* Monticello, Ind., 1899.

Clark, Charles T., *Opdycke Tigers, 125th O.V.I.,* Columbus: Spahr & Glenn, 1895.

Cope, Alexis, *The Fifteenth Ohio Volunteers and its Campaigns,* Columbus: Press of the Edward T. Miller Co., 1916.

Douglas, Lucia R., editor, *Douglas's Texas Battery, CSA,* Tyler, Texas: Smith County Historical Society, 1966.

Gottschalk, Phil, *In Deadly Earnest: The History of the First Missouri Brigade, CSA,* Columbia: Missouri River Press, 1991.

Grecian, Joseph, *History of the Eighty-Third Regiment Indiana Volunteer Infantry,* Cincinnati: John F. Uhlhorn Printer, 1865.

Hinman, Wilbur F. *The Story of the Sherman Brigade,* Alliance, Ohio: Press of Daily Review, 1897.

Kerwood, Asbury L., *Annals of the Fifty-Seventh Regiment Indiana Volunteers,* Dayton: W.J. Shuey, 1868.

Kinnear, John R., *History of the Eighty-Sixth Regiment Illinois Volunteer Infantry,* Chicago: Tribune Company's Book and Job Print Office, 1866.

McAdams, F.M., *Every-day Soldier Life, or A History of the One Hundred and Thirteenth Ohio Volunteer Infantry,* Columbus: Charles M. Cott & Co., 1884.

Merrill, Samuel, *The Seventieth Indiana Volunteer Infantry in the War of the Rebellion,* Indianapolis: The Bowen-Merrill Company, 1900.

Miller, Rex, *Hundley's Ragged Volunteers: A day-by-day account of the 31st Alabama Infantry Regiment, CSA 1861-1865,* Depew, N.Y.: Patrex Press, 1991.

Newlin, William H., *A History of the Seventy-Third Regiment of Illinois Infantry Volunteers,* Springfield, 1890.

Payne, Edwin W., *History of the Thirty-Fourth Regiment of Illinois Volunteer Infantry,* Clinton, Iowa: Allen Printing Co., 1902.

Remington, Cyrus K., *A Record of Battery I, First N.Y. Light Artillery Vols.,* Buffalo: Press of the Courier Company, 1891.

Rogers, Robert M., *The 125th Regiment Illinois Volunteer Infantry,* Champaign: Gazette Steam Print, 1882.

Rood, Hosea W., *Story of the Service of Company E, and of the Twelfth Wisconsin Regiment of Veteran Volunteer Infantry, in the War of the Rebellion,* Milwaukee: Swain & Tate Co., 1893.

Smith, Daniel P., *Company K, First Alabama Regiment, or Three Years in the Confederate Service,* Philadelphia: Burk & McFetridge, 1885.

Stewart, Nixon B., *Dan. McCook's Regiment, 52nd O.V.I.,* Alliance, Ohio: Review Print, 1900.

The "Dutchess County Regiment" (150th Regiment of New York State Volunteer Infantry) in the Civil War: Its Story as Told by its Members, Danbury, Conn.: The Danbury Medical Printing Co., 1907.

The Story of the Fifty-Fifth Regiment Illinois Volunteer Infantry in the Civil War 1861-1865, Huntington, W.Va.: Blue Acorn Press, 1993.

Tracie, Theodore C., *Annals of the Nineteenth Ohio Battery Volunteer Artillery,* Cleveland: J.B. Savage, 1878.

Woodruff, George H., *Fifteen Years Ago: or the Patriotism of Will County,* Joliet, Ill.: Joliet Republican Book and Job Steam Printing House, 1876.

Worsham, William J., *The Old Nineteenth Tennessee,* Knoxville: Press of Paragon Printing Co., 1902.

Wright, Henry H., *A History of the Sixth Iowa Infantry,* Iowa City: State Historical Society of Iowa, 1923.

Official records & government publications

Bates, Samuel P., *History of Pennsylvania Volunteers 1861-5,* five volumes, Harrisburg: B. Singerly, 1869.

Davis, George B., Perry, Leslie J. & Kirkley, Joseph W., Board of Publication. Cowles, Calvin D., compiler, *Atlas to Accompany the Official Records of the Union and Confederate Armies,* Washington, D.C.: Government Printing Office, 1891-1895.

Henderson, Lillian, compiler, *Roster of the Confederate Soldiers of Georgia, 1861-1865,* Hapeville: Longino & Porter, 1959-1964.

Illinois. *Report of the Illinois Adjutant General containing Reports for the Years 1861-66,* nine volumes, Springfield: Phillips Bros. State Printers, 1900-1902.

Iowa. *Roster and Record of Iowa Soldiers in the War of the Rebellion,* five volumes, Des Moines: Emory H. English State Printer, 1908-1911.

Kelly, Dennis & Bearss, Edwin C., *Map of the Battlefields of Kennesaw Mountain and Kolb's Farm, Georgia 1864* and *The Battlefields of Kennesaw Mountain and Kolb's Farm, Georgia 1864,* Kennesaw Mountain Historical Association, Inc., 1994.

Kentucky. *Report of the Adjutant General of the State of Kentucky,* two volumes, Frankfort: John H. Harney, Public Printer, 1866-1867.

Ohio. Roster Commission. *Official Roster of the Soldiers of the State of Ohio in the War of the Rebellion, 1861-1866,* 12 volumes, Akron, Cincinnati, Norwalk, 1886-1895.

Phisterer, Frederick, compiler, *New York in the War of the Rebellion 1861 to 1865,* five volumes, Albany: J.B. Lyon Company, State Printers, 1912.

Tennessee. *Tennesseans in the Civil War,* two parts, Nashville: Civil War Centennial Commission, 1964-1965.

Terrell, W.H.H., *Report of the Adjutant General of the State of Indiana,* eight volumes, Indianapolis: W.R. Holloway State Printer, 1865-1868.

United States War Department. *War of the Rebellion: A Compilation of the Official Records of the Union and Confederate Armies,* 128 volumes, Washington, D.C.: Government Printing Office, 1891-1902.

Wisconsin. *Wisconsin Volunteers, War of the Rebellion 1861-1865,* Madison: Democrat Printing Company, 1914.

Military histories, biographies & reference works

Castel, Albert, *Decision in the West: The Atlanta Campaign of 1864,* Lawrence: University Press of Kansas, 1992.

Cox, Jacob D., *Atlanta,* Dayton: Press of Morningside Bookshop, 1987.

Dawes, Ephraim C., "The Confederate Strength in the Atlanta Campaign," *Battles and Leaders of the Civil War,* vol. 4, New York: The Century Company, 1886.

Fox, William F., *Regimental Losses in The American Civil War 1861-1865,* Dayton: Press of Morningside Bookshop, 1985.

Johnson, Kathy, *Colonel Frederick Bartleson,* Joliet: Will County Historical Society, 1983.

Kelly, Dennis, *Kennesaw Mountain and the Atlanta Campaign: A Tour Guide,* Marietta: Kennesaw Mountain Historical Association, Inc., 1990.

Lindsley, John B., *The Military Annals of Tennessee. Confederate,* Nashville: J.M. Lindsley & Co., 1886.

Polk, William M., *Leonidas Polk: Bishop and General,* vol. II, New York: Longmans, Green and Co., 1915.

Strayer, Larry M. & Baumgartner, Richard A., *Echoes of Battle: The Atlanta Campaign,* Huntington, W.Va.: Blue Acorn Press, 1991.

The National Cyclopaedia of American Biography, vol. IV, New York: James T. White & Company, 1897.

Warner, Ezra J., *Generals in Gray,* Baton Rouge: Louisiana State University Press, 1959.

Warner, Ezra J., *Generals in Blue,* Baton Rouge: Louisiana State University Press, 1992.

Welsh, Jack D., *Medical Histories of Confederate Generals,* Kent, Ohio: The Kent State University Press, 1995.

Miscellaneous

Bierce, Ambrose G., "The Crime at Pickett's Mill," *The Collected Works of Ambrose Bierce,* vol. I, New York: Gordian Press, 1966.

Proceedings of the Twenty-Third Reunion of the Eighty-Sixth Regiment Illinois Volunteer Infantry, Peoria, 1909.

Proceedings of the Twenty-Fourth Reunion of the Eighty-Sixth Regiment Illinois Volunteer Infantry, Peoria, 1910.

Proceedings of the Thirty-Ninth Annual Encampment of the Department of Ohio, Grand Army of the Republic, Lima: Republican-Gazette Print, 1905.

Society of the Seventy-Fourth Illinois Volunteer Infantry: Sixth Reunion Proceedings and History of the Regiment, Rockford: W.P. Lamb, 1903.

INDEX

Page numbers appearing in boldface indicate photographs or illustrations.

Other Civil War Titles Published by Blue Acorn Press

Blue Lightning

Wilder's Mounted Infantry Brigade in the Battle of Chickamauga

Richard A. Baumgartner

With a potent combination of rapid-firing Spencer rifles, aggressive and determined leadership, and unlimited confidence in themselves, the soldiers of Colonel John T. Wilder's mounted Lightning Brigade solidified a reputation in the savage 1863 battle of Chickamauga as one of the Union Army's hardest fighting and most effective combat organizations. His five Indiana and Illinois regiments, along with the 18th Indiana Battery, confronted troops from five different Confederate brigades during three days of fighting, and badly bloodied them all. Author Richard Baumgartner skillfully blends dozens of first-person narratives with more than 150 photographs to vividly depict a major segment of the Lightning Brigade's proud history during the Civil War.

"Through tight organization, careful transitions and clear prose, *Blue Lightning* offers the reader a goldmine of carefully selected passages from letters, diaries and reports, not to speak of a rich array of photographs."
Blue & Gray Magazine

"Scores of previously unpublished photographs of the brigade add much value and character to this book. *Blue Lightning* is a fine look at an under-appreciated unit and provides important insight into the evolution of warfare and the influence of repeating weapons on battlefield tactics."
Civil War Magazine

"The narrative crackles along with the implied speed of the title. Baumgartner's book is an excellent addition to the Civil War bookshelf, and will undoubtedly emerge as one of the best of 1997."
America's Civil War Magazine

Hardcover with dust jacket, 256 pages, 156 photographs, notes, bibliography, index. $30

Blood & Sacrifice

The Civil War Journal of a Confederate Soldier

William Pitt Chambers

A schoolteacher turned soldier, Mississippian William Pitt Chambers served three years in the Army of Vicksburg and the Army of Tennessee, rising in rank from private to sergeant, orderly sergeant, sergeant major and acting adjutant. His 1862-1865 journal, edited with notes by historian Richard Baumgartner, provides an open window to the hopes, dreams and fears of an intelligent, thoughtful and observant Confederate enlisted man. Chambers' journal chronicles nearly the entire history of the 46th Mississippi Volunteer Infantry through life and death in camp, on the march and in battles fought at Vicksburg, Port Gibson, Dallas, Kennesaw Mountain, Atlanta, Allatoona and Fort Blakely.

"Chambers left a memorable record that is noteworthy for its setting, quality of style and content. *Blood & Sacrifice* is a cut above the typical memoir. It has the style of Mary Boykin Chesnut's *Diary from Dixie* and the drama of Sam Watkins' *Co. Aytch*."
Rod Gragg, author of *The Illustrated Confederate Reader*

"This unpretentious, honest account is a must for anyone who wants to understand the war from the front-line Confederate soldier's perspective."
John Michael Priest, author of *Antietam: The Soldiers' Battle*

Softcover, 288 pages, illustrated, notes, bibliography, index. $18

BLUE ACORN PRESS

P.O. Box 2684 • Huntington, West Virginia 25726 • (304) 733-3917

Other Civil War Titles Published by Blue Acorn Press

Loyal West Virginia 1861-1865

Theodore F. Lang

Ably describing events and personalities responsible for West Virginia's creation as America's 35th state midway through the Civil War, Lang's primary attention focuses on military operations involving West Virginia and its soldiers who remained loyal to the Union. In addition to his experiences as a combat and staff officer, the author details successes and failures of military leaders serving in the state or under West Virginia banners on bloody battlefields in Virginia, Maryland and Pennsylvania. Skirmishes and bitter fighting at Philippi, Rich Mountain, Moorefield, Harpers Ferry and Droop Mountain share equally with West Virginians' participation in major battles at 2nd Manassas, Antietam, Vicksburg, Chattanooga, the Shenandoah Valley and Appomattox. Soldiers from the Mountain State battled "Stonewall" Jackson at Cross Keys, helped repel a Confederate assault on East Cemetery Hill at Gettysburg, tangled with Early at Winchester and Cedar Creek, and smashed through Rebel resistance under Custer at Five Forks. Histories of every West Virginia military organization with complete officer rosters are supplemented by 63 photographic portraits, greatly enhancing Lang's rare original 1895 edition.

Hardcover with dust jacket, 450 pages, 63 photographs, full regimental index. $35

Echoes of Battle

The Struggle For Chattanooga

Richard A. Baumgartner & Larry M. Strayer

Unparalleled in its blending of photographic imagery and riveting accounts of soldier-participants, *Echoes of Battle* offers a unique portrayal of the Civil War's strategically important Tullahoma, Chickamauga and Chattanooga campaigns. The authors draw from hundreds of 1863 diaries, journals, letters and official reports, as well as memoirs, reminiscences and regimental histories to provide in-depth insight into the experiences of Union and Confederate enlisted men, and their commanding officers. Combining personal narratives with 465 wartime photographs — many of them from private collections and never before published — continues an unsurpassed standard previously set by Baumgartner and Strayer with their critically acclaimed volume *Echoes of Battle: The Atlanta Campaign,* recipient of 1994's Richard B. Harwell Award.

"This book is simply must reading for anyone who is a student of Civil War history. The photographs and personalized accounts are fantastic, and I can't imagine anyone not being very impressed by the research and work performed. By combining vivid visual images and excellent personal narratives Baumgartner and Strayer have produced a 'hands on' style of history that is particularly meaningful."
Wiley Sword, author of *Embrace An Angry Wind*

"*Echoes of Battle* tells the story of a major western campaign with an artfully composed string of first-person accounts, connecting narratives, maps and — a sheer delight — hundreds of photographs of individual soldiers. This is history of the Civil War's common soldier at its best."
***Military Images* Magazine**

"Blue Acorn Press has scored another coup. *Echoes of Battle: The Struggle for Chattanooga* is a blockbuster. The authors have a talent for winnowing the seed from the chaff found in multitudes of disparate Civil War sources and weaving it into a well-organized and balanced book."
Edwin C. Bearss, former chief historian of the National Park Service

Hardcover with dust jacket, 484 pages, 465 photographs, notes, bibliography, index. $40

BLUE ACORN PRESS

P.O. Box 2684 • Huntington, West Virginia 25726 • (304) 733-3917